I0795650

IMAGES
of America

ENFIELD
1950–1980

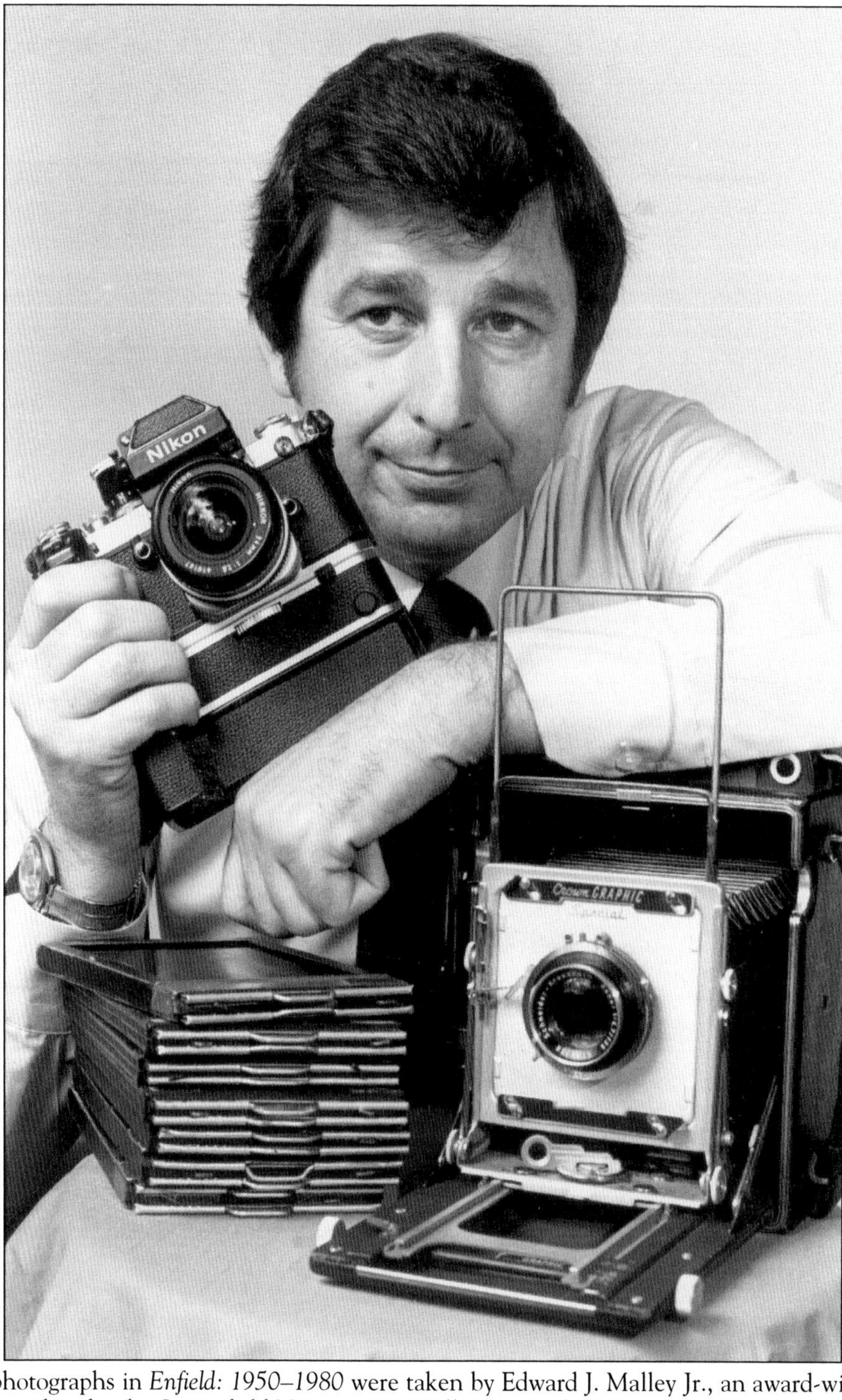

The photographs in *Enfield: 1950–1980* were taken by Edward J. Malley Jr., an award-winning photographer for the Springfield Newspapers. Malley covered major news events in the region for over 25 years. He was a photographer for the *Daily News* beginning in 1955. Later in his career, he became photo editor of the Springfield Newspapers—the *Daily News*, *Morning Union*, and *Sunday Republican*. (Photograph by Kevin Twombly.)

IMAGES
of America

ENFIELD
1950–1980

James M. Malley

ARCADIA
PUBLISHING

ISBN 978-0-7385-1158-0

Published by Arcadia Publishing
Charleston, South Carolina

Printed in the United States of America

Library of Congress Catalog Card Number: 2002116099

For all general information contact Arcadia Publishing at:
Telephone 843-853-2070
Fax 843-853-0044
E-mail sales@arcadiapublishing.com
For customer service and orders:
Toll-Free 1-888-313-2665

Visit us on the Internet at www.arcadiapublishing.com

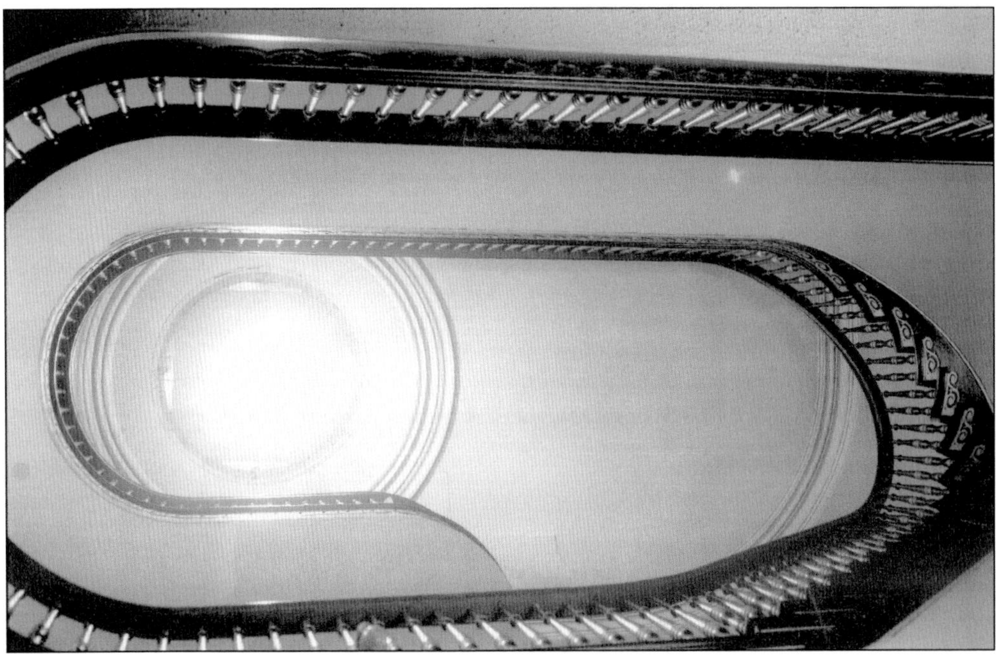

The Enfield Inn spiral staircase, shown in the 1960s, was made of solid cherry and trimmed with gold leaf. The historic inn was located on Enfield Street, across the street from the present-day Enfield High School driveway. It was built c. 1845 as the home of Col. Augustus Hazard, owner of the Hazard Powder Company. The mansion was a French Colonial design. Hazard received noted politicians of the 1800s, including Jefferson Davis and Daniel Webster. In 1969, a major fire destroyed the inn.

CONTENTS

ACKNOWLEDGMENTS

This book is the result of personal interviews with many people who shared their memories and helped identify the people, places, and events of Enfield's recent past: Michael Blaney, J. Francis Browne III, Paul Censki (Thompsonville fire marshal), Jack Cerrato, Nick DellAquila, Carol Donle, John Gual, Stanley Dynia, Charles "Chick" Egan, Herbert Foy (Enfield police chief), Ted Furey, Eleanor Malley, John Malley, Jeff Moody, Sue Neville, George Noble, Barbara Nosal, Jack O'Brien, Art Potter, Pat Reilly, Jim Reveruzzi, Edward N. Richards (Enfield fire chief), John Riley, Bob Rookey, Frank Rudolf, Bill Spanswick, Mary Lou Strom, Richard Sunter, Bob Tanguay, Phyllis Tanguay, Frank Troiano, and Yvonne Wollenberg.

I would like to recognize the people who assisted me with gathering source material, publishing information, and editing of the book: Rosalie Fiore, Susan M. Gray, Michael K. Miller, Suzanne Olechnicki, Frank Poirot, Eileen Russell, and Dr. Frank G. Taylor.

I would like to thank my wife, Karla; my two children, Justin and Erin Malley; my mother, Helene Malley; and my brother, Michael Malley, for all their assistance during the research of this book. I would also like to give special thanks to the Enfield Central Library and staff for hosting a special viewing of the photographs in November 2002. Many people and places were identified by library patrons. The Enfield Press, Journal Inquirer, and the Hartford Courant newspapers publicized the library event and ran photographs for their readers to help identify people, places, and events.

The photographs in the collection were taken by my father, photographer Edward J. Malley Jr. I would like to thank Bill Moran of the Thompsonville Fire Department for loaning photographs and Rev. John Gwozdz for loaning newspaper photographs. Many of the photographs were printed by Thomas O. Panaccione.

During the research of this book, conflicting information on Enfield's recent history was discussed during my personal interviews with local residents. Some pieces of information were verified from a number of sources. Information that could not be substantiated was not used in the book.

Dedicated in memory of my father, Edward J. Malley Jr.

Introduction

The fascinating images featured in this volume were taken by award-winning photographer and newspaperman Edward J. Malley Jr. Born on February 27, 1938, in Springfield, Massachusetts, he was the son of Edward J. Malley Sr. and Clare (Provencher) Malley. He grew up in Thompsonville on Russell Street and, in the mid-1940s, moved to the Highland Park neighborhood. His interest in photography began as a hobby in the late 1940s, when he was a student at St. Joseph's School on Cross Street in Thompsonville. By age 12, he was developing his own pictures in the darkroom that he built at his home on Francis Avenue.

He continued his education at Cathedral High School in Springfield, Massachusetts. He became a staff photographer for the *Cathedral Chronicle* student newspaper and was always seen with a camera by his side. He also played Catholic Youth Organization (CYO) basketball for St. Patrick's Church in Thompsonville and played junior varsity basketball and football for Cathedral High School. At the age of 17, when he was a senior, he took photographs of Cathedral High School events during the day and held a full-time position as a staff photographer for the Springfield *Daily News* in the evening.

Malley's sharp black-and-white newspaper photographs usually took a local slant on Enfield. He took most of these photographs with a four- by five-inch Speed Graphics press camera, the professional camera of newsmen through the 1950s. Later in his career, he used a Nikon 35-millimeter single-lens reflex camera. He would do anything to get a better shot. Sometimes, he could be seen on the rafters at Cathedral High School or at the end of a boom on a crane, 200 feet in the air over a construction site.

In the past half-century, Enfield has undergone a transformation from a rural mill-and-farming town of 15,000 to a substantial suburban community of 45,000. Located in north-central Connecticut on the eastern side of the Connecticut River, the town was once known as the Carpet City. In the 1950s and 1960s, new housing developments increased rapidly, with homebuilder Leger Starr leading the way. With a continuing increase in the population, a new school was constructed every year. This population growth led to new public facilities, including the Enfield Town Hall, the Enfield Central Library, and the Enfield Public Works facility.

In August 1955, Malley recorded the destructive forces of Hurricane Diane. On August 18 and 19, downtown Thompsonville was inundated with water. The flood resulted from a combination of the volume and duration of precipitation. On August 20, some Thompsonville residents woke up to flooded cellars and the sight of downtown streets ripped apart.

In 1956, Malley captured the process of carpet making at the Bigelow-Sanford Carpet Company in Thompsonville. The carpet mill played a vital role in workers' lives, providing employment and housing, as well as leisure activities, such as sports teams and craft clubs. Many labor strikes took place over wages in the 1900s. By 1960, the carpet company started moving production down south. The carpet company closed its doors in 1971.

In the late 1950s, Malley became involved in local community organizations. He was a member of the Enfield Hunter's Club and Knights of Columbus, Washington Irving Council No. 50. In the early 1960s, he was involved with local government as a chairman of the Enfield Planning and Zoning Commission. He was also a member of the National Press Photographers Association and the Connecticut News Photographers Association.

In addition to his duties as a newspaper photographer, Malley was a freelance photographer for the Enfield Road Construction Company. By the late 1950s, he began documenting the changes to the rural landscape. The construction of the Hartford-Springfield Expressway (later named Interstate 91) led to land taking by eminent domain from the state line to the East Windsor border. The construction of four exits led to development of five shopping malls in the 1960s and early 1970s. The population soared to 46,189.

Malley covered the five town fire departments in action throughout his career. The fire departments were established in Enfield by legislative act, including Thompsonville (1839), Hazardville (1892), Enfield (1896), North Thompsonville (1914), and Shaker Pines (1941). He recorded three major fires, including the Enfield Inn fire (January 3, 1969), the Osborn Prison Farm fire (July 8, 1971), and the Browne Building fire (March 12, 1979).

Malley covered the entire sports gamut, from sandlot pickup games to national sports teams in Boston. He took photographs of youths playing ice hockey on local ponds and youths playing games at the Enfield Youth Center, Greys Club reunions, and major-league sports celebrities at the Knights of Columbus. He captured local rising stars, some of whom made it to the professional level.

Malley photographed local businesses, politicians, community leaders, schools, and special events in Enfield. New businesses were documented in annual town reports and in the daily pages of the newspaper. He covered local, state, and national political elections.

Malley's interest in people and things brought him numerous awards, including three top prizes in the 1973 United Press International regional photograph competition for newspapers. He also received recognition by the Associated Press, the Enfield Fire Chiefs Association, and the National Press Photographers Association.

Malley became the *Daily News* photo editor in May 1978. He was promoted to photo editor of the Springfield Newspapers—the *Daily News*, *Morning Union*, and *Sunday Republican*—in January 1980. After a battle with cancer, he passed away on May 18, 1982.

The images on the following pages cover the major news events over a 30-year period. The photographs depict Enfield's major transition from a small rural community in 1950 to a new suburban community in 1980.

One

THOMPSONVILLE

The village of Thompsonville was named after Orrin Thompson, owner of the Thompsonville Carpet Company, in 1828. Business and industry grew rapidly around its main industry. By the early 1900s, private commercial development and residential construction by the carpet company increased, which led to the current grid layout of streets and housing stock of today. The center of Thompsonville was a busy place in the 1950s. Workers headed off early in the morning to work at the carpet mill or walked toward Commerce Street to catch a train to Hartford or Springfield. Most of the daily needs of families were located in Thompsonville. Residents shopped in a variety of stores and used the pond and the youth center building for recreation. They were educated in public and parochial schools and were entertained in theaters. They dined in restaurants and attended church services. All of it was within walking distance of residential neighborhoods in Thompsonville.

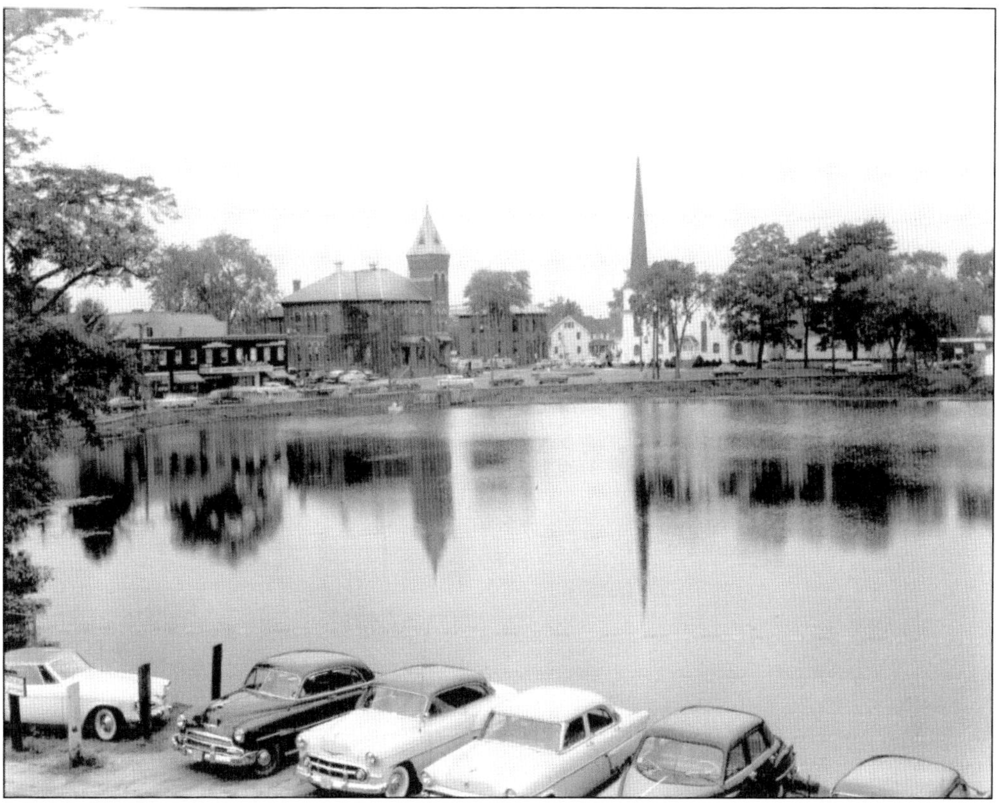

The Strand Theatre, the courthouse building, the town hall, and the First Presbyterian Church create a mirror image on Freshwater Pond in front of a row of cars in 1954. Freshwater Pond was much larger in 1954 compared to today, as the edge of North Main Street was right up next to the sidewalk in front of the Strand, the courthouse, and the pond.

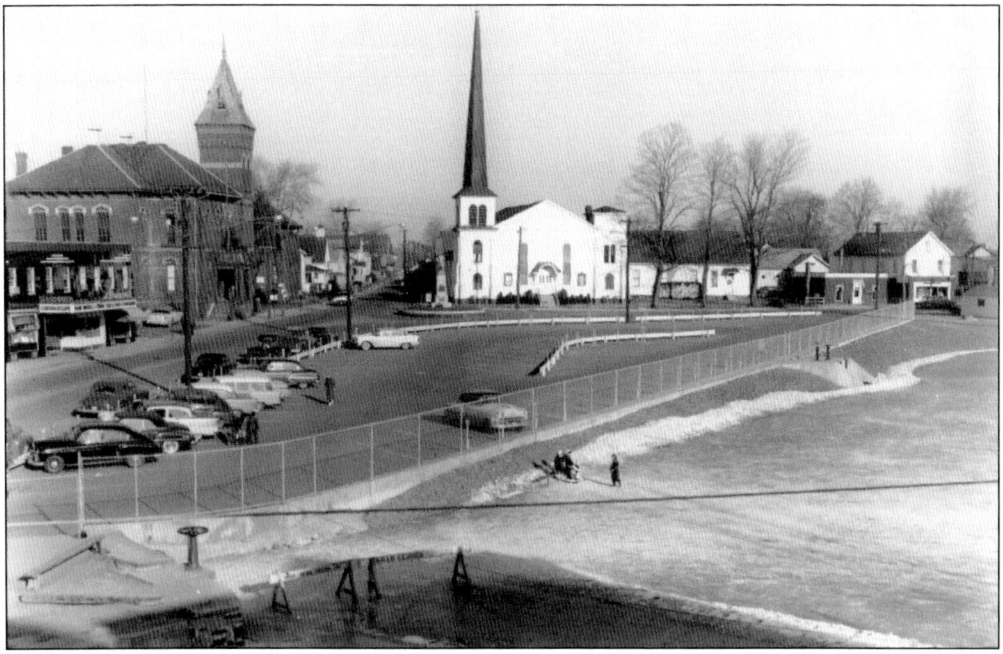

Thompsonville youths take advantage of a cold winter day as they get ready to ice-skate on Freshwater Pond in 1955. A new 87-car municipal parking lot was constructed by the Enfield Road Construction Company (later named Della Construction) in 1955. The northwest portion of Freshwater Pond was filled in to build the parking lot. The Strand Theatre, the courthouse building, the First Presbyterian Church, the Dressmaker Shop (owned by Clementine Pagano), and the Mid-Nite Spa were located on North Main Street. The Mid-Nite Spa, owned by Louis P. Salier, was a local hangout for teenagers in the 1950s.

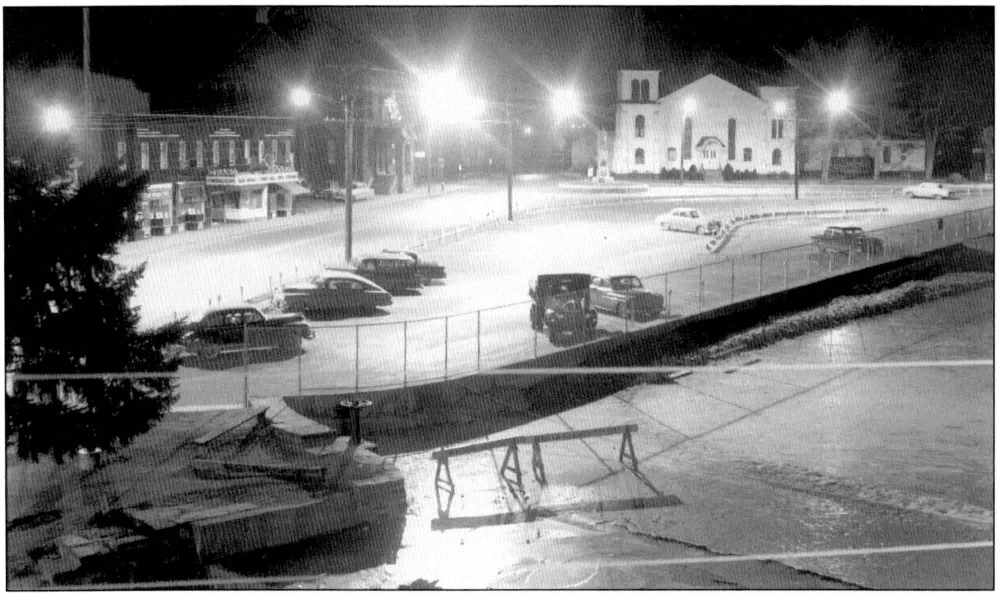

The Strand Theatre, the courthouse building, the First Presbyterian Church, and Freshwater Pond are illuminated on a winter night in 1955. This photograph was taken on the same day as the previous view.

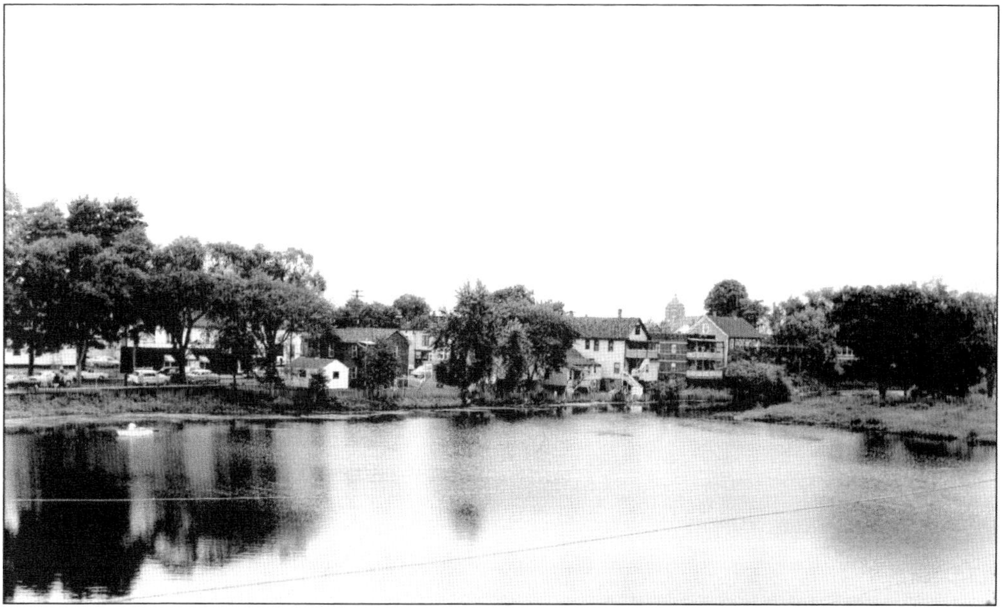

North Main Street businesses and apartments along the edge of Freshwater Pond are shown in the early 1950s. The pond continues to be the site of the annual Enfield Park and Recreation Fishing Derby. The pond was also used by the Bigelow mill. The mill used water from the pond to clean wool, because it was cleaner than the Connecticut River. The pond was dredged every five years, to remove silt and sedimentation.

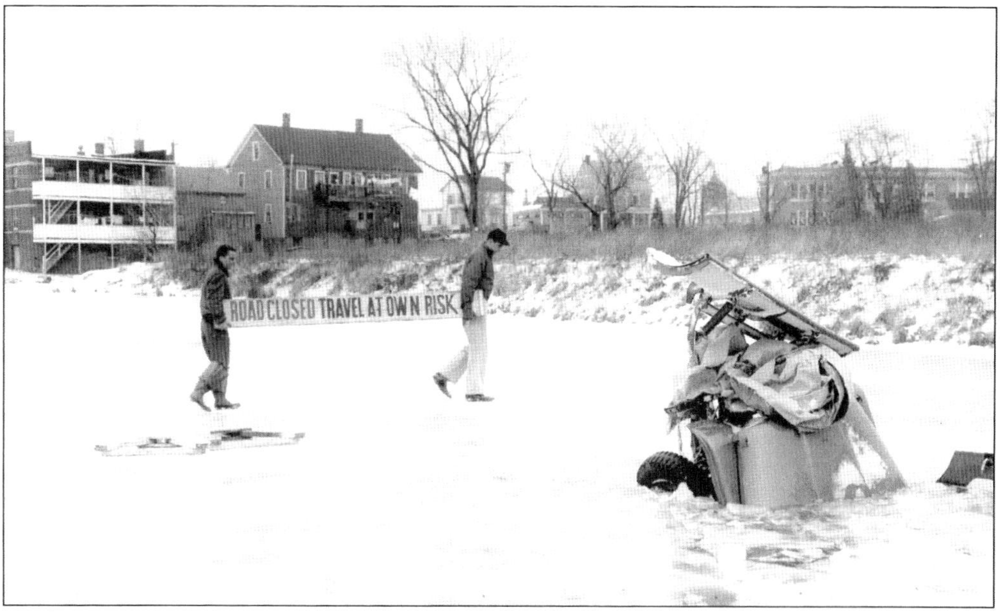

In this 1960s view, Enfield Park and Recreation employees Karl Russotto (left) and Bill Spanswick carry a sawhorse to keep skaters away from a partially submerged Jeep. Enfield Parks and Recreation director Angelo Lamagna routinely plowed Freshwater Pond after a snowstorm but was not so fortunate, as the Jeep he was driving crashed through the ice. Lamagna survived the crash, and the Jeep was later pulled out of the ice by a large crane and placed along the edge of the pond.

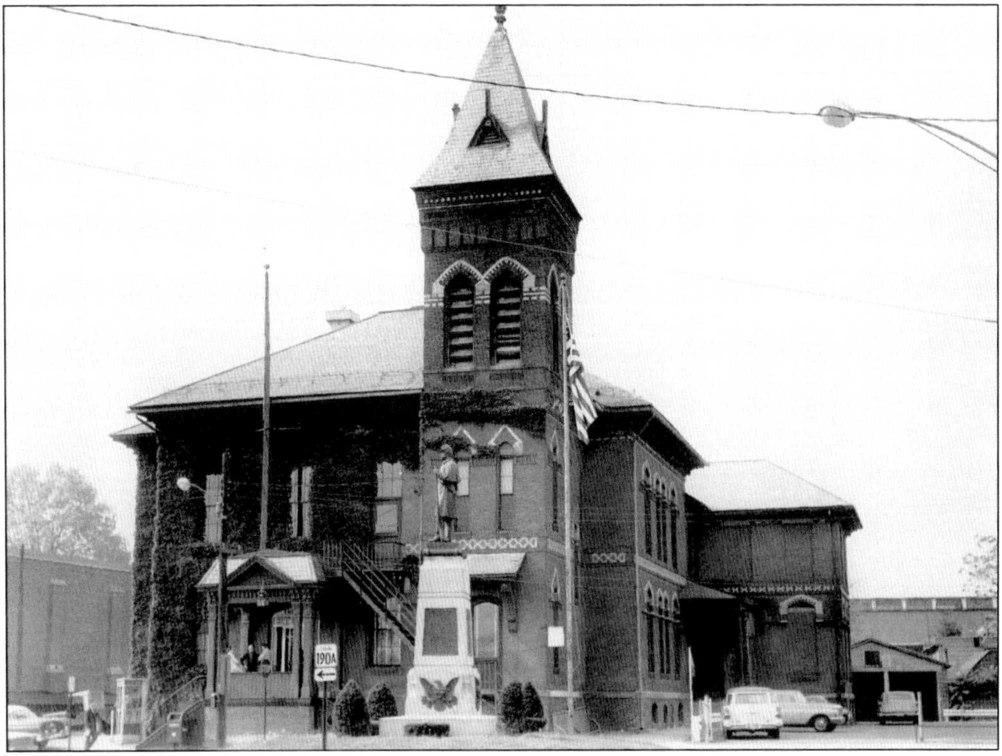

The Thompsonville Civil War Monument stands in front of a building that housed the courthouse, the Enfield Police Department, and the Enfield Youth Center on North Main Street in the 1950s. The building was demolished in the early 1970s and was replaced by the Enfield Neighborhood Center in the mid-1970s.

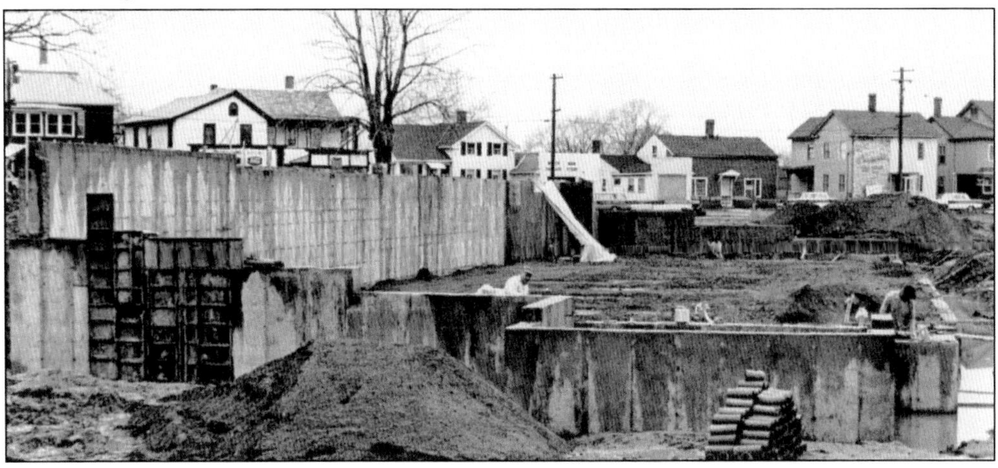

Construction of the Enfield Town Hall took place in the early 1960s. Businesses along North Main Street can be seen in the background. The businesses were later torn down as part of the urban renewal project in the 1970s. The Enfield Town Building Committee for the project included James W. Sherman (chairman), Chester F. Brainard Jr. (secretary), R. Dudley Bridge, Charles H. Gatto, and Dr. Carl L. Scavotto. The project's architects were Olson and Miller. The project superintendent was Dominic C. Cimino, and the contractor was Horn Construction. The town hall was completed in 1964.

Photographer Edward J. Malley Jr. was known for his sense of humor. When the Enfield Town Hall was under construction in 1964, he climbed up to the roof and leaned a sign against the cupola: "For Sale Reilly Real Estate." At the time, William Reilly was a town councilman and owned a real estate business in Thompsonville.

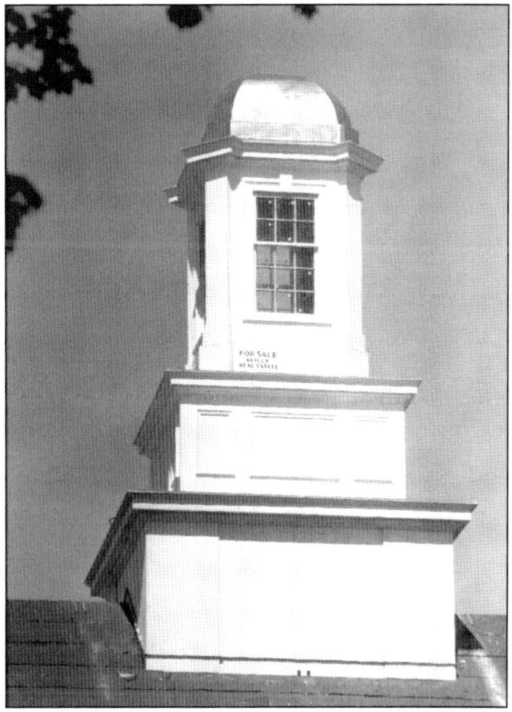

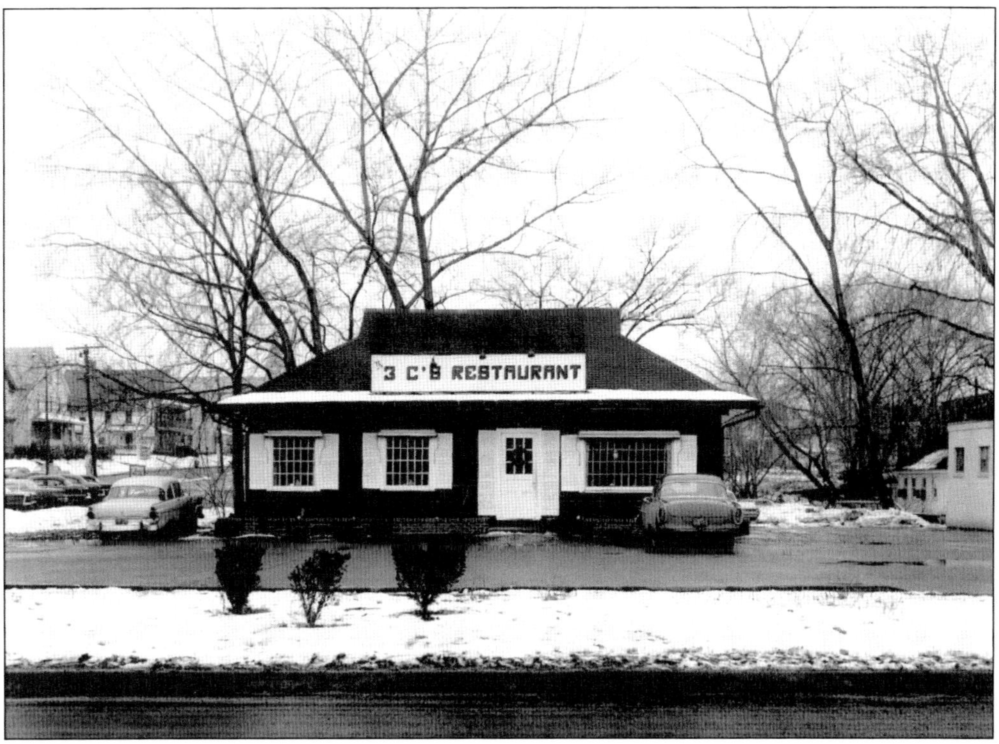

Pictured in the 1950s is the 3 C's Restaurant, located on the west side of Enfield Street, just north of High Street and Freshwater Brook. The restaurant was owned by Tony Almeida. The current site is home to Freshwater Plaza.

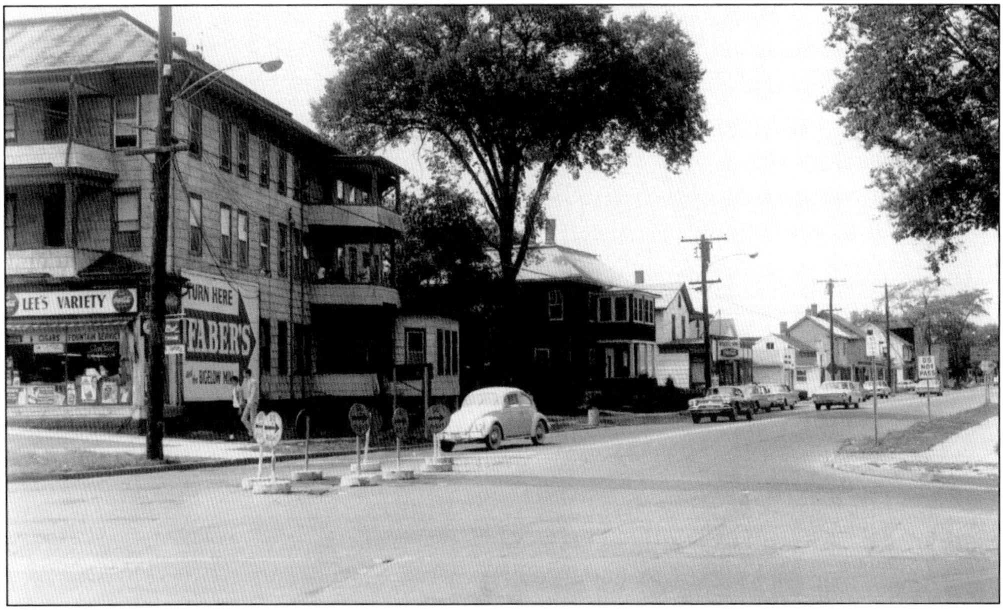

This 1960s view shows Lee's Variety, owned by Robert and Eugene Lee and located at the intersection of Enfield and North Main Streets. D'Aleo & Sons grocers and the North Main Street Package Store were located on the south side of North Main Street. The buildings were demolished as part of the urban renewal project in the 1970s. The current site is part of the town hall green.

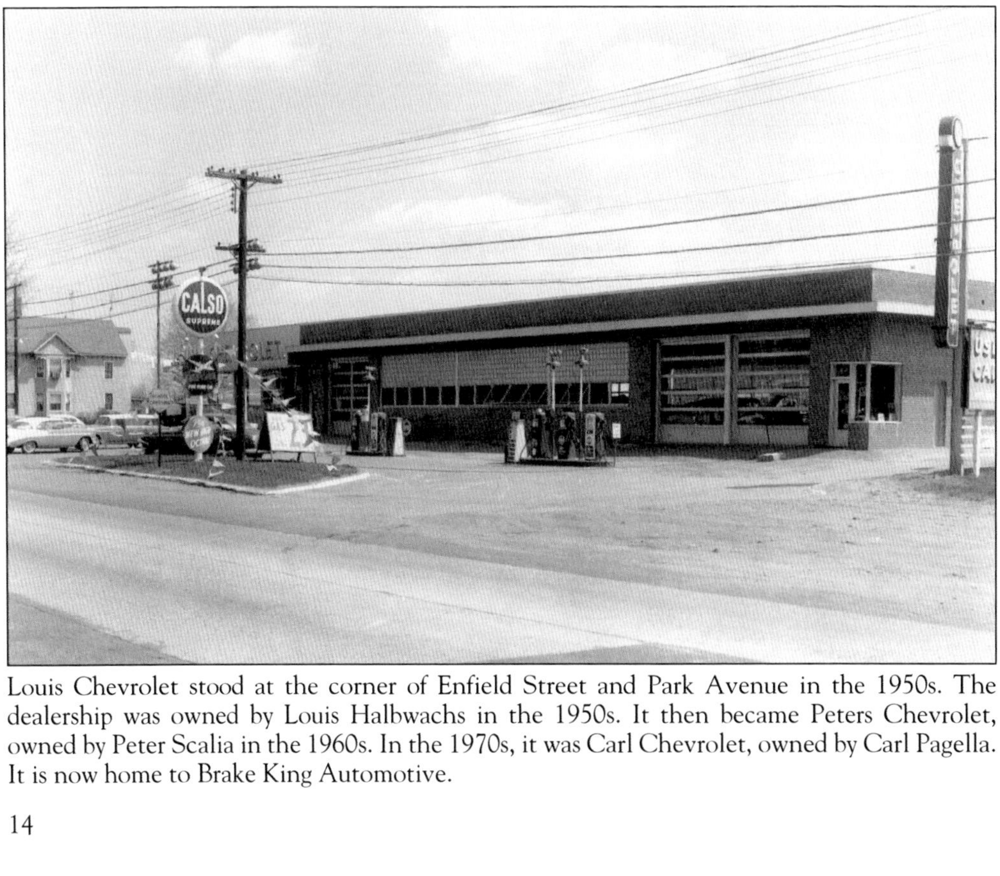

Louis Chevrolet stood at the corner of Enfield Street and Park Avenue in the 1950s. The dealership was owned by Louis Halbwachs in the 1950s. It then became Peters Chevrolet, owned by Peter Scalia in the 1960s. In the 1970s, it was Carl Chevrolet, owned by Carl Pagella. It is now home to Brake King Automotive.

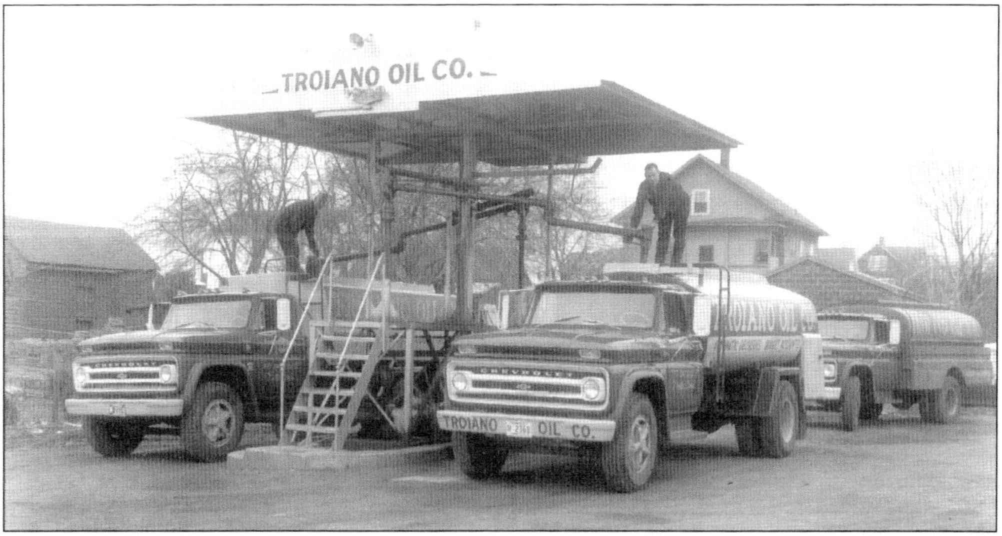

Two unidentified men fill Troiano Oil Company trucks on Enfield Street in the 1960s. In 1934, the business, owned by Anthony Troiano Sr., moved to the Enfield Street site. Troiano opened a welding and radiator-repair shop and, a year later, started selling gasoline. In the 1950s, his two sons, Frank Troiano and Anthony Troiano Jr., became active in the business and eventually became business partners. In 1996, Anthony Troiano Jr.'s son Frank Troiano became active in the family business.

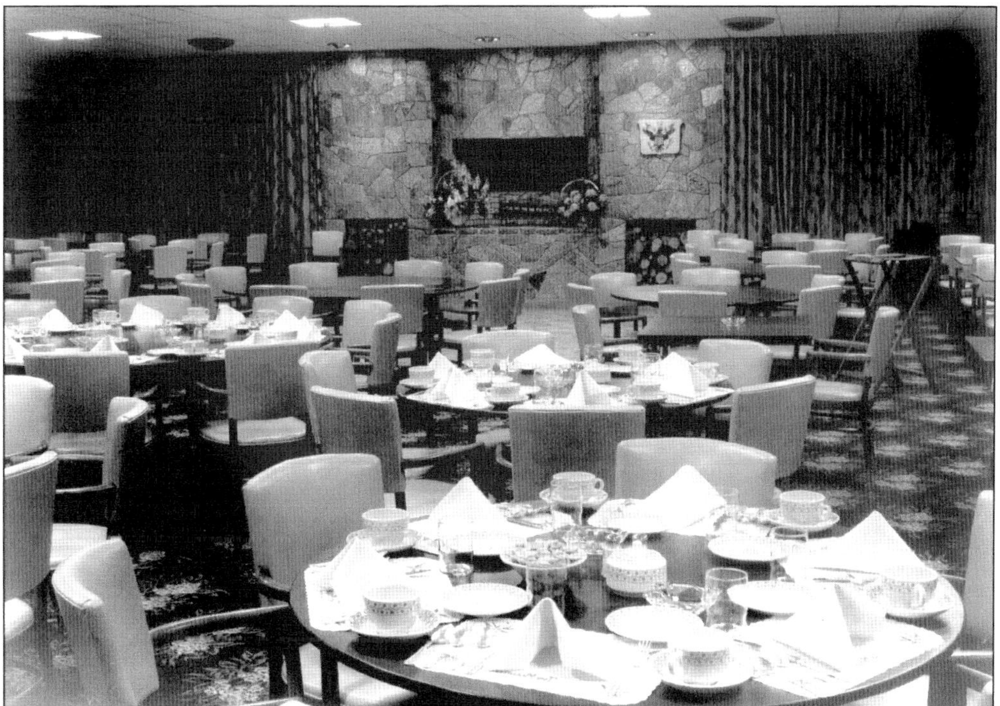

The Mountain Laurel Restaurant dining room is pictured in 1962. Notice that the carpet had a mountain laurel flower pattern, designed by the Bigelow-Sanford Carpet Company. The popular restaurant, owned by Hugo Trappe, was located on Enfield Street.

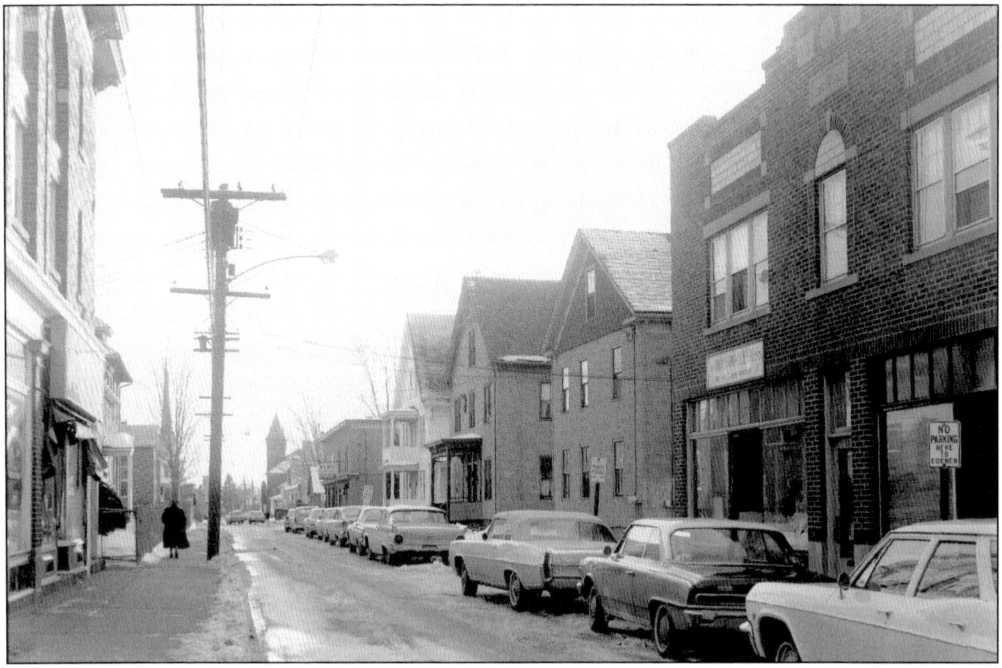

This 1960s view, looking south on Church Street, shows the American Legion John Maciolek Post No. 154, Nowak's Pharmacy, and the First Presbyterian Church steeple on the left. On the right are the Thompsonville Press, Ted's Package Store, and the courthouse tower.

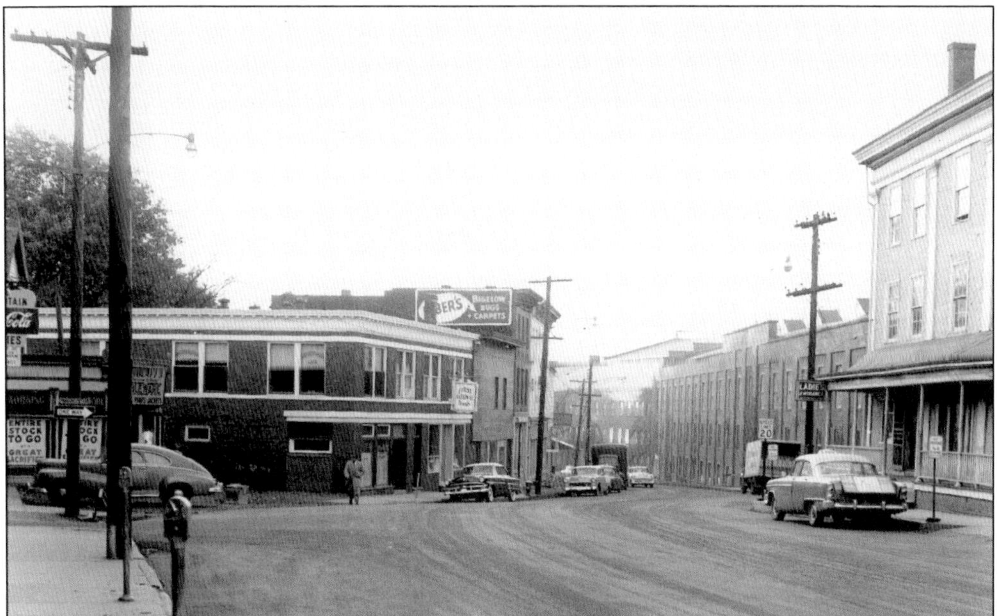

Looking west on Main Street in the 1950s, this view shows, on the left, Greenblatt's clothing store, the First National Bank, Metropolitan Life, the Greys Club, and the Faber's carpet store. On the right are the Thompsonville Hotel, and the Bigelow-Sanford Carpet Company. Notice the Ladies Entrance sign on the porch of the Thompsonville Hotel.

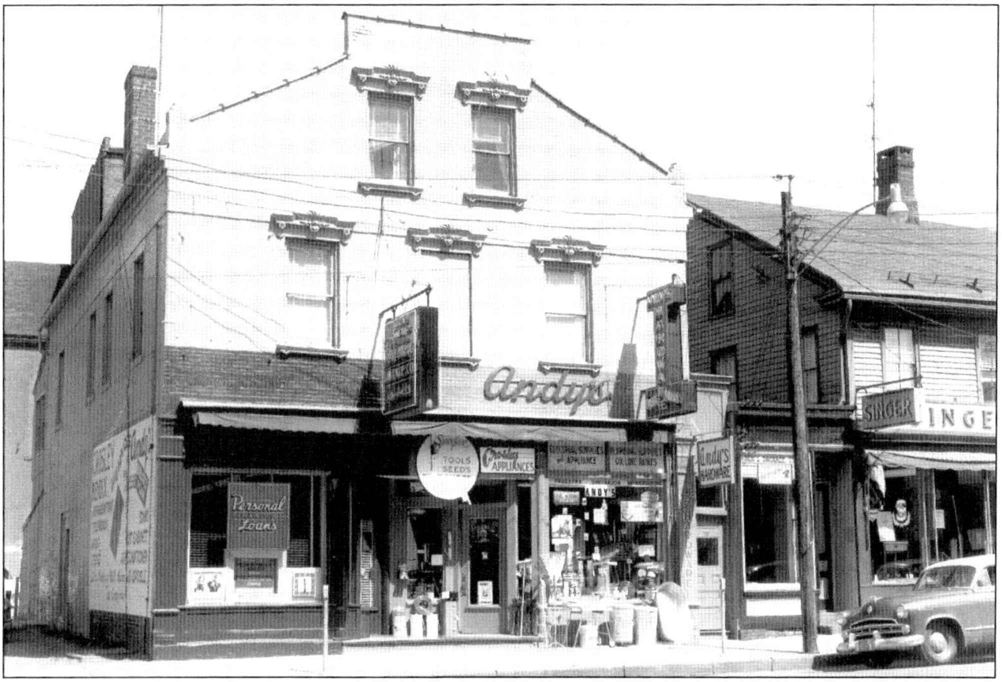

Andy's Hardware, pictured in the 1950s, was located on Main Street next to the Thompsonville Hotel. The store was owned and operated by Andy Liucci. This building was torn down during the urban renewal project in the 1970s.

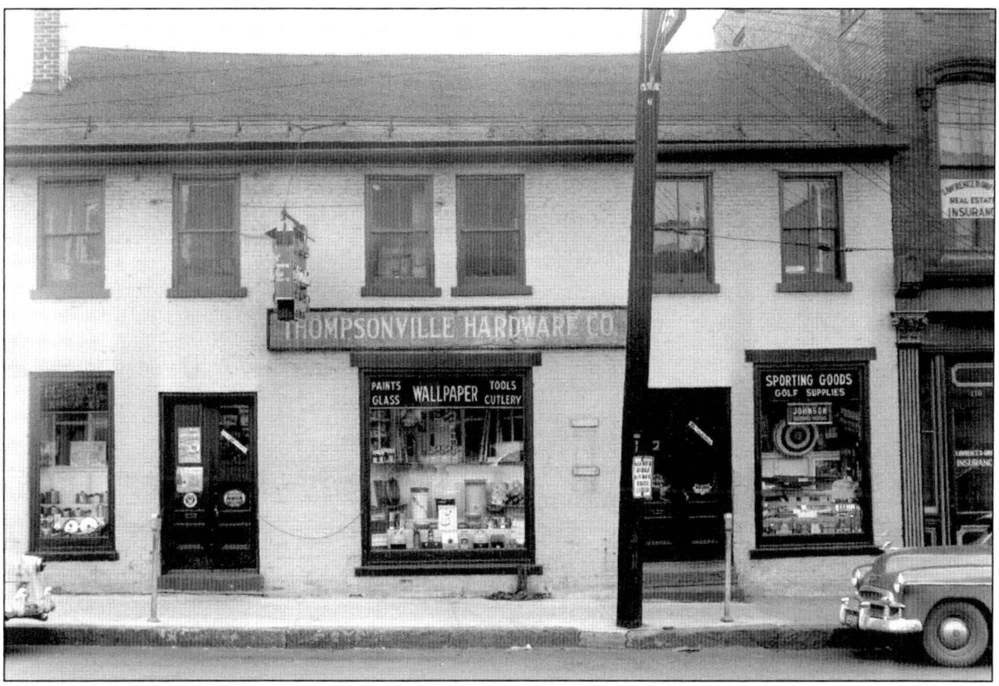

This 1950s view shows Thompsonville Hardware, located on the south side of Main Street. The store was owned by two brothers, Frank and George Stuart. The building was torn down under the urban renewal project in the 1970s.

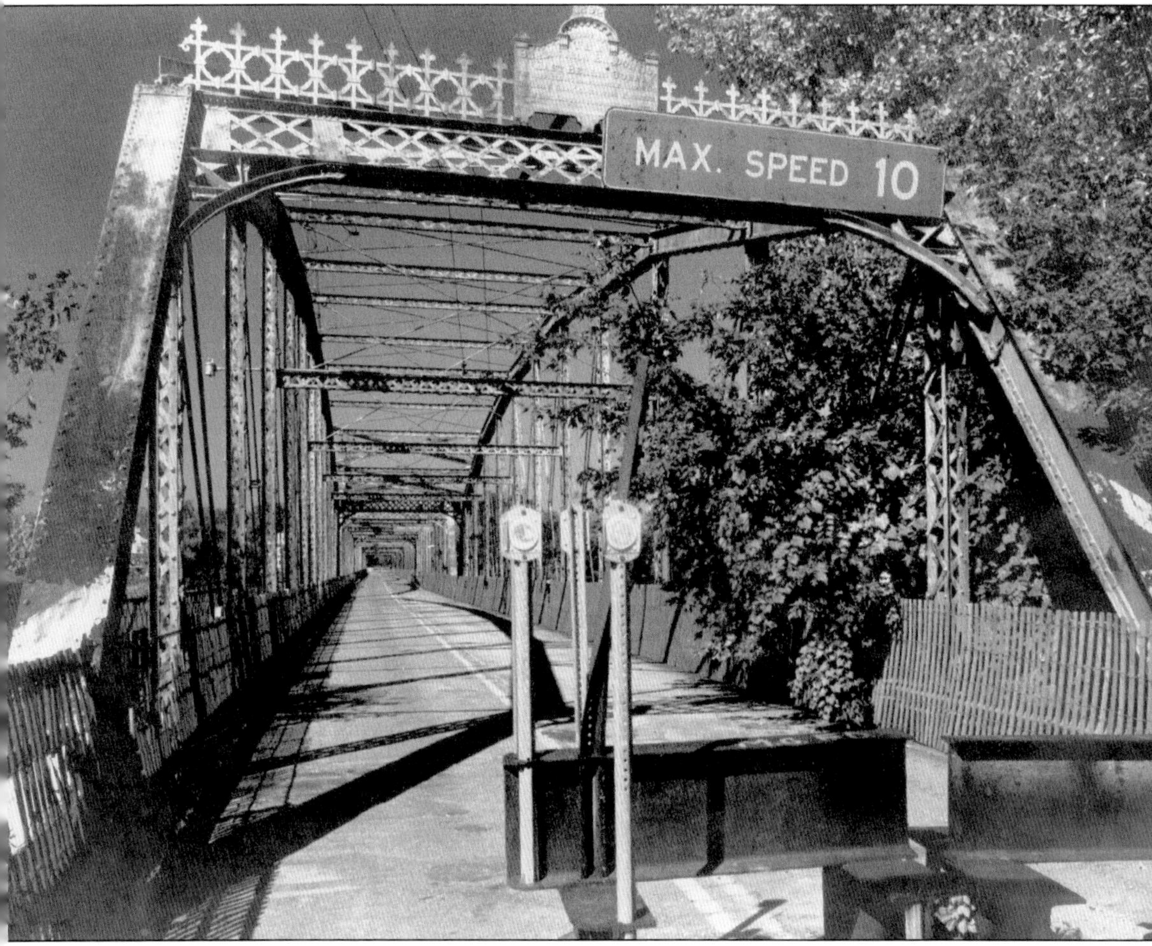

The Thompsonville–Suffield bridge is shown in disrepair during the 1960s. The bridge was closed to vehicular traffic in December 1966, when the new Route 190 bridge opened to traffic between Enfield and Suffield. The old iron bridge over the Connecticut River (the center span) was dynamited and dropped into the water in July 1971. The second and third spans were demolished in August 1971. The stone piers were left standing in the event a pedestrian bridge was built in the future. The Thompsonville Revitalization Committee master plan in the 1990s included a project using the stone abutments for a fishing pier and viewing area. At the present time, the pier has not been constructed.

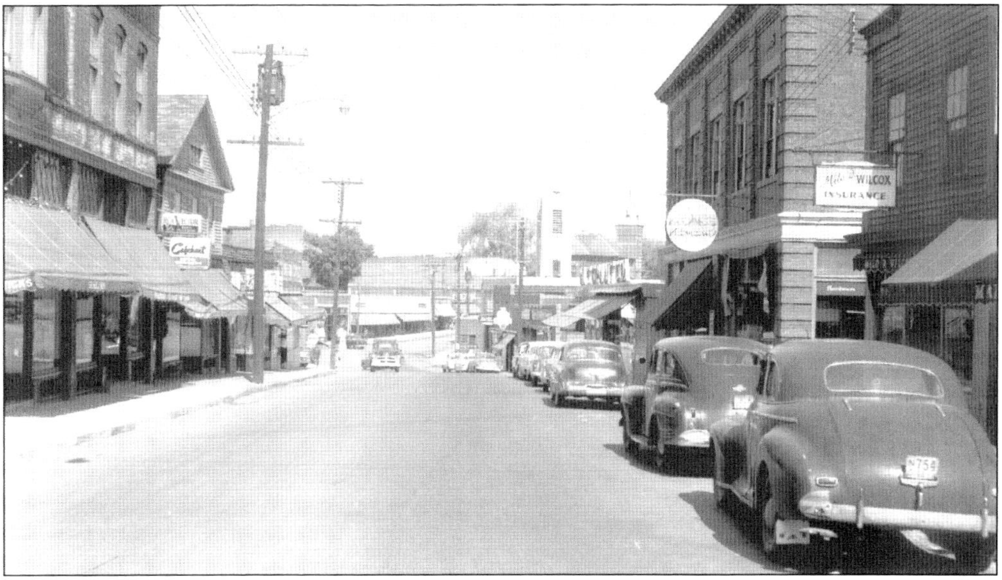

This 1950s view, looking north on Pearl Street, shows Graham's, the Ernest Shop, Gatto's Music Center and Appliances, Spaulding Gardens Florists, Reilly's Package Store, and the First National Stores on the left. J.C. Penney is in the center on North Main Street. On the right are Mary's Dress Shop, Milo D. Wilcox Insurance, Hydack Hardware, Craig's Kiddie Centre, the W.T. Grant store, Burn's Supermarket, Pascucci's Package Store, Marek Jewelers, the Van Doren Service Bureau, the Thompsonville Fire Department, and the bus station.

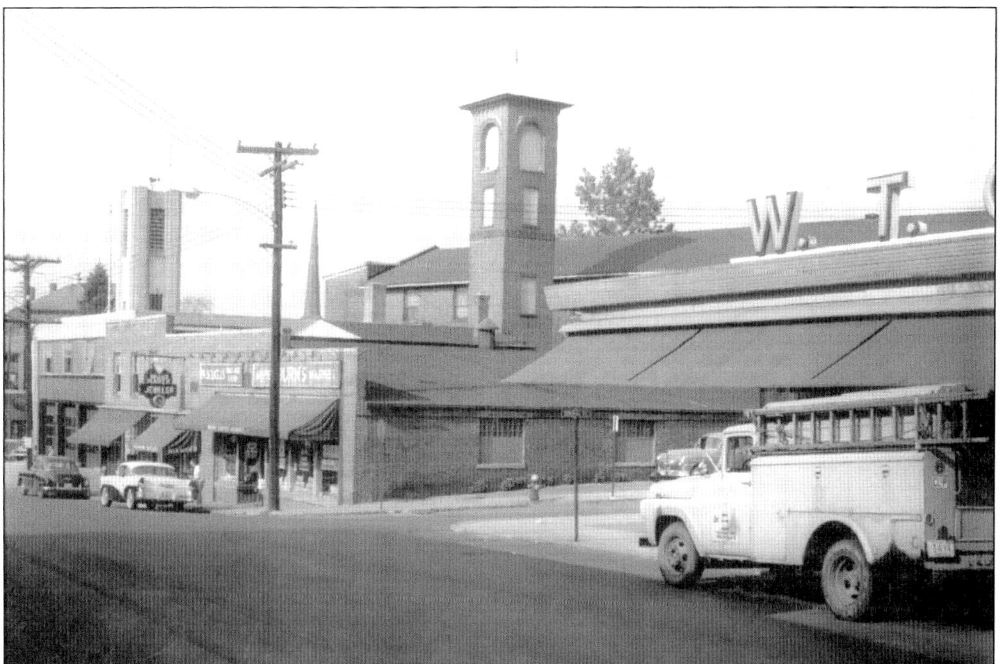

Pictured on the right in the 1950s are the W.T. Grant store, Burn's Supermarket, Pascucci's Package Store, Marek Jewelers, and the Thompsonville Fire Department. The former fire department bell tower stands behind Burn's Supermarket.

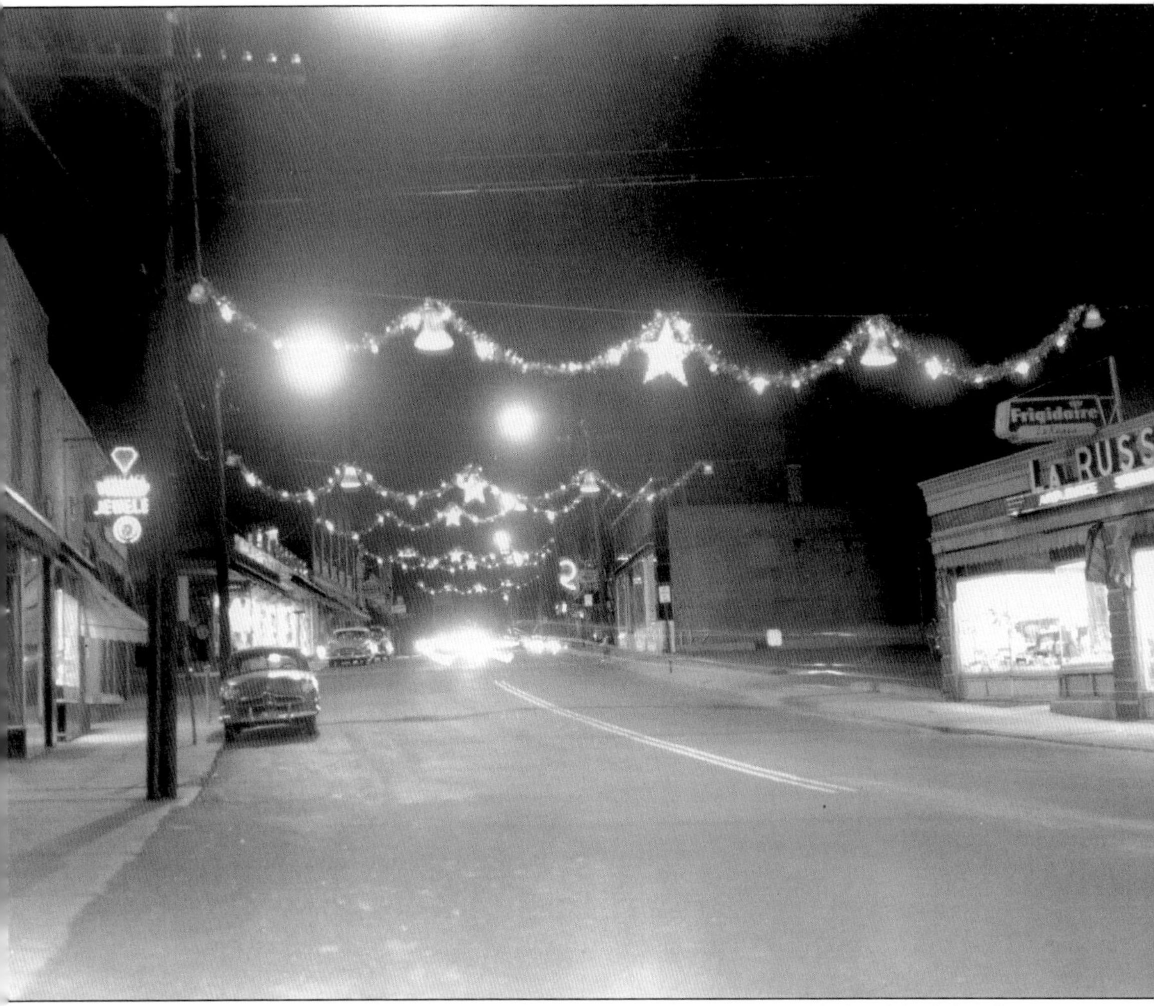

Looking south on Pearl Street, this 1950s view shows a series of lighted holiday decorations across the street. A committee of downtown Thompsonville merchants coordinated the annual event. Committee members included Al LaRussa, owner of the LaRussa Appliance Store; Vincent Sferrazza, owner of Vincent's Apparel; Myron Marek, owner of Marek Jewelers; and Robert Gray, manager of Faber's. The event was sponsored by the Greater Enfield Chamber of Commerce and the Downtown Merchants Association. From the 1950s to the 1970s, the lighting ceremony took place near Freshwater Pond, next to the falls and on the Enfield Street town hall green. Santa Claus was called upon to turn a master switch to turn on the holiday lights.

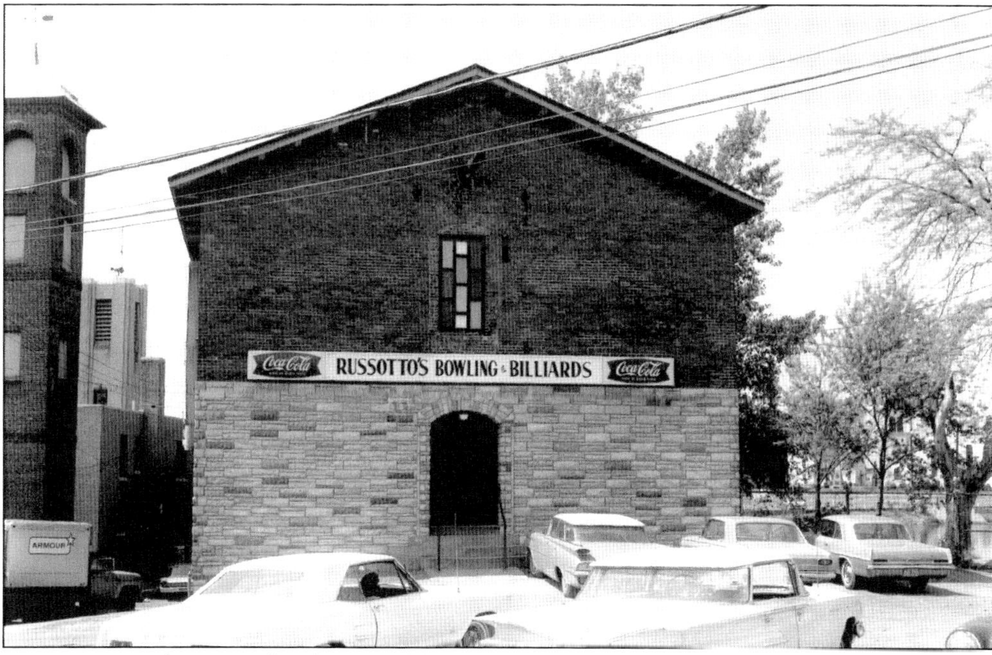

Russotto's Bowling & Billiards, owned by Joseph B. Russotto, was located on Central Street. The building once housed the Enfield Police Department on the first floor. The former Thompsonville Fire Department bell tower is shown to the left of the bowling alley in this 1960s photograph.

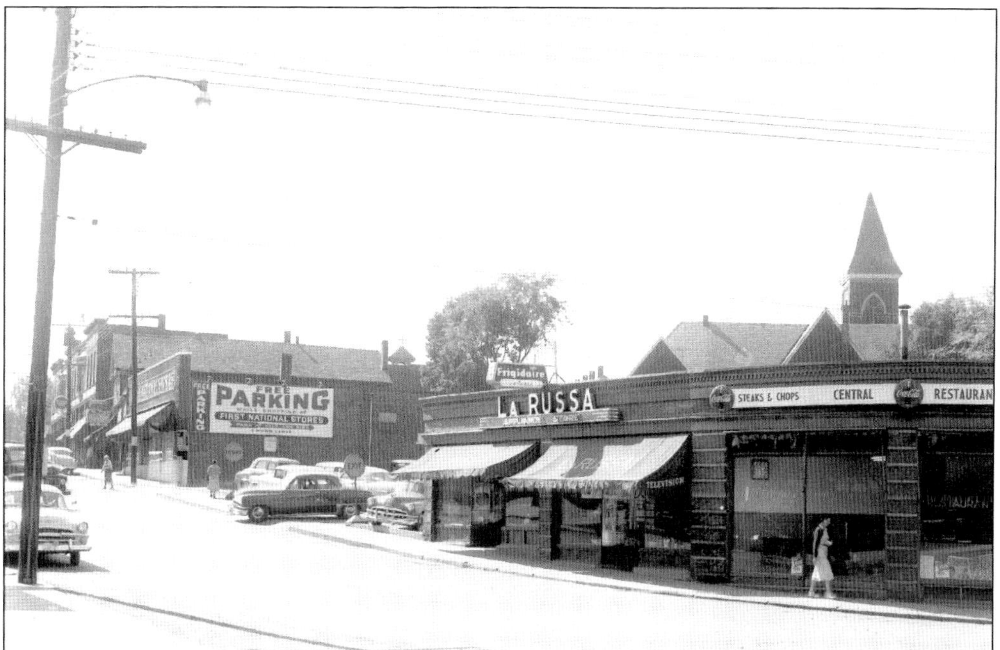

The LaRussa Appliance Store and the Central Restaurant on Pearl Street are pictured in the 1950s. The appliance store was owned by Al LaRussa and later by his son Ron LaRussa. Nicholas Bobersky owned the Central Restaurant in the 1950s.

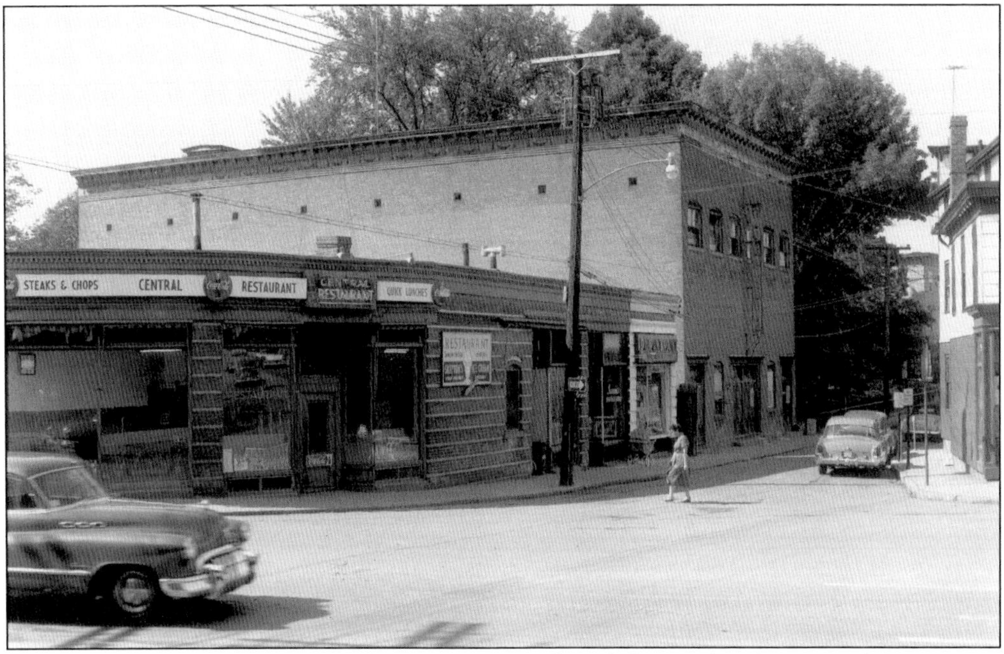

This view on Pearl and Asnuntuck Streets shows, from left to right, the Central Restaurant, Lamont's Barber Shop, the Thompsonville Paint Center, and the Majestic Theater (vacant since the 1930s). Notice that Asnuntuck Street was a one-way street when this photograph was taken in the 1950s.

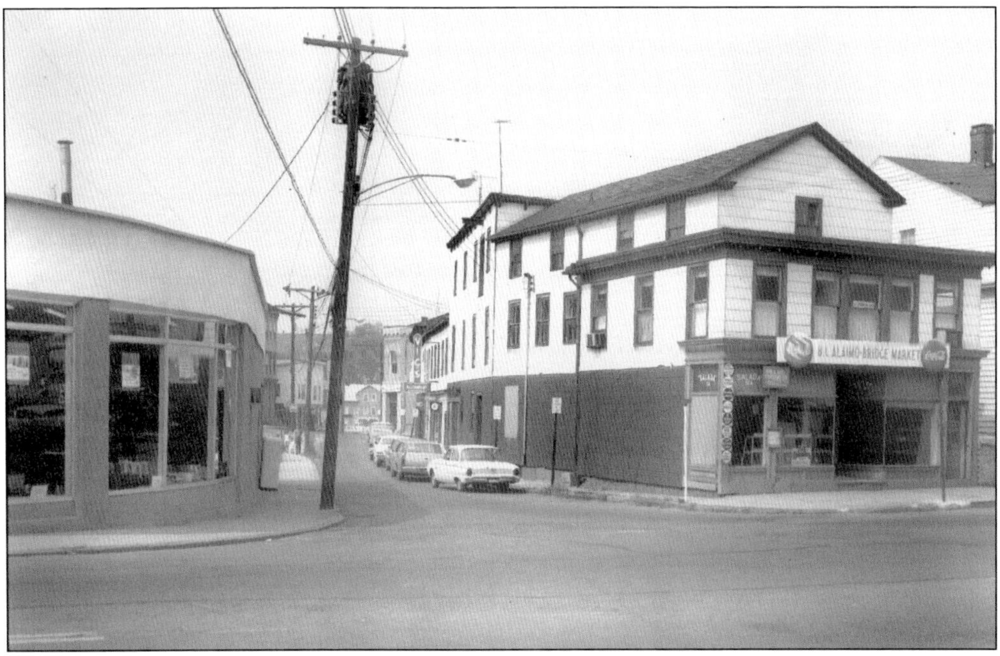

This 1960s view on Pearl and Asnuntuck Streets shows the LaRussa Appliance Store on the left, Vic's Restaurant on Asnuntuck Street, and the B.C. Alaimo-Bridge Market, owned by Benjamin H. Alaimo, on Pearl Street. All of these businesses were torn down as part of the urban renewal project in the 1970s.

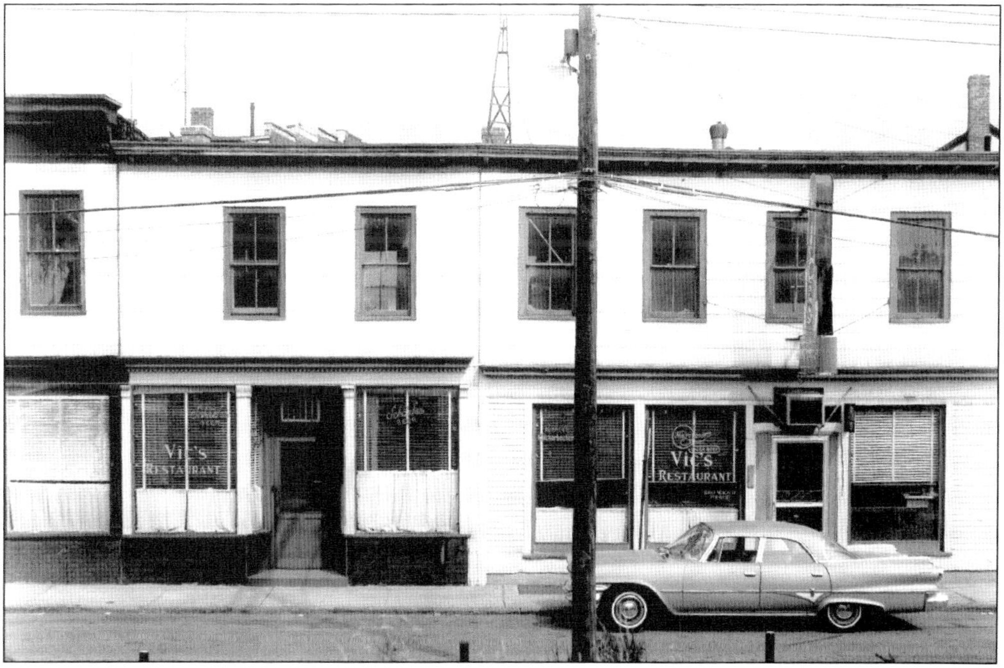

Vic's Restaurant is pictured in the 1950s. Located on Asnuntuck Street, it was owned and operated by Vic Moschetti.

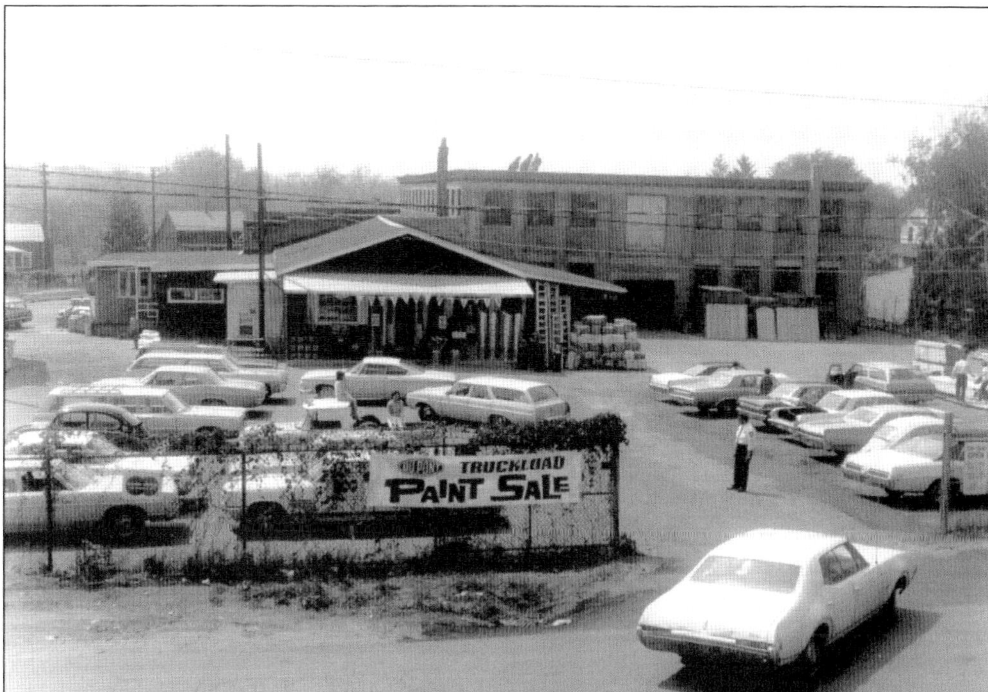

This 1960s view shows Kelly-Fradet Lumber Marts, on Prospect Street. The store was operated by Lloyd W. Fradet and Clarence "Red" Weeks. In the 1970s, Weeks took over the operation of the lumber store.

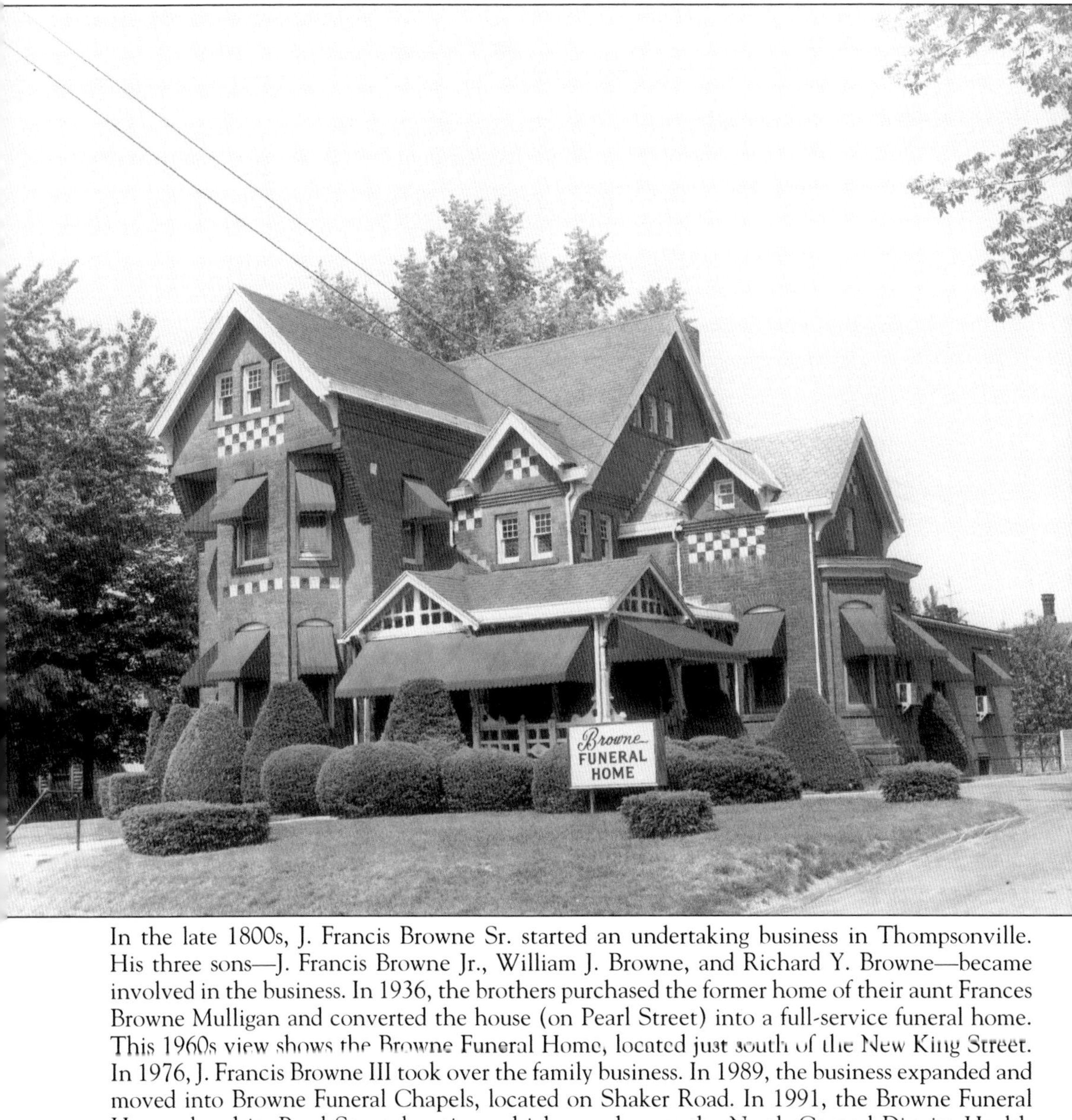

In the late 1800s, J. Francis Browne Sr. started an undertaking business in Thompsonville. His three sons—J. Francis Browne Jr., William J. Browne, and Richard Y. Browne—became involved in the business. In 1936, the brothers purchased the former home of their aunt Frances Browne Mulligan and converted the house (on Pearl Street) into a full-service funeral home. This 1960s view shows the Browne Funeral Home, located just south of the New King Street. In 1976, J. Francis Browne III took over the family business. In 1989, the business expanded and moved into Browne Funeral Chapels, located on Shaker Road. In 1991, the Browne Funeral Home closed its Pearl Street location, which now houses the North Central District Health Department.

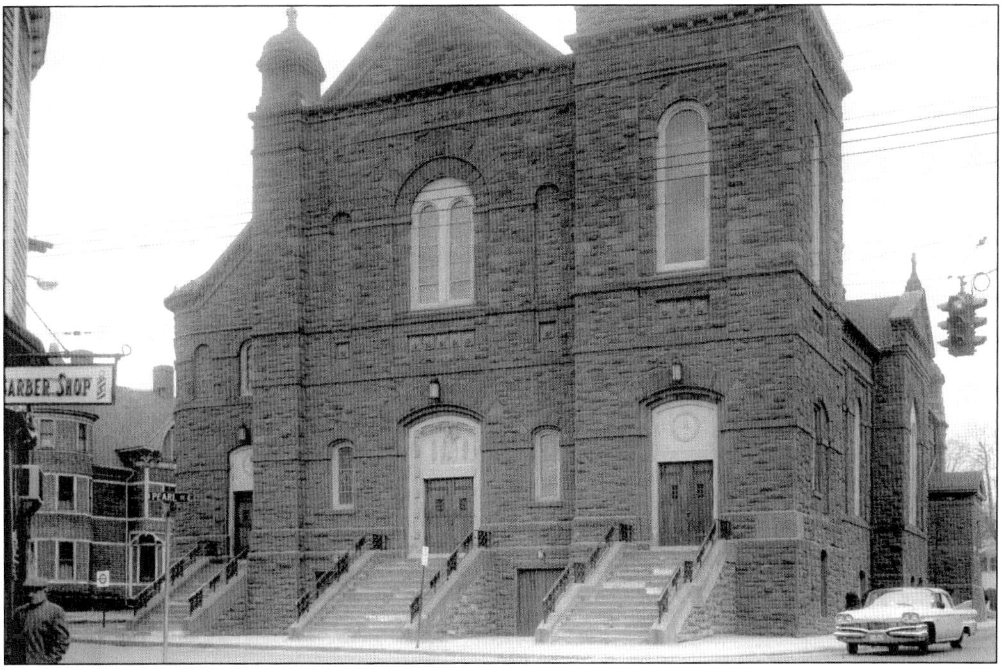

St. Patrick's Church, at the intersection of High and Pearl Streets, is pictured in the 1950s. In 1949, a fire destroyed everything except for the brownstone walls. New interior designs of the church required construction workers to replace the stained-glass window openings with brownstone. Notice the traffic signal over the busy intersection.

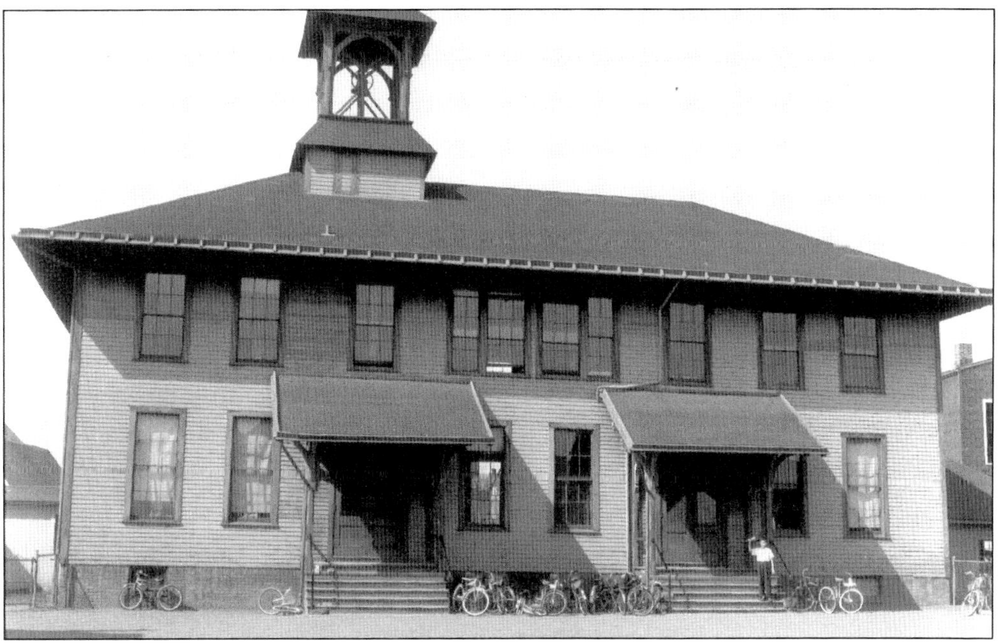

A boy rings a bell at St. Joseph's School, located on Cross Street, in the 1950s. The building became inadequate to the needs of the students and was closed in 1958. A new school building was constructed on lower Pearl Street, near the intersection of Hathaway Avenue. The new school opened in September 1958.

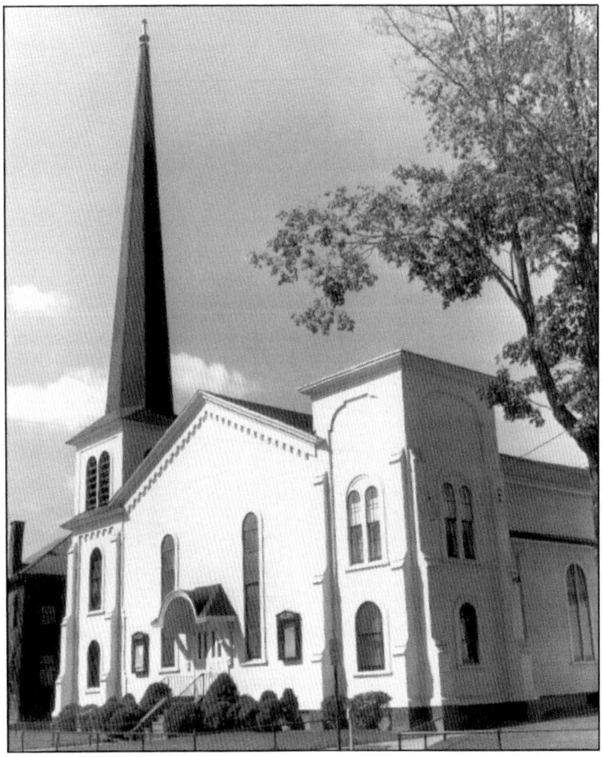

The First Presbyterian Church, at the intersection of North Main and Church Streets, is shown in the 1950s. The congregation was organized in 1839, and the church was built in 1840, with additions built in the later 1800s. By 1960, the church had fallen into disrepair, and the congregation decided to build a new church. The old building was torn down in 1967. The site is the current home to Silvia's Catering.

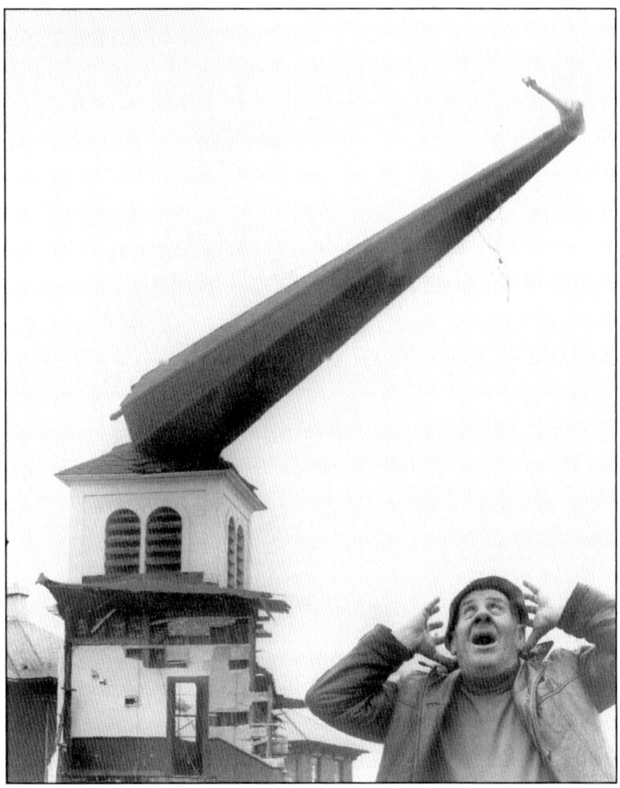

This 1967 view shows Herman Hare of the Enfield Road Construction Company in apparent fear of the falling First Presbyterian Church steeple. Hare directed a crane to pull down the steeple after previous plans to take the steeple down in sections had failed.

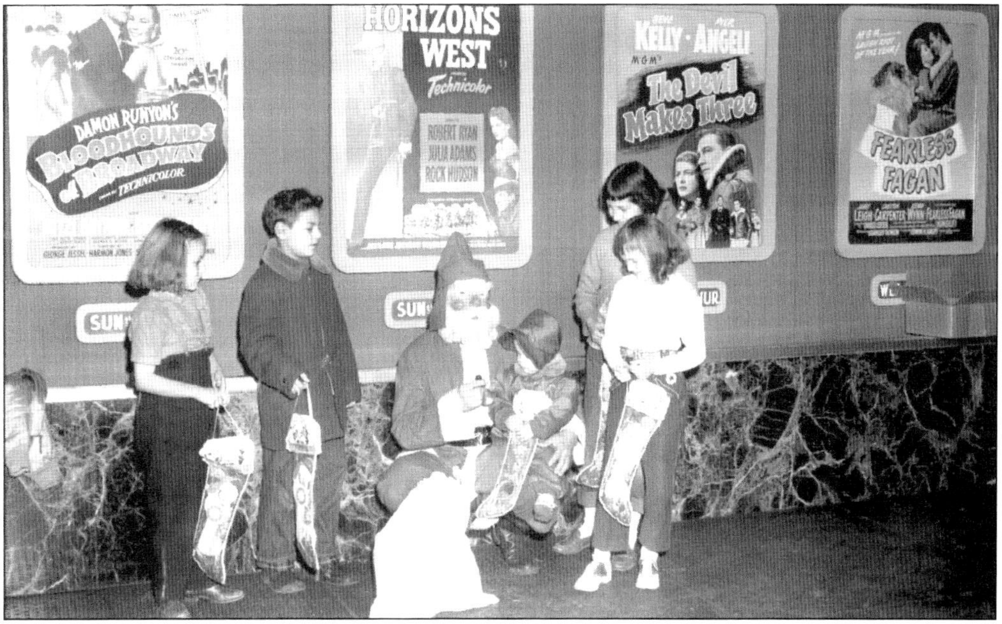

Children look on as Santa Claus listens to a little girl's Christmas wish in the Strand Theatre lobby in December 1952. The movie posters in the background feature the Hollywood stars of the 1950s.

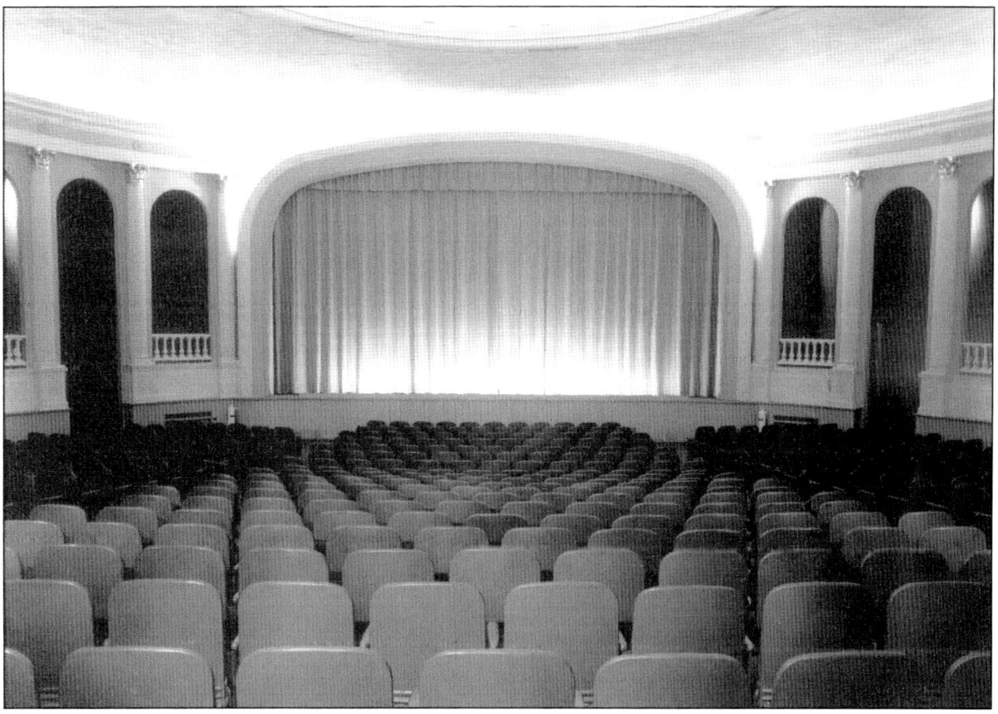

This 1960s view shows the interior of the Strand Theatre, located on North Main Street. The theater was built in 1937. It closed in the 1970s and reopened in the 1980s for a short time before it closed again. The Save Our Strand committee was formed in the 1990s to restore the theater back to its original prominence.

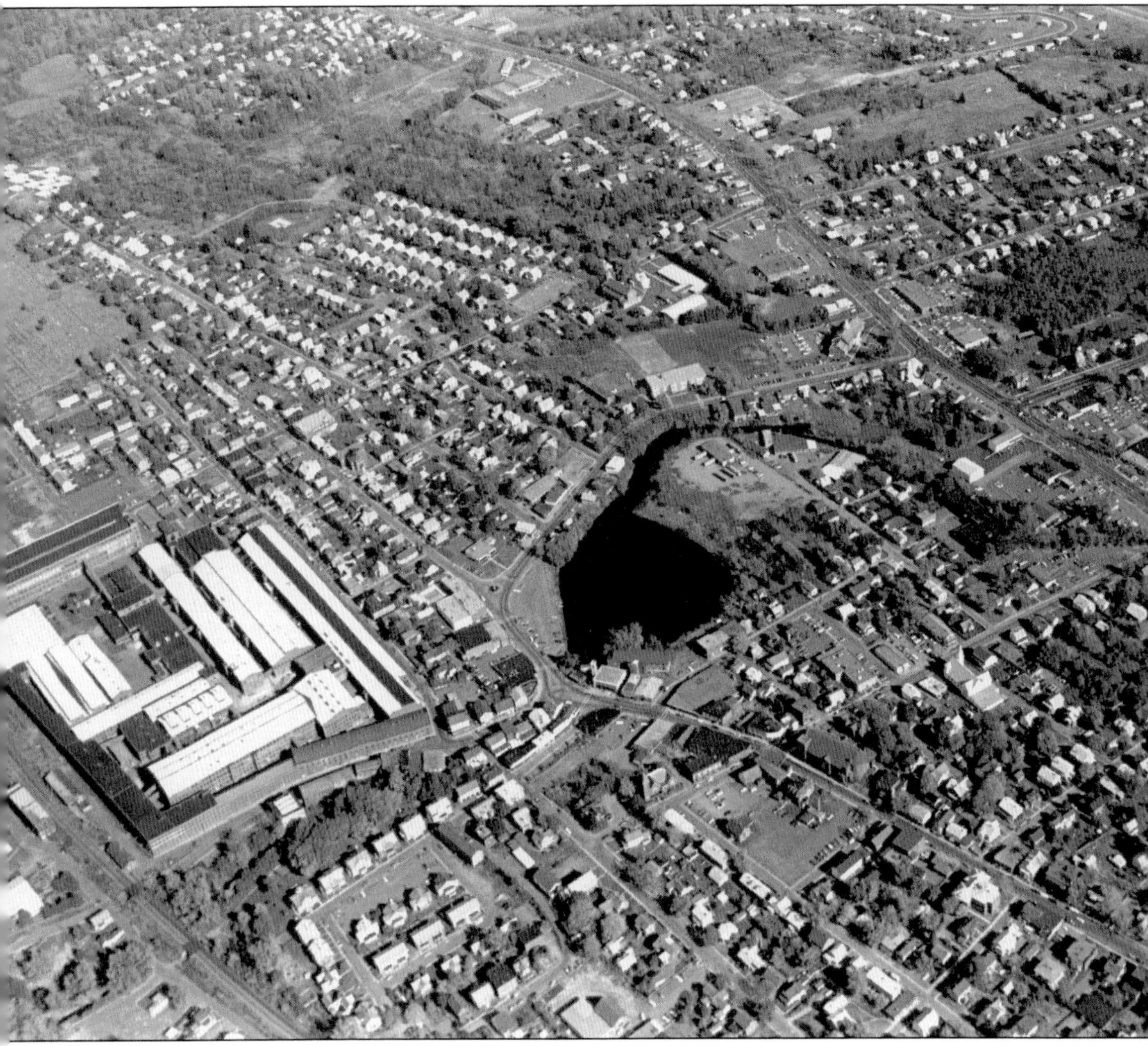

Pictured in the 1970s are the carpet plant and mill housing (left), the Freshwater Brook and Pond (center), and Enfield Street, cutting through the business district (top right). The village of Thompsonville is shown prior to the urban renewal project around Freshwater Brook and Pond. The selling of the carpet mill in 1958 and the eventual closing in 1971 led to the deterioration of buildings in Thompsonville. In addition, the closing of the Thompsonville–Suffield bridge in 1966, the construction of Interstate 91, and development of shopping malls took business away from downtown merchants. Town officials targeted Thompsonville as an urban renewal area. Businesses and homes along Freshwater Brook and Pond were torn down, but some were not replaced. North Main Street was realigned to connect to the Elm Street intersection and to enlarge the town hall green. A landscaped walkway was also constructed along Freshwater Brook and Pond. In 1979, Thompsonville received another setback when a major fire led to the razing of the Browne Building, located at the intersection of High and Pearl Streets.

Two

The Bigelow-Sanford Carpet Company

Thompsonville's carpet industry was founded by Orrin Thompson in 1828. Erastus B. Bigelow, John and Stephen Sanford, and Alvin D. Higgins were instrumental in the evolution of the Bigelow-Sanford Carpet Company as the largest and oldest carpet company in the United States in 1929. The carpet mill played an integral role in workers' lives, providing employment, housing, and leisure activities, such as sports teams and craft clubs. The carpet mill employed thousands of people in Thompsonville through the mid-1950s. Many labor strikes took place in the early 1900s—a contributing factor for Bigelow officials to move production south by the late 1950s. The carpet company closed its doors in 1971.

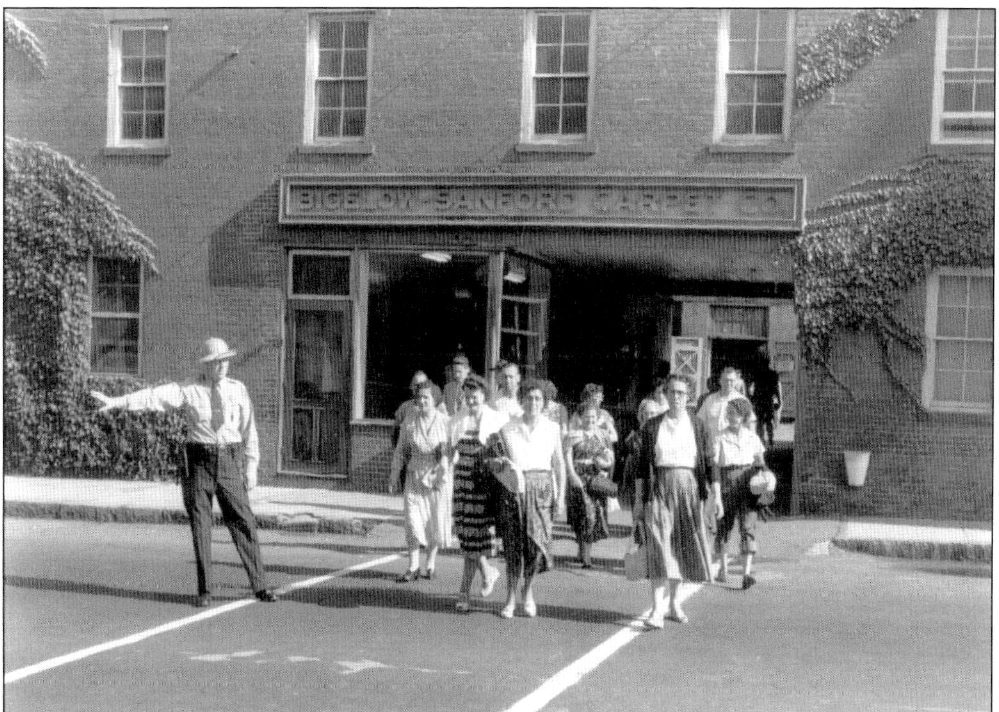

Bigelow security guard Thomas P. Quinlan halts traffic to allow employees to leave the main entrance of the Bigelow-Sanford Carpet Company, located on Main Street (state Route 190), in 1956. In the 1950s, Main Street was a busy thoroughfare. Route 190 made its way through the center of Thompsonville, past the carpet mill on Main Street, and over the Thompsonville–Suffield bridge to Suffield.

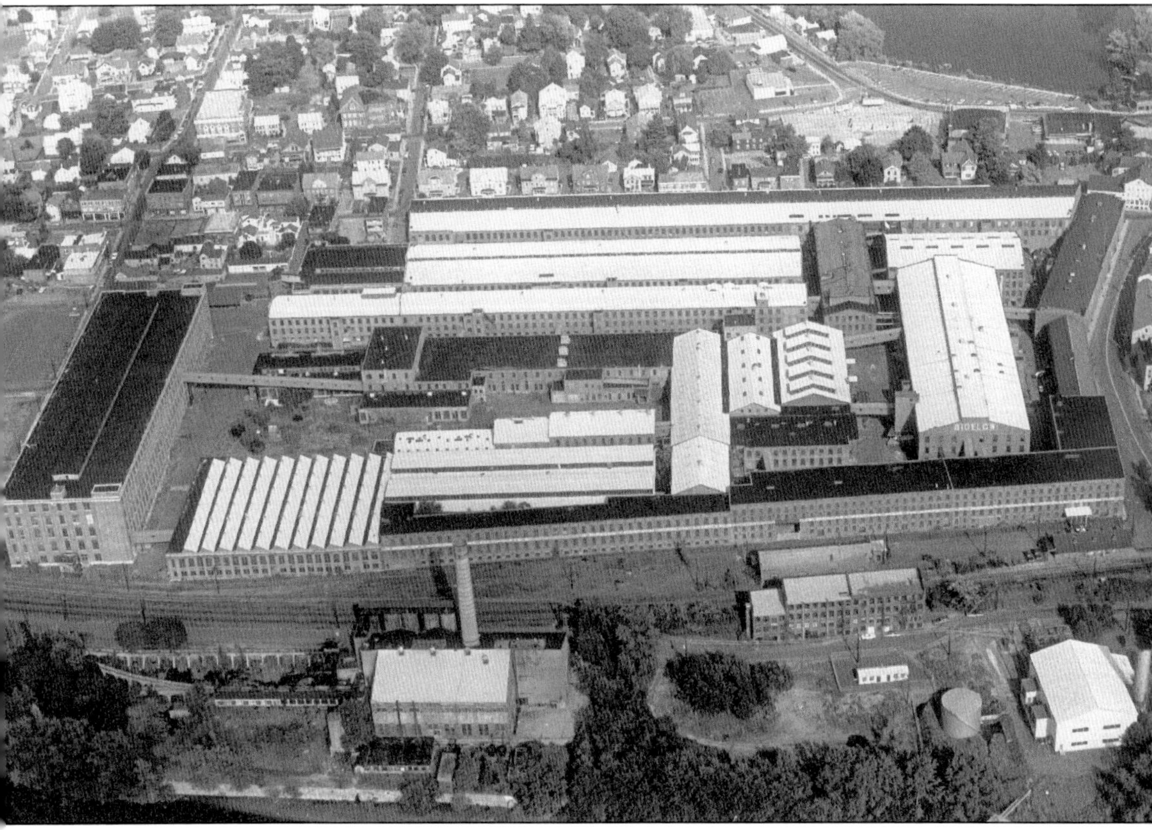

Looking east, this 1974 aerial view shows the former Bigelow-Sanford Carpet Company and the surrounding Thompsonville neighborhood. The 26-acre mill site was leased to numerous companies before falling into disrepair in the 1980s. More than half of the buildings were taken down in the 1980s to make room for a $65 million transformation of the former mill to luxury apartments. The John M. Corcoran Company restored six buildings, housing 471 apartments, a health club, an indoor swimming pool, and office space.

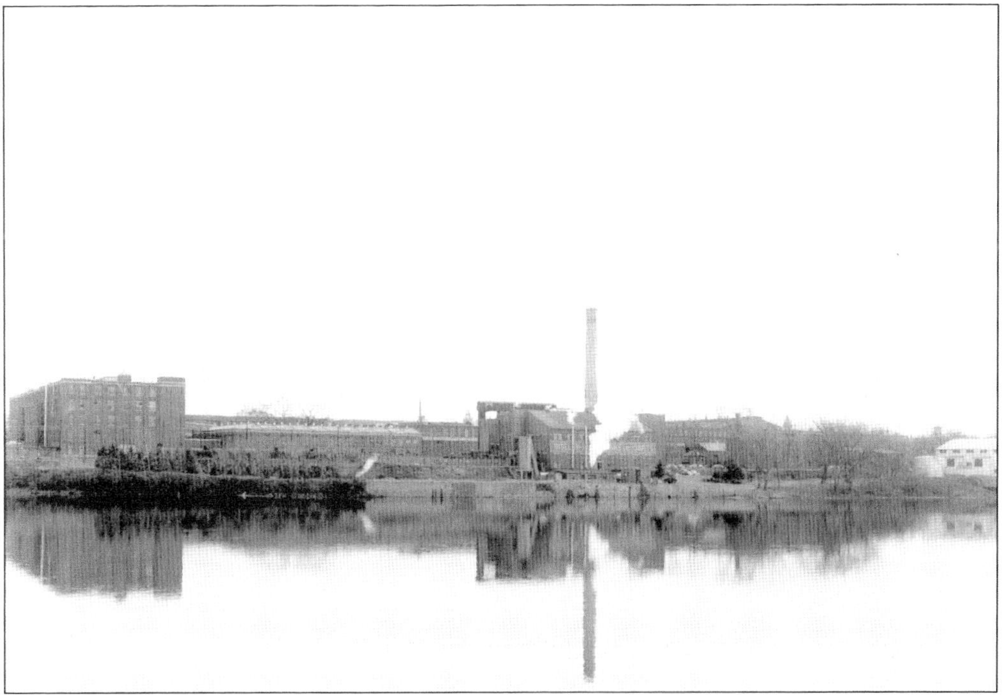

The Bigelow-Sanford Carpet Company created a mirror image on the Connecticut River in the 1950s. The photograph was taken near the banks of the Connecticut River in Suffield.

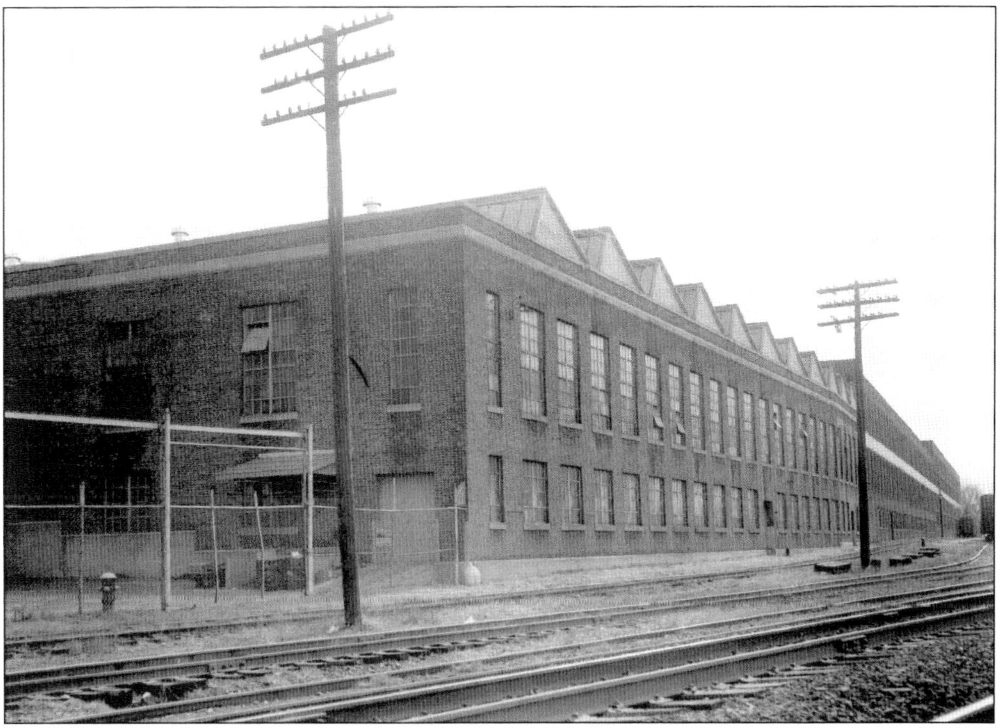

This 1950s view, looking south, shows the railroad tracks next to the Jacquard building, nicknamed the "Sawtooth Building" because of the sawlike roofline.

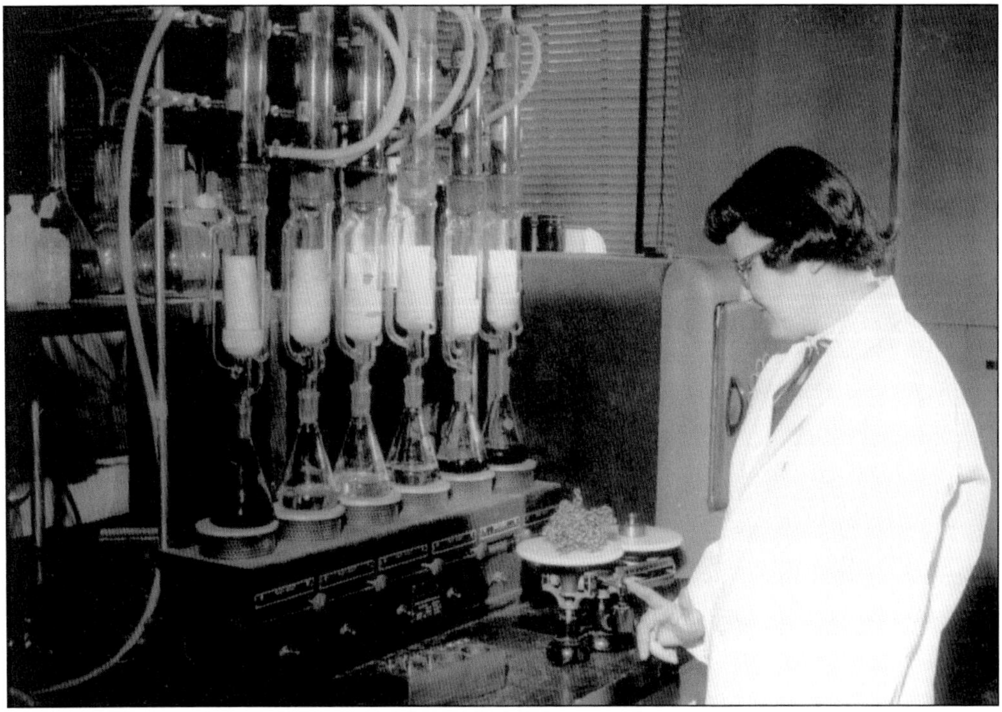

Theresa Proux is shown in a modern quality-control laboratory in 1956. Bigelow laboratory technicians completed a variety of experiments on wool and yarn.

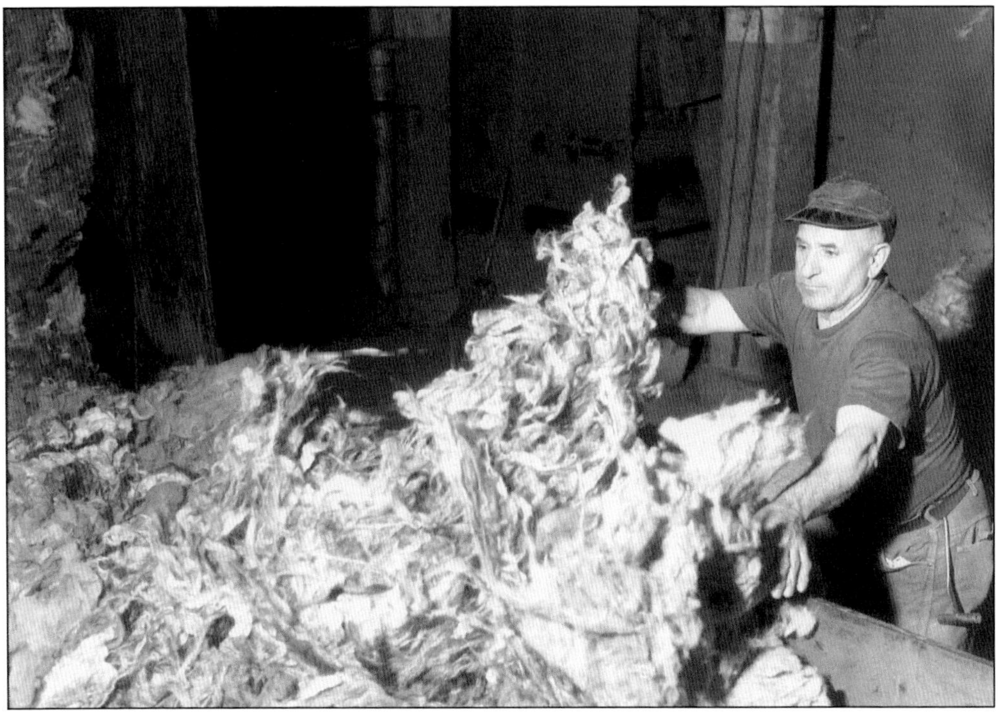

Jack Lorino pulls apart the wool to rid it from any foreign matter before it is transferred to a scouring bath in 1956. This initial step started the rug-making process at the carpet mill.

Sam Misuraca operates a baling machine in this 1956 photograph. After the wool was cleaned and dried, it was transferred to storage bins until it was needed.

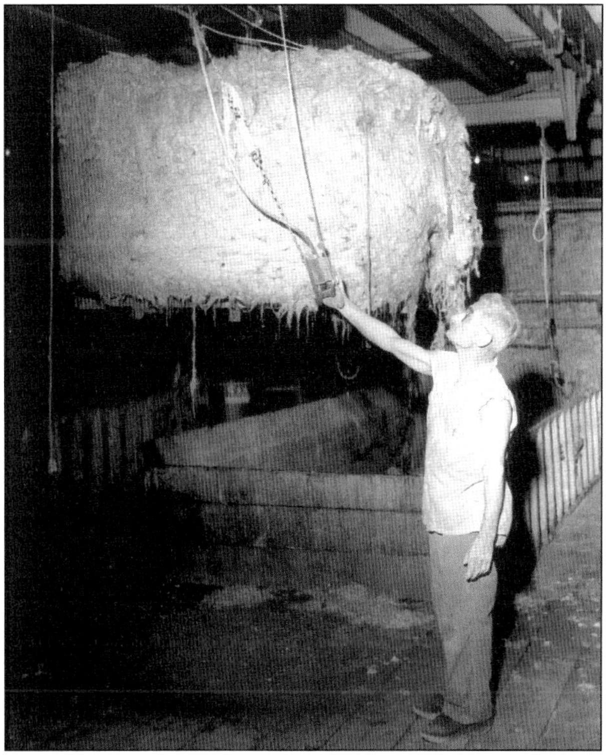

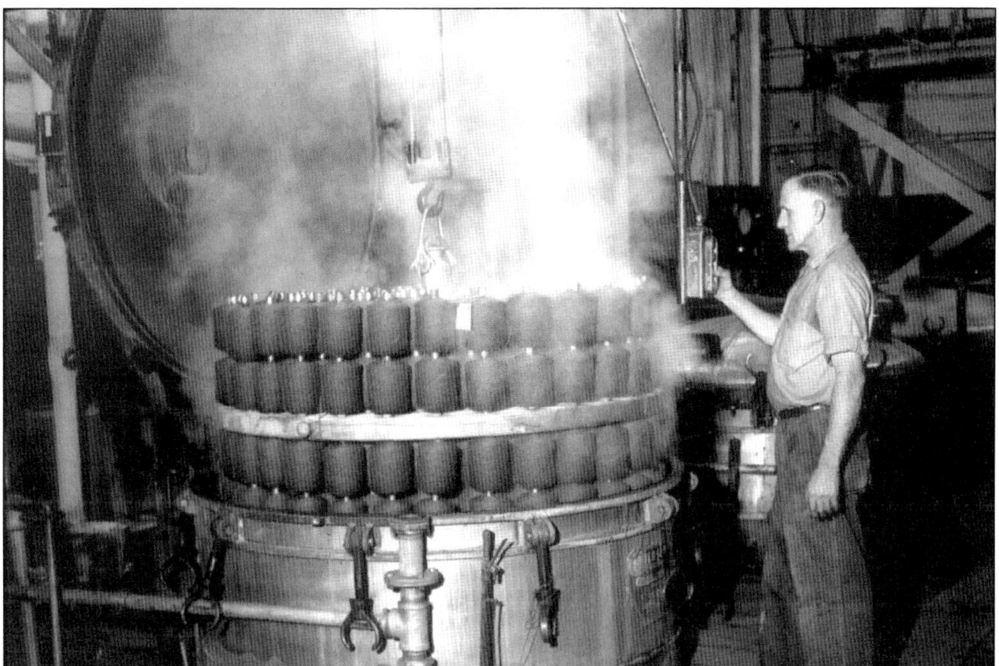

Arthur Putnam raises a huge batch of dyed yarn from a vat dyeing machine in 1956. Bigelow dyed more than 4,000 hues to use in its carpets. The dye house was one of the buildings restored for luxury apartments at the Bigelow Commons.

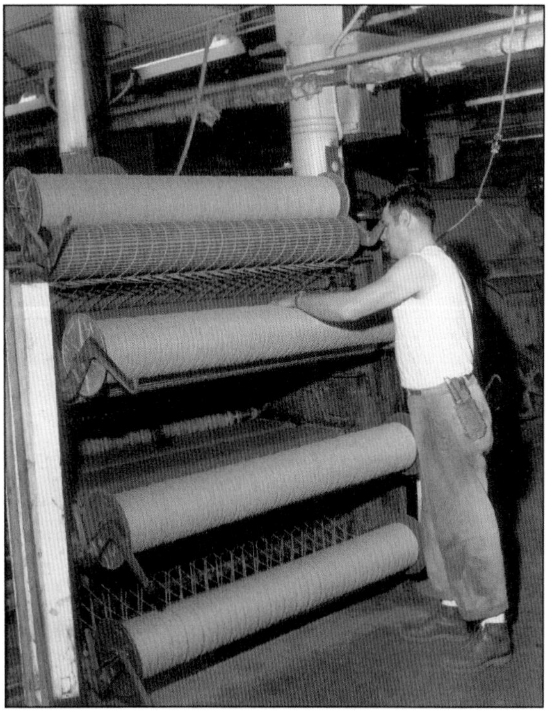

Fred Middlebrook is shown operating a carding machine in 1956. Carding separated the wool and prepared the wool for spinning.

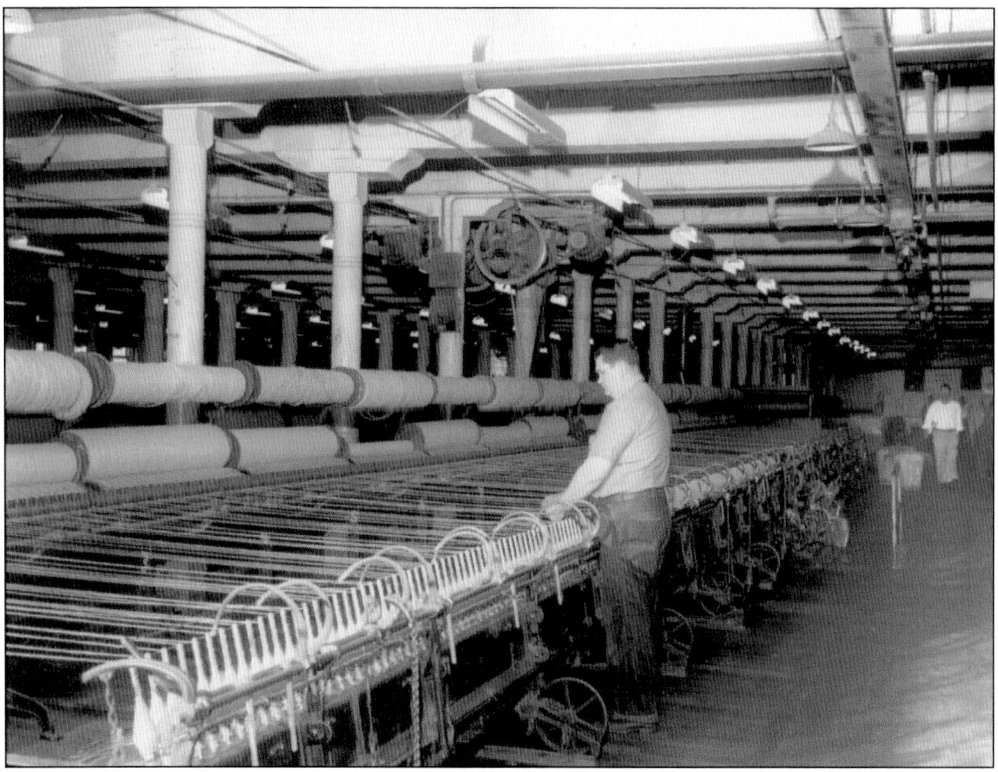

This 1956 view shows Albert Weller working on a mule spinning machine. In this process, the operator stretches the loose wool while bobbins twist it into yarn.

Josephine Dunaj operates a twisting frame in 1956. This operation added strength to the yarn and also combined two or more strands of yarn at a time.

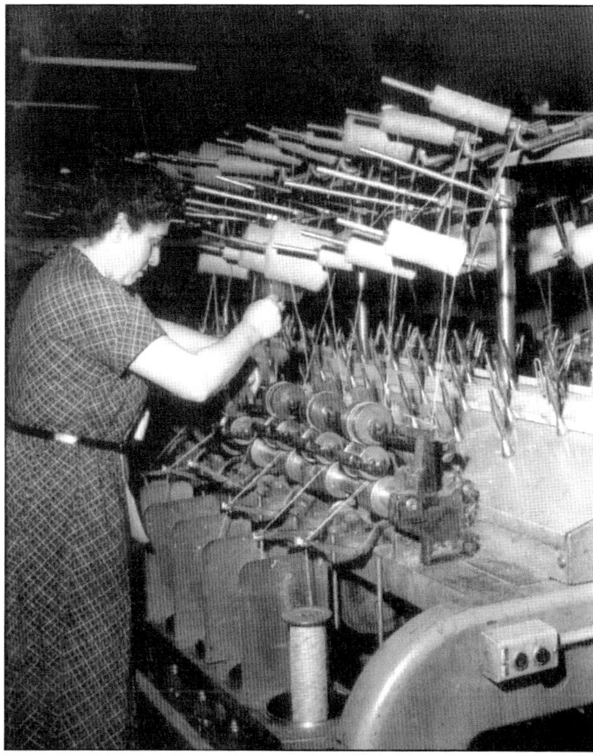

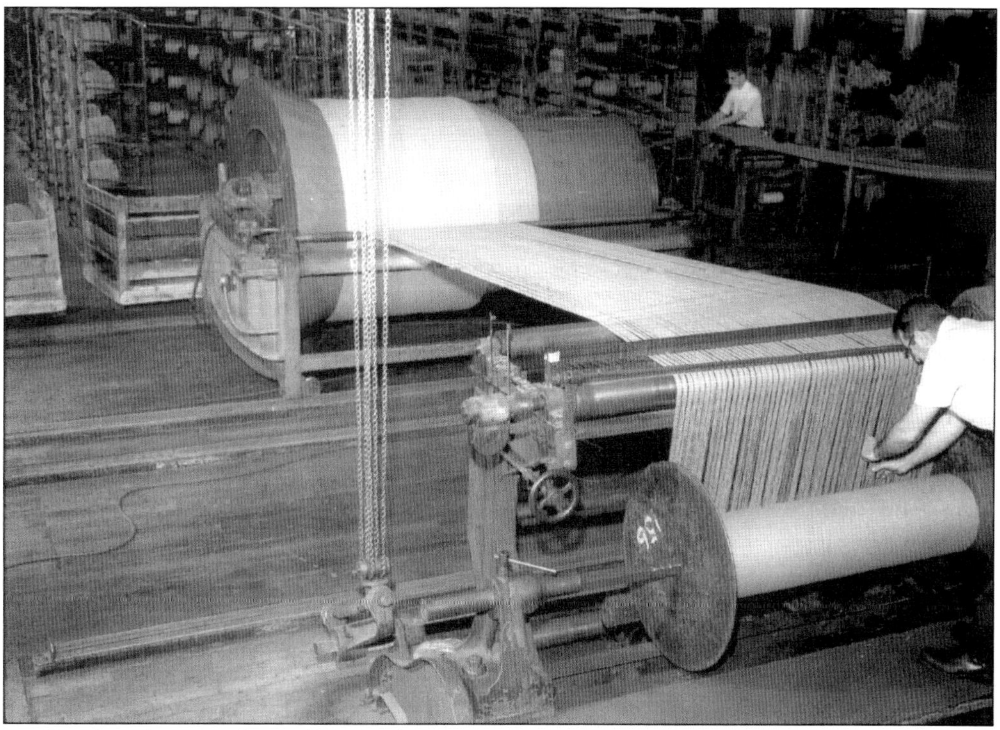

Joe Buczkowski rewinds smaller spools of yarn for the velvet loom onto larger spools to give them an even tension in 1956. Pete Bellico is in the background.

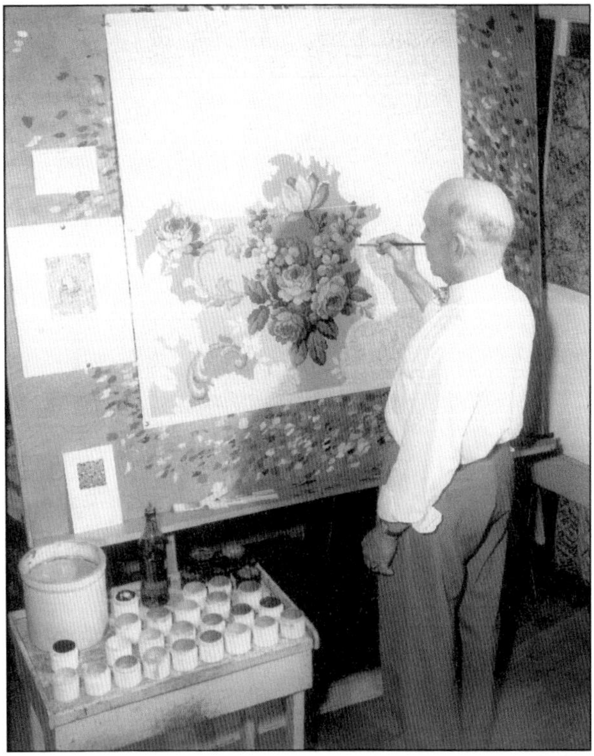

Henry Landry, a veteran master designer, is shown painting a carpet design in 1956.

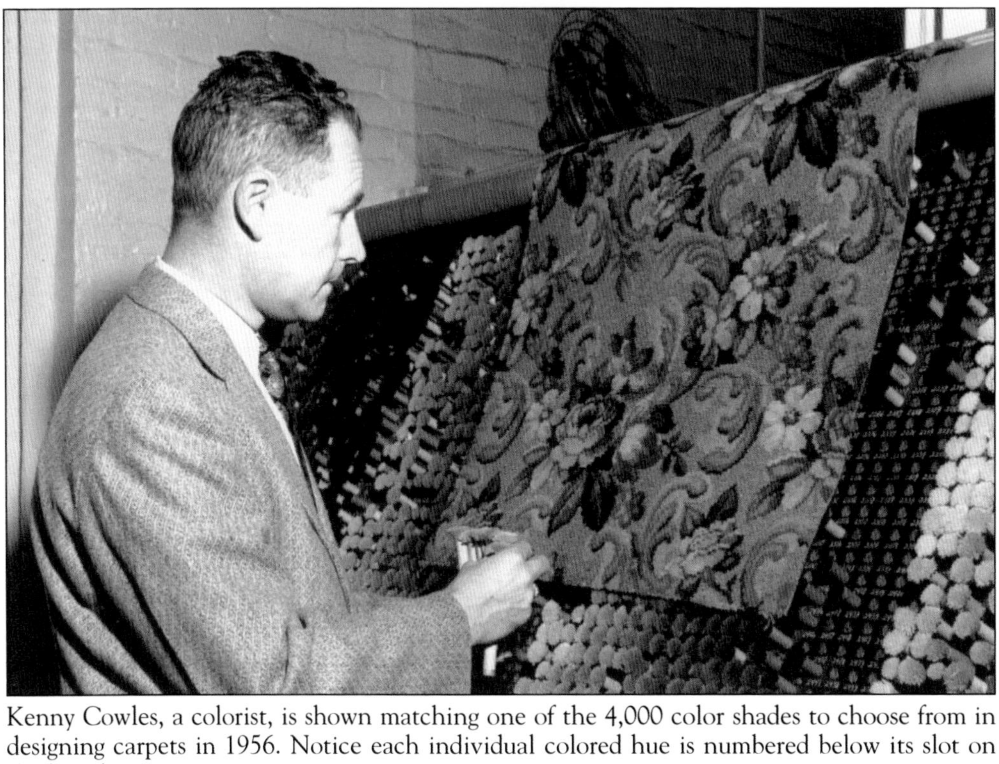

Kenny Cowles, a colorist, is shown matching one of the 4,000 color shades to choose from in designing carpets in 1956. Notice each individual colored hue is numbered below its slot on the board.

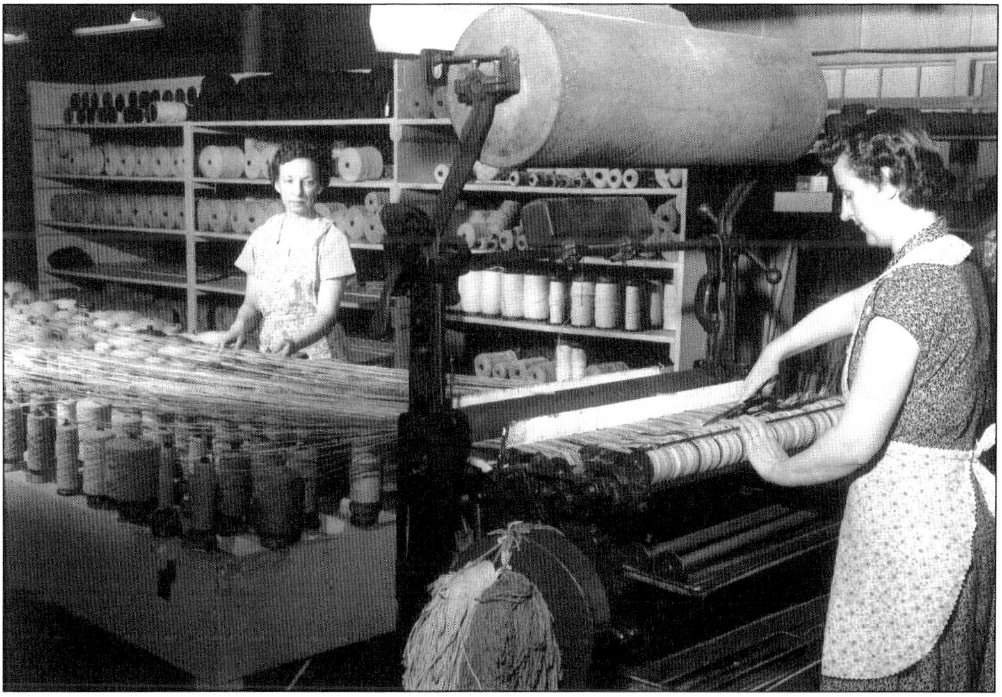

Freida (left) and Rosalie Prayzner are shown arranging colored yarns, which will set the pattern of an Axminster carpet in 1956. The co-workers were also sisters-in-law.

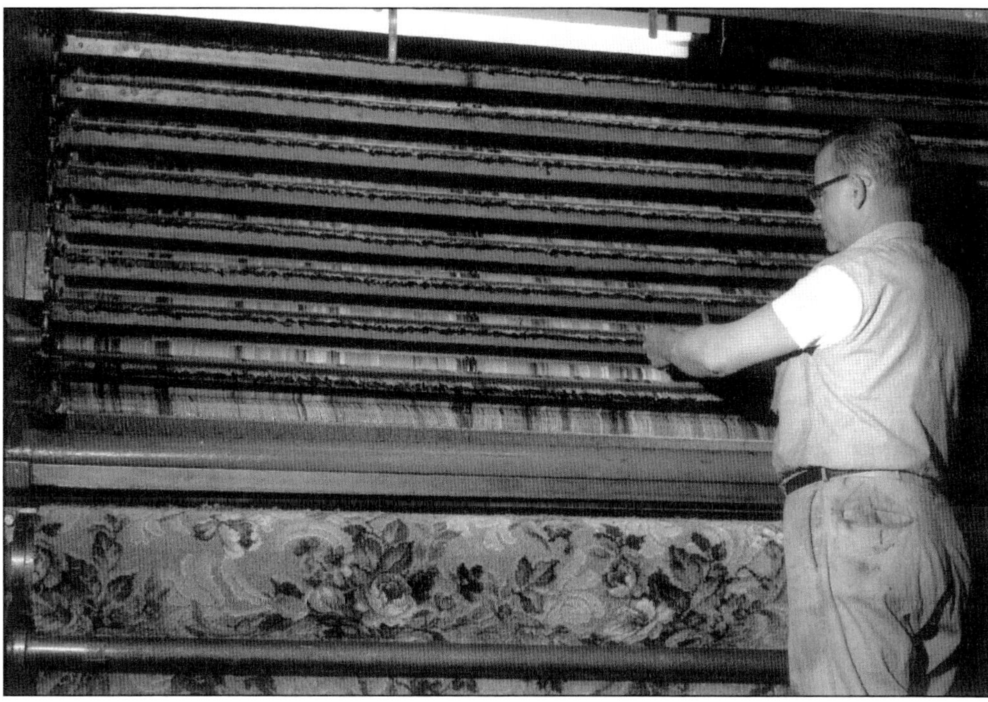

Teofile Marut operates an Axminster loom in 1956. The Axminster carpet design is closely related to Oriental carpets but costs a fraction of the price. The Axminster building was one of the buildings restored for luxury apartments at the Bigelow Commons.

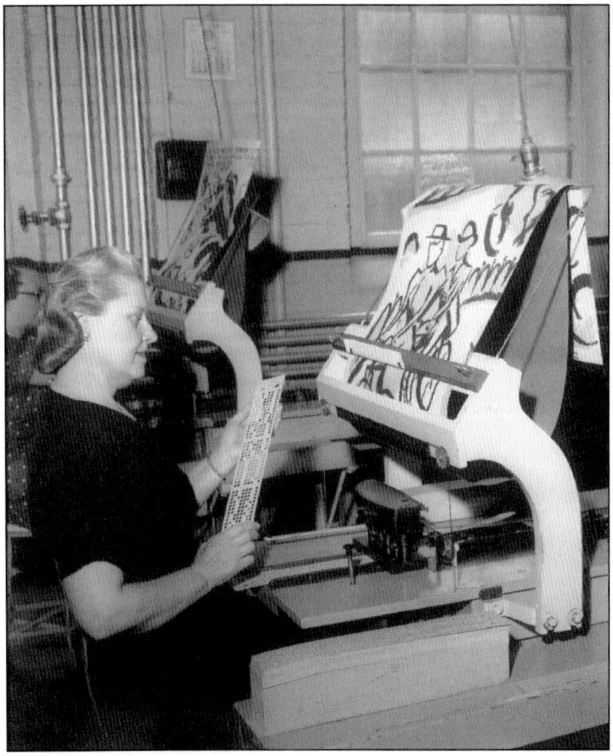

Catherine Kvajauskas, a Jacquard card cutter, translates the color rows in the design to perforated cards in 1956. The Jacquard building was one of the buildings restored for office space at the Bigelow Commons complex.

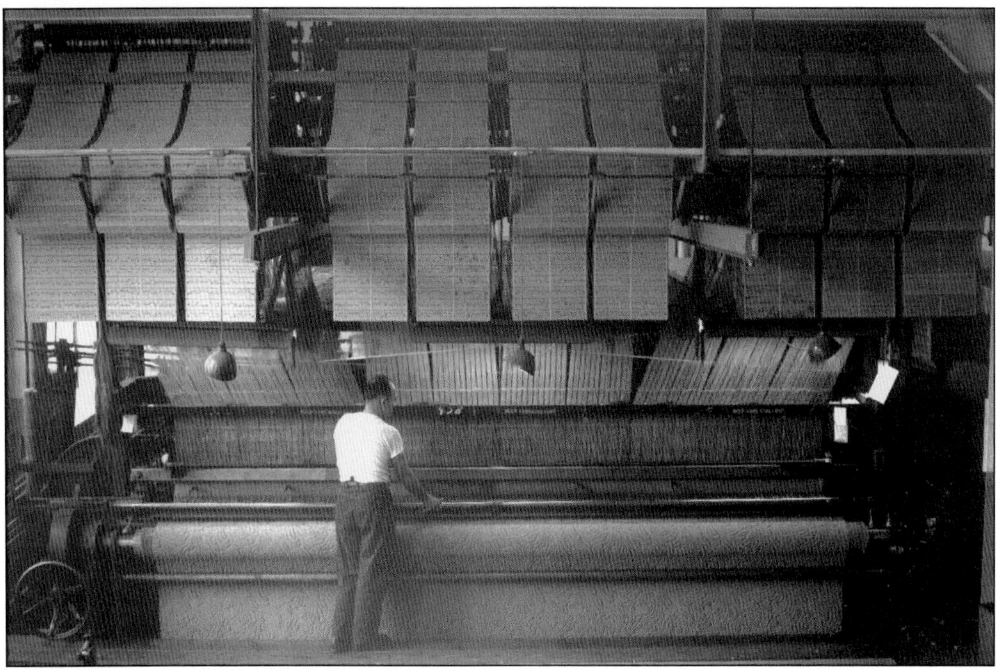

Theodore Kula Sr., a Jacquard weaver, operates a Jacquard loom in 1956. The loom was controlled by punch cards that allowed certain colored strands of yarn into the carpet design. The Jacquard design was featured in high-quality carpets that were installed at some of the best hotels in the United States.

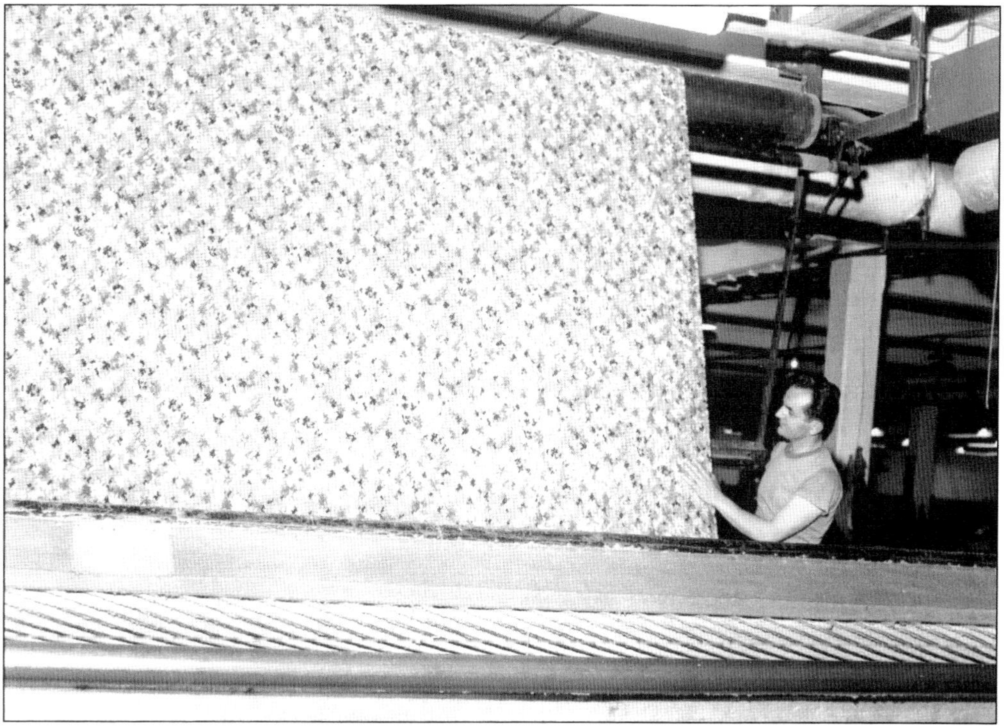

Henry Paolini, a shearing operator, is shown cutting the pile height of a completed carpet in 1956.

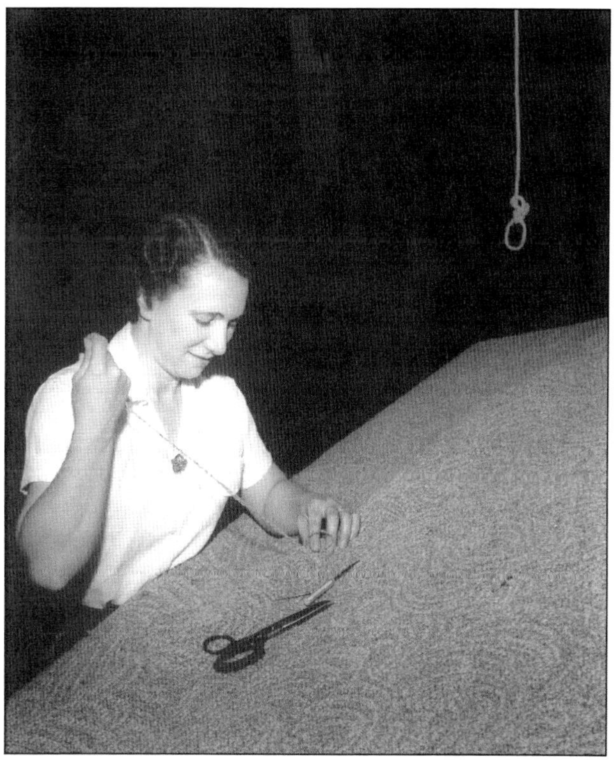

Mary Kelly, a rug inspector, removes a loose strand from a carpet in 1956. Rug inspection was the last operation in the carpet-making process before shipment. The Bigelow-Sanford Carpet Company had 25 district offices from coast to coast.

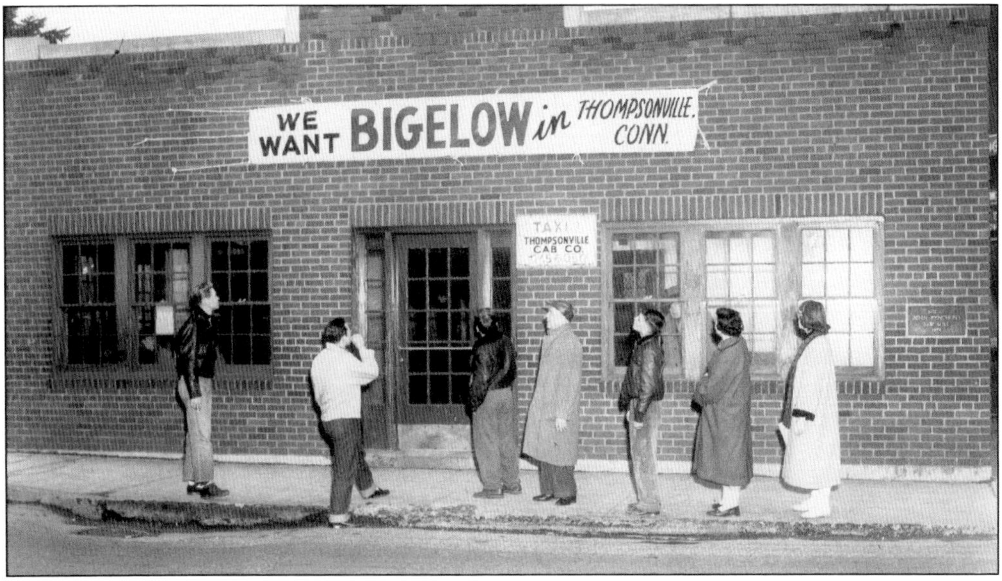

Thompsonville residents look up at the banner on the Thompsonville bus station in disbelief at the possibility of Bigelow leaving town in the 1950s. The concerns of the residents became a reality. By the late 1950s, Bigelow officials moved production down south. The carpet company closed its doors in 1971. The bus station was torn down as part of urban renewal in the 1970s. The site now serves as a viewing area of the Freshwater Pond dam area.

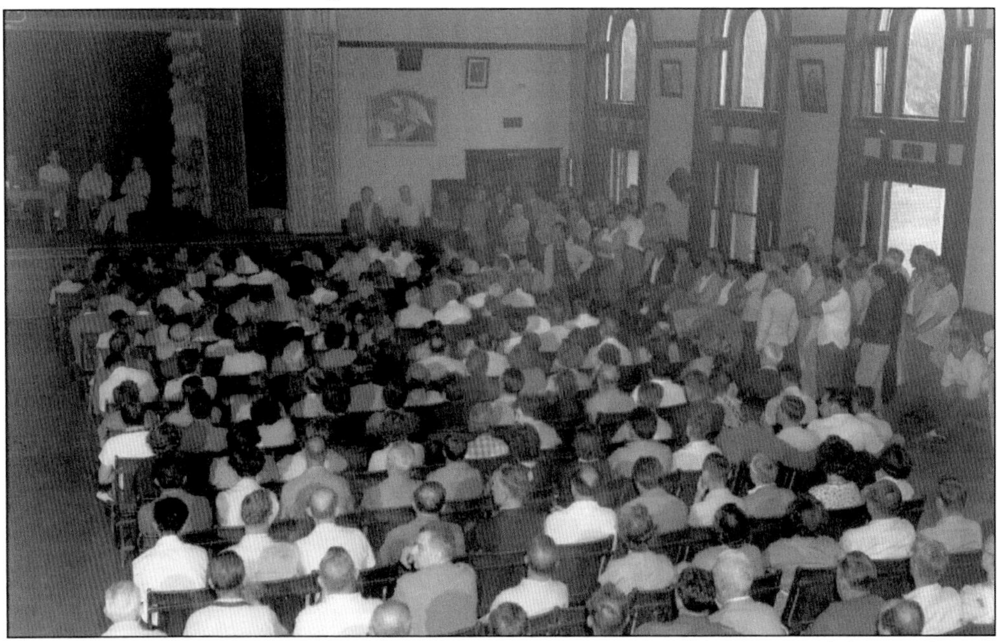

This August 1954 view shows Bigelow-Sanford Carpet Company employees of the Local 2188 Textile Workers Union of America, CIO, at a strike meeting held at the Polish National Home, located at the intersection of Alden Avenue and Church Street. A walkout by Jacquard workers was caused by disciplinary action by a Jacquard superintendent against a veteran Jacquard weaver. Five days later, the manufacturing of carpets came to a complete halt when other departments also staged a walkout to show solidarity.

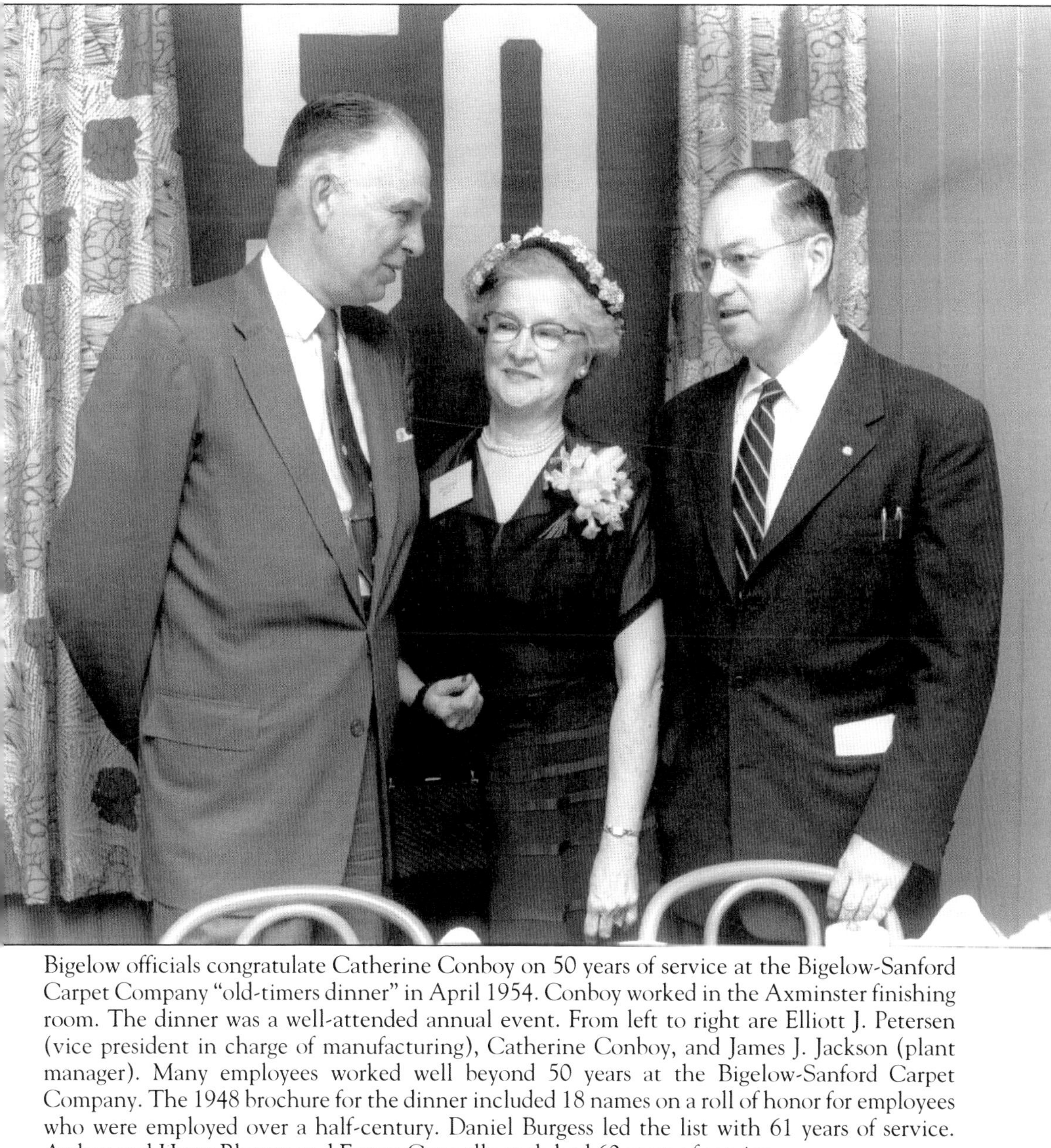

Bigelow officials congratulate Catherine Conboy on 50 years of service at the Bigelow-Sanford Carpet Company "old-timers dinner" in April 1954. Conboy worked in the Axminster finishing room. The dinner was a well-attended annual event. From left to right are Elliott J. Petersen (vice president in charge of manufacturing), Catherine Conboy, and James J. Jackson (plant manager). Many employees worked well beyond 50 years at the Bigelow-Sanford Carpet Company. The 1948 brochure for the dinner included 18 names on a roll of honor for employees who were employed over a half-century. Daniel Burgess led the list with 61 years of service. Arthur and Harry Blowen and Emma Connelly each had 60 years of service.

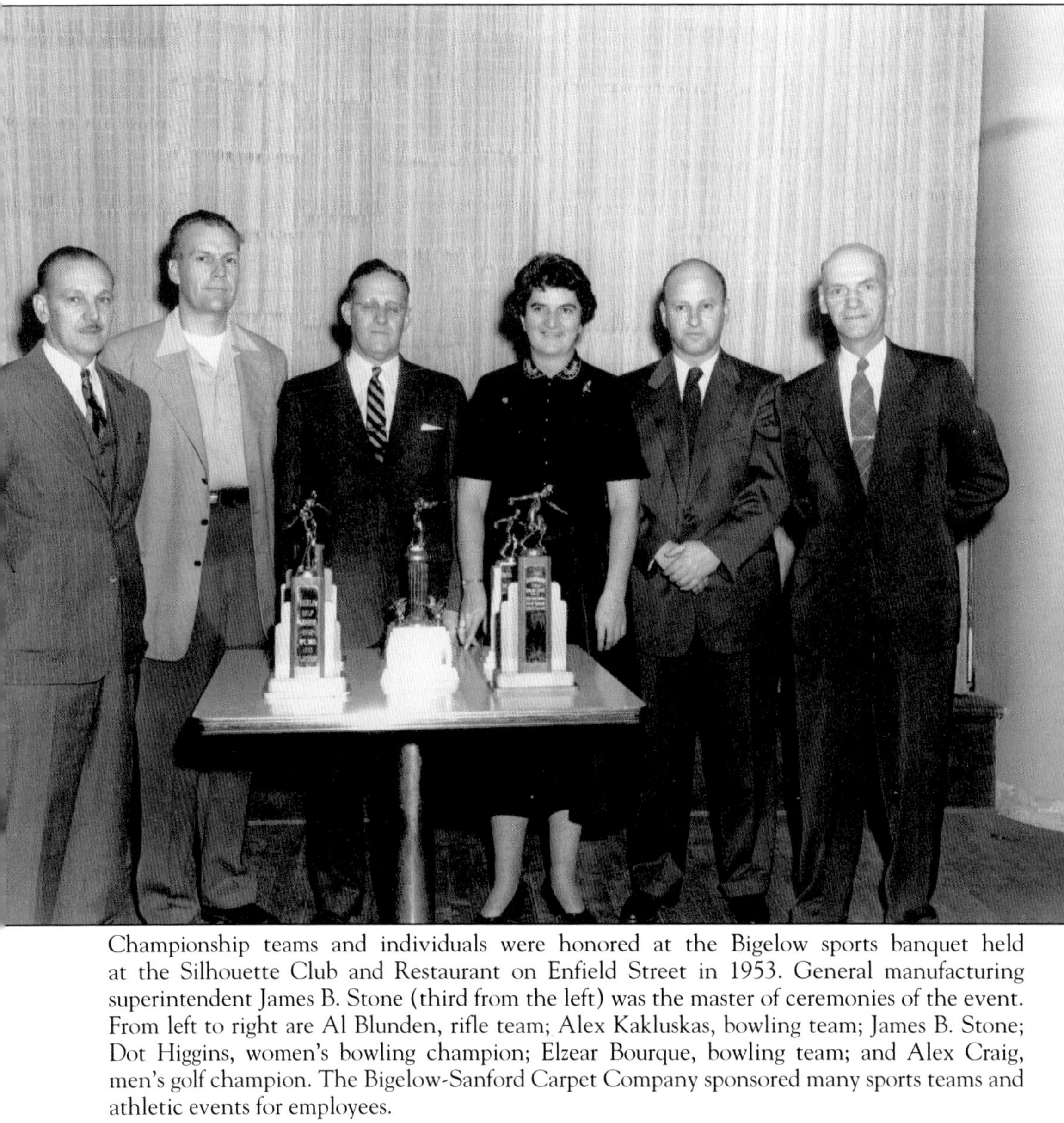

Championship teams and individuals were honored at the Bigelow sports banquet held at the Silhouette Club and Restaurant on Enfield Street in 1953. General manufacturing superintendent James B. Stone (third from the left) was the master of ceremonies of the event. From left to right are Al Blunden, rifle team; Alex Kakluskas, bowling team; James B. Stone; Dot Higgins, women's bowling champion; Elzear Bourque, bowling team; and Alex Craig, men's golf champion. The Bigelow-Sanford Carpet Company sponsored many sports teams and athletic events for employees.

Three

THE 1955 FLOOD

In August 1955, Edward J. Malley Jr. recorded the destructive forces of Hurricane Diane. During a 24-hour period between August 18 and 19, some 19 inches of rain fell on downtown Thompsonville. The flood resulted from a combination of the volume and duration of precipitation. Another cause of the flood was the building of the parking lot on North Main Street near Freshwater Pond, which lowered the height of the bank and increased the water runoff onto Asnuntuck, Main, North Main, and Pearl Streets. The damage exceeded $1 million in Thompsonville. There was no loss of life in Enfield. The rest of the state did not fare that well; 87 deaths occurred throughout the state.

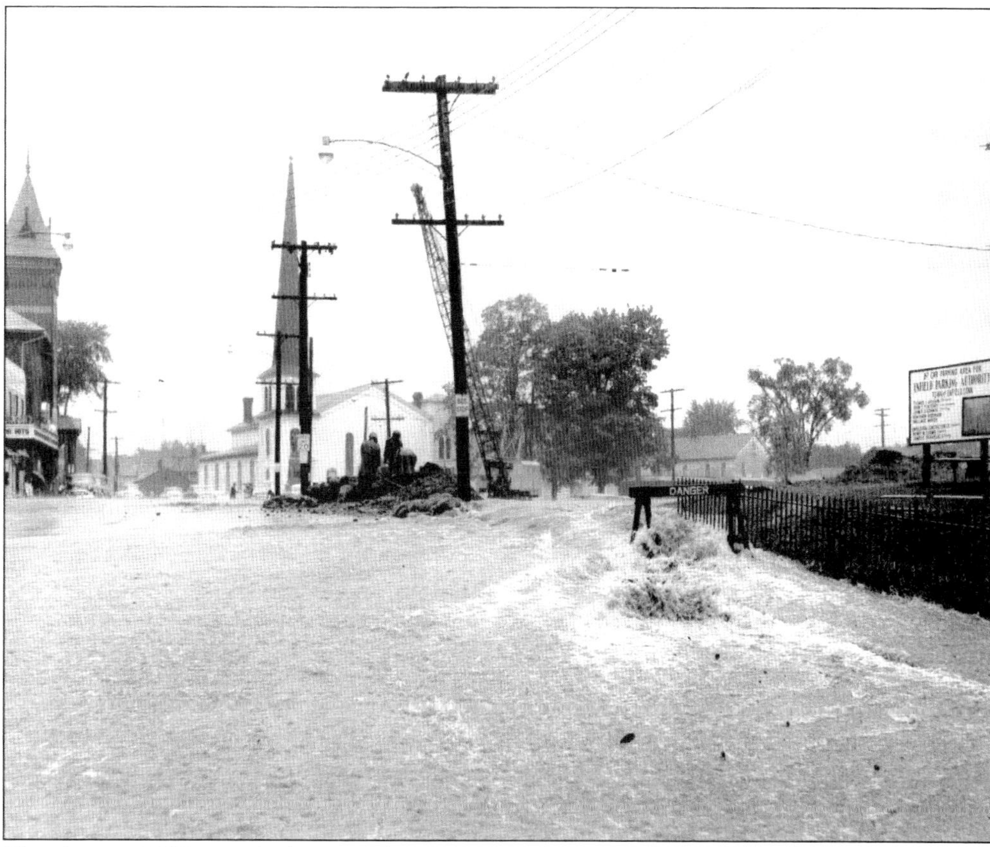

This August 1955 view, looking north on North Main Street, shows Enfield Road Construction Company workers trying to build a barrier along the construction site of the new municipal parking lot along North Main Street. The workers' efforts became fruitless against the torrents of water. Five hundred yards of fill were washed away from the parking lot. The floodwaters are shown raging down North Main Street.

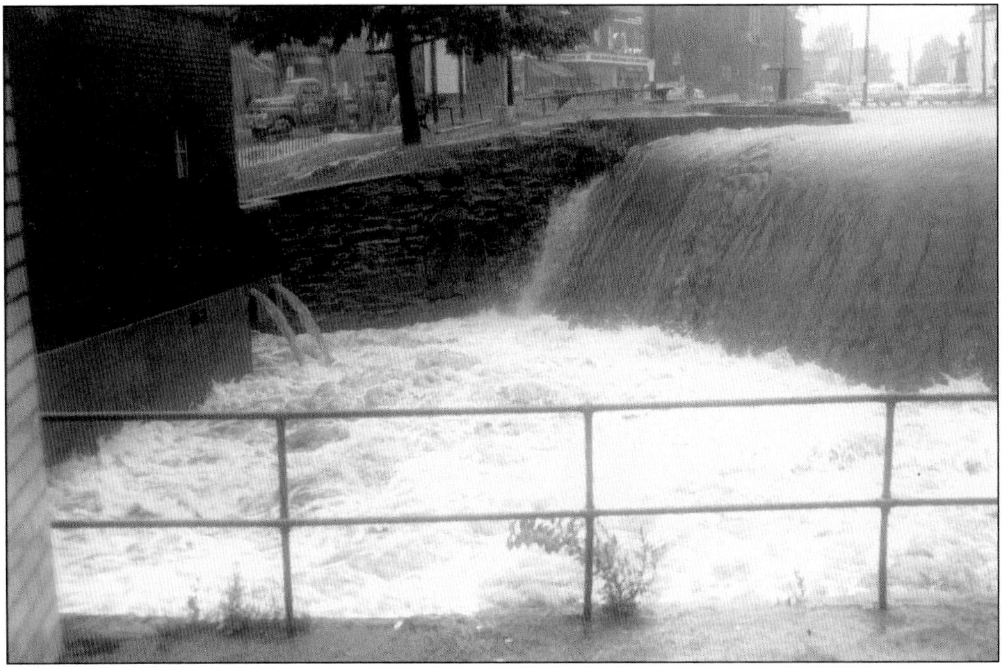

Taken from behind the Thompsonville Fire Department, this photograph shows Freshwater Pond waters cascading over the dam behind the Thompsonville bus station. The Strand Theatre and the courthouse building are in the background.

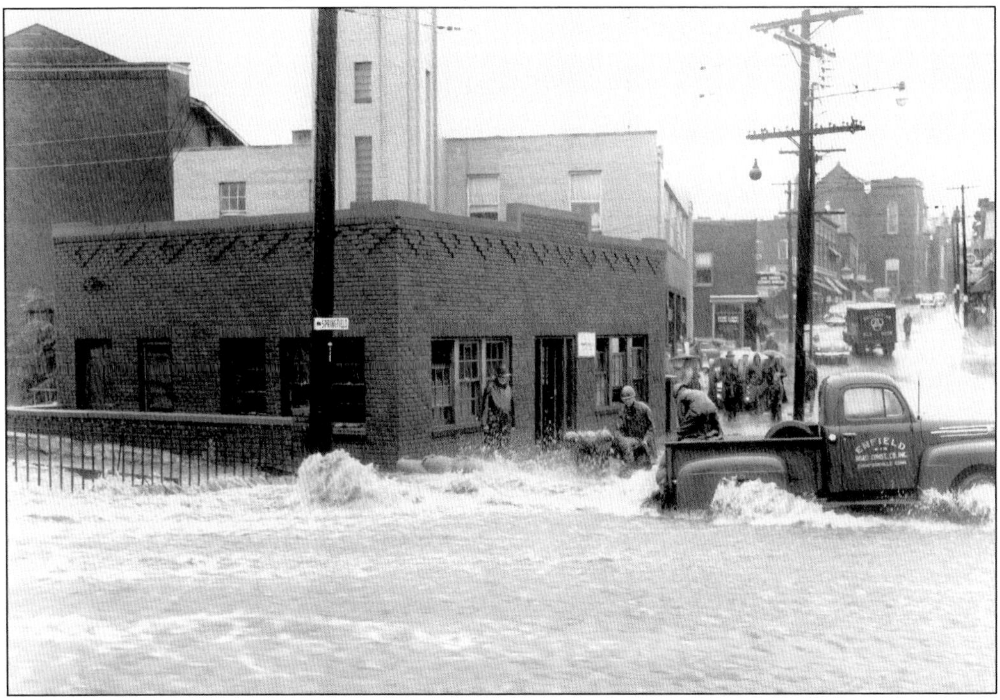

Enfield Road Construction Company workers grab sandbags from the company truck to divert the overflow of water from Freshwater Pond away from the bus station in 1955. Concerned Thompsonville residents in front of the Thompsonville Fire Department look on in disbelief.

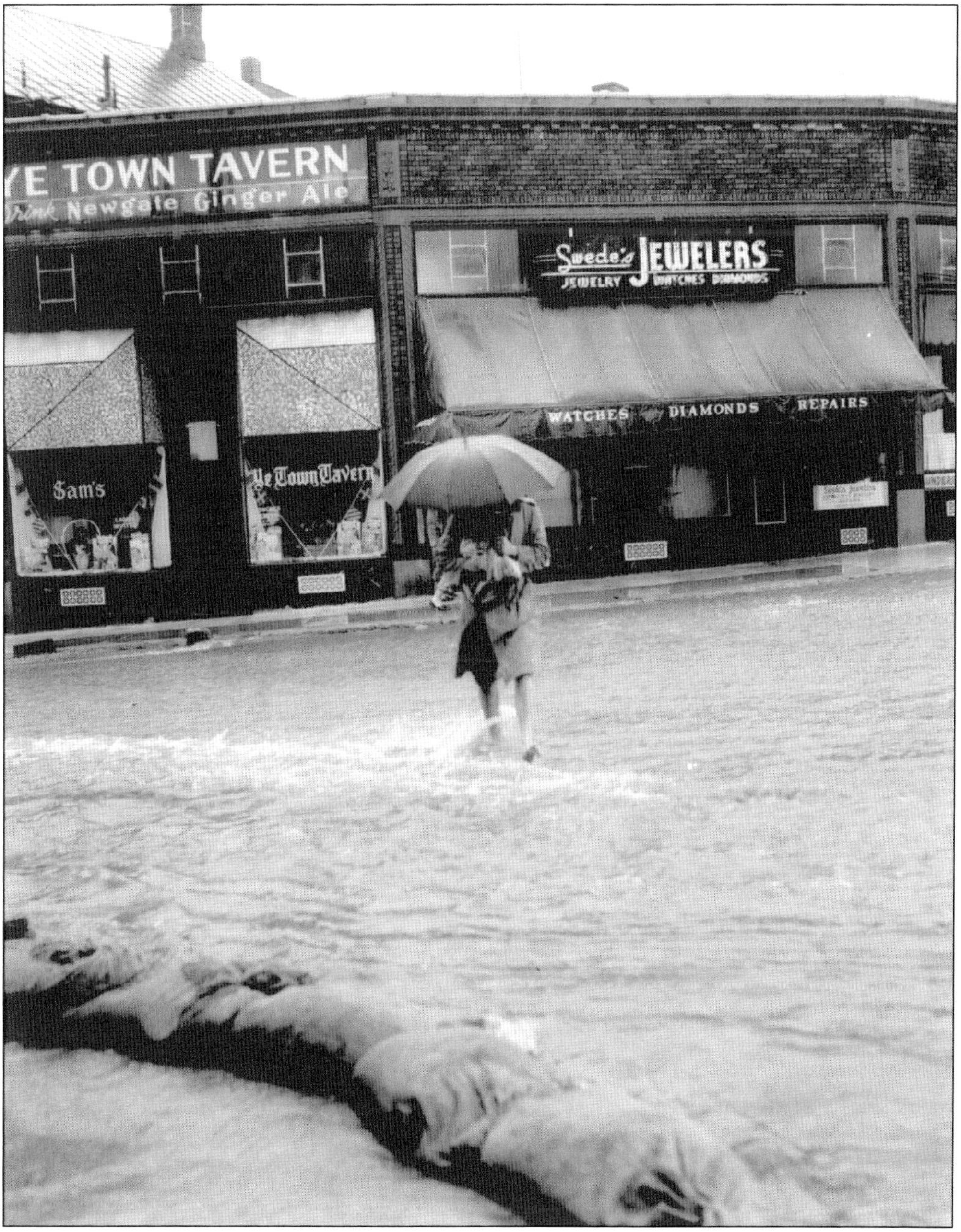

Floodwaters pass by the Ye Town Tavern and Swede's Jewelers while an unidentified woman receives a foot bath as she makes her way around a sandbagged Main Street on August 19, 1955. The Ye Town Tavern was run by Sam and Mitzi Labendick. Swede's Jewelers was owned by Stanley A. Swede. The building was torn down as part of the urban renewal plan in the 1970s. The Swede's Jewelers store is currently located in the Warehouse Point section of East Windsor.

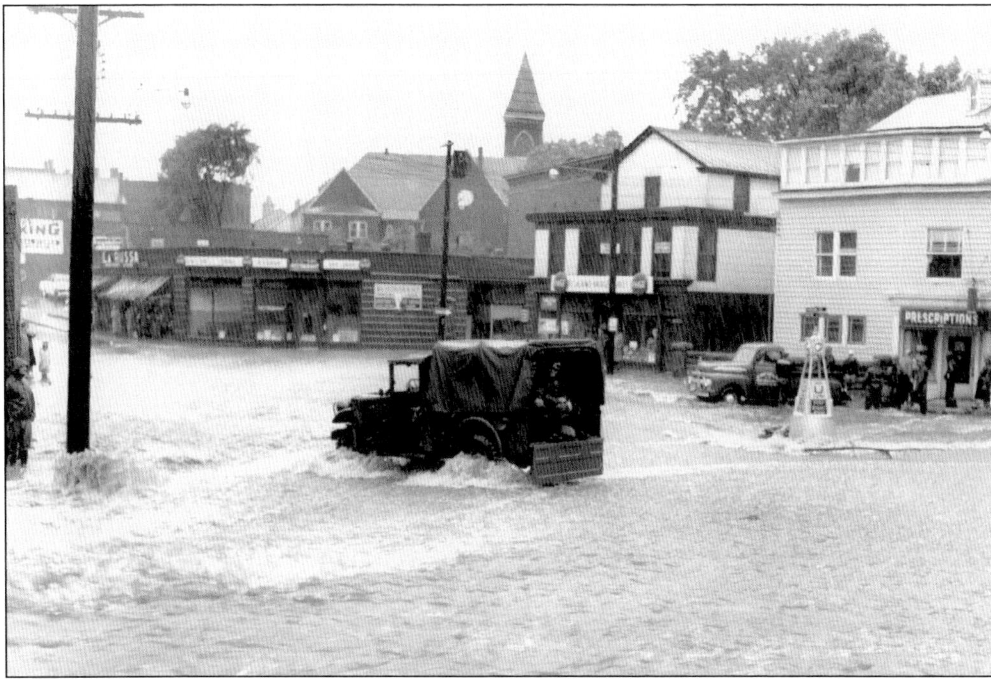

A National Guard Jeep makes it way through the overflow of water from Freshwater Pond. To the right, Enfield Road Construction Company employees discuss their next move in front of the Thompsonville Drug Store, located on Main Street.

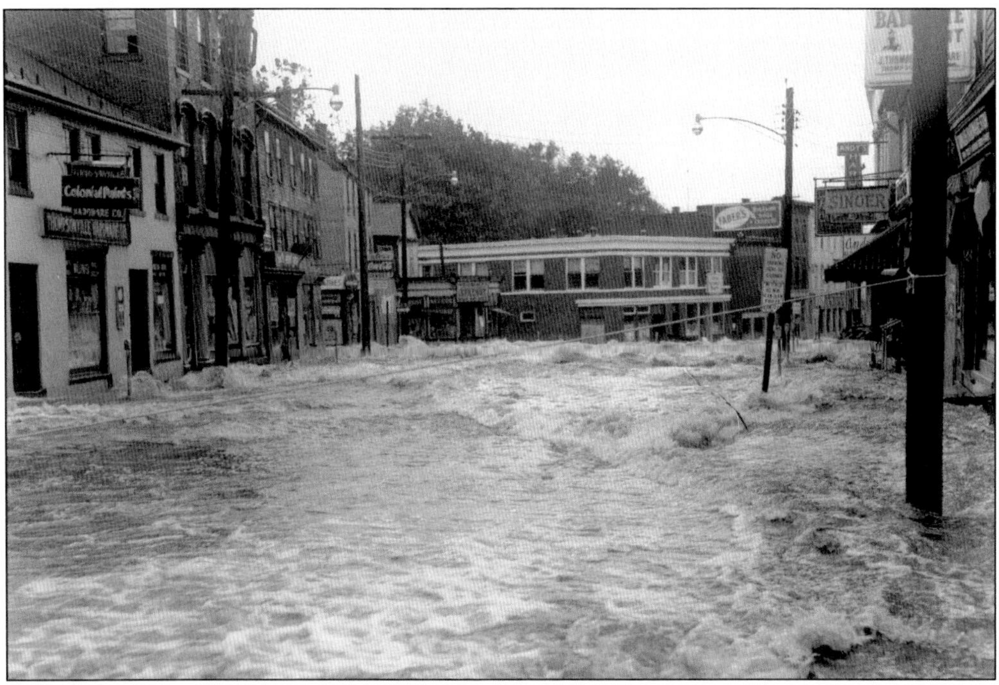

This view, looking west on Main Street, shows raging waters at the peak of the flood. Notice the safety rope tied to the telephone pole. Public safety officials carried trapped workers from the south side of Main Street across the street to safety.

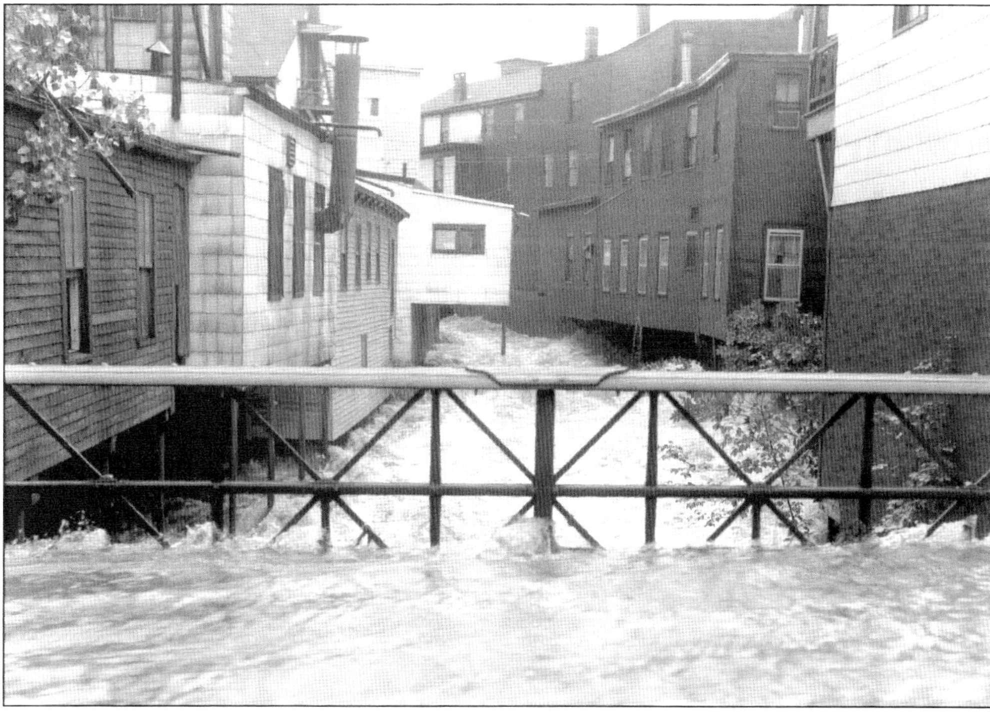

This view, looking east from the Prospect Street bridge, shows Freshwater Brook's raging waters below the rear side of buildings behind Main and Asnuntuck Streets. All of the buildings and the bridge were torn down as part of the urban renewal plan in the 1970s.

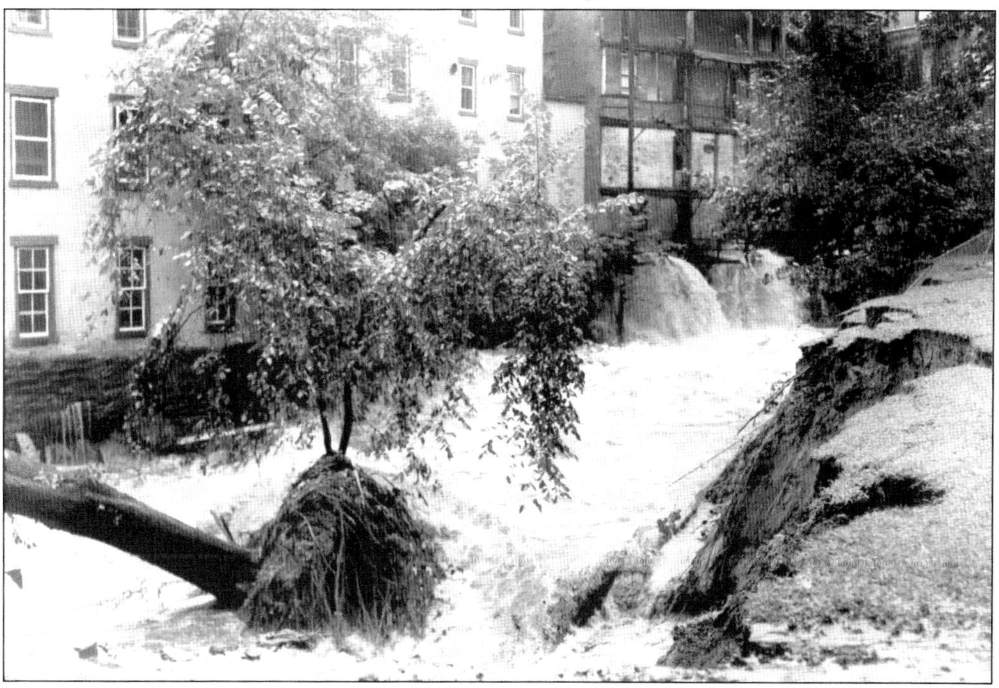

Freshwater Brook uproots a large tree and erodes property along Asnuntuck Street. The rear side of the Bigelow office building is in the background.

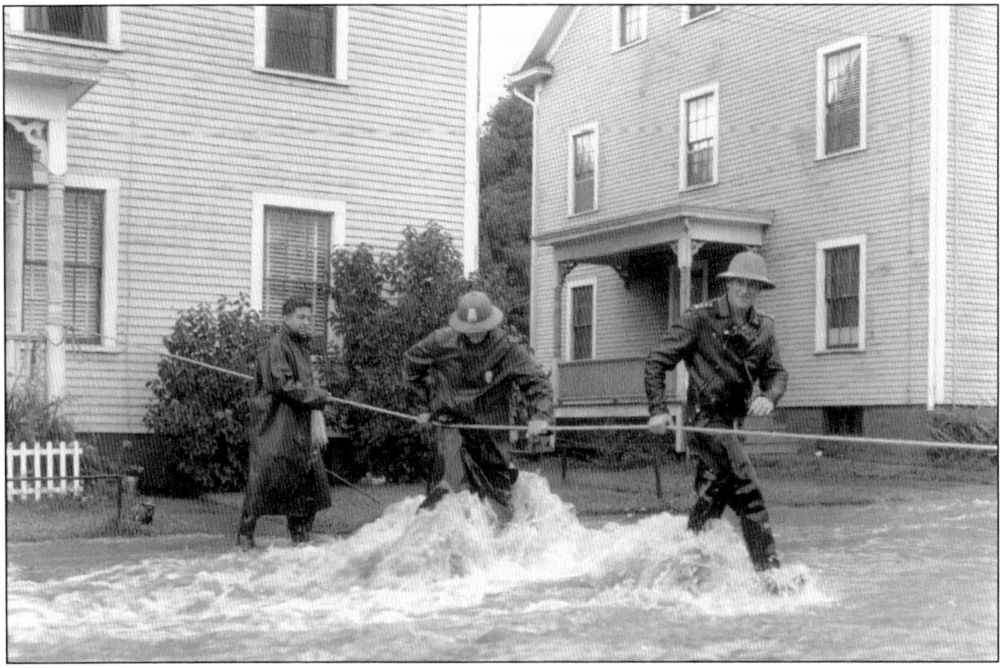

Public safety officials struggle as they walk across Asnuntuck Street with the aid of a safety rope. To the left is Thompsonville volunteer fireman Roy Frangiamore. The other two men are unidentified.

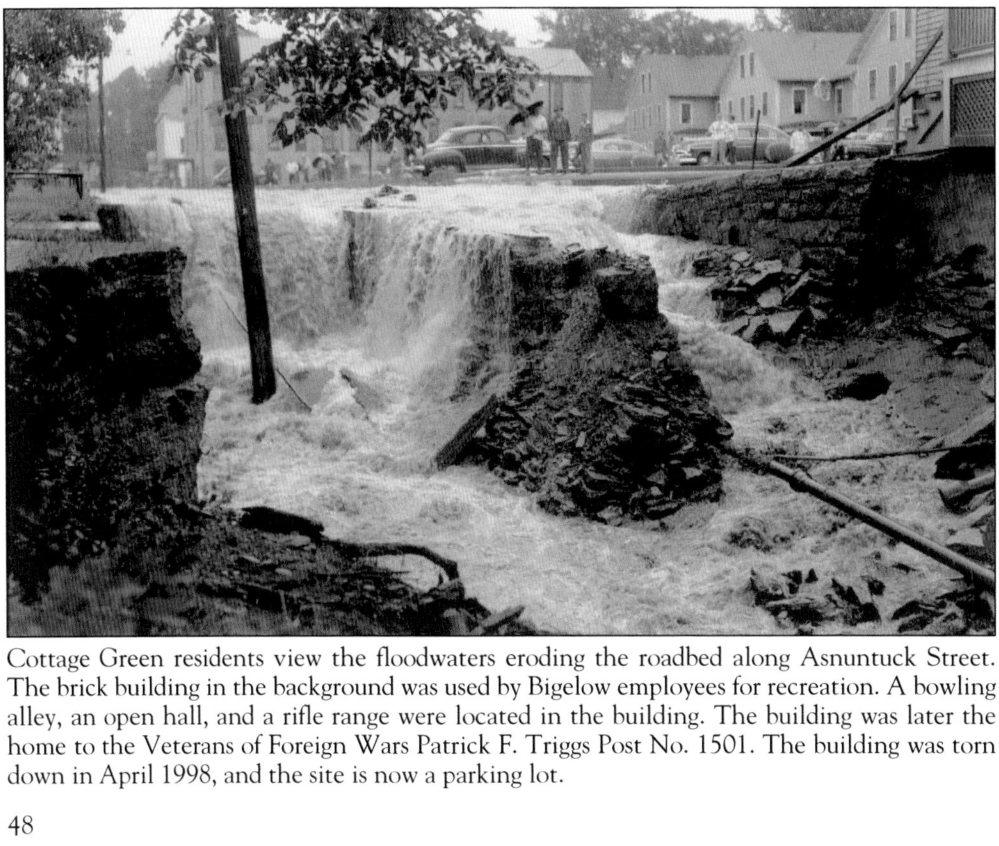

Cottage Green residents view the floodwaters eroding the roadbed along Asnuntuck Street. The brick building in the background was used by Bigelow employees for recreation. A bowling alley, an open hall, and a rifle range were located in the building. The building was later the home to the Veterans of Foreign Wars Patrick F. Triggs Post No. 1501. The building was torn down in April 1998, and the site is now a parking lot.

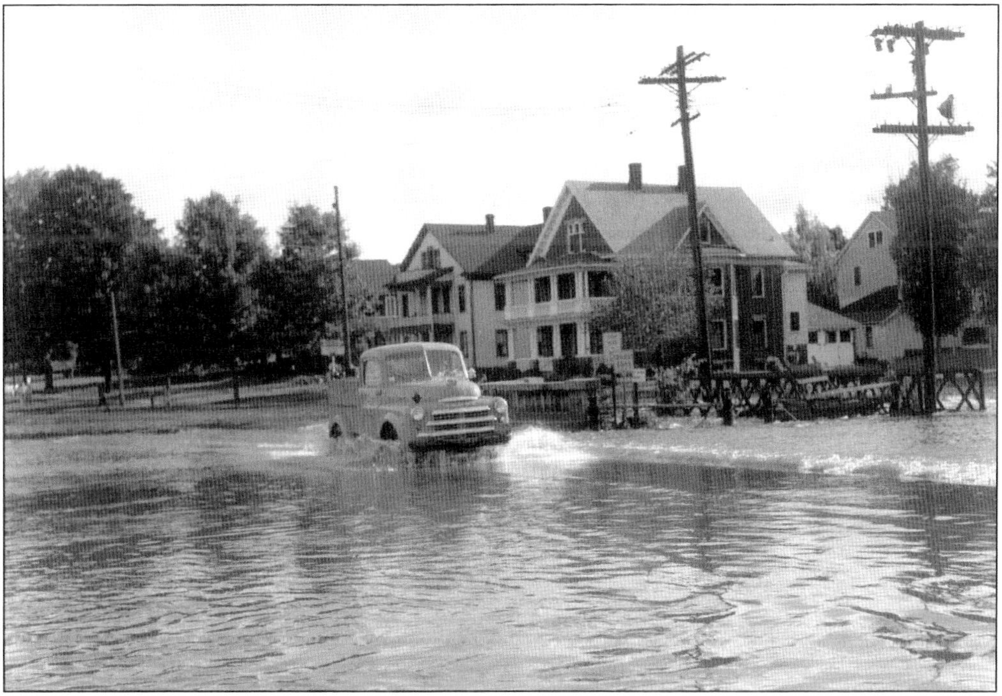

Freshwater Brook overflowed its banks at the intersection of Enfield and High Streets in the 1955 flood. A truck crosses over Freshwater Brook bridge overpass, heading north of Enfield Street.

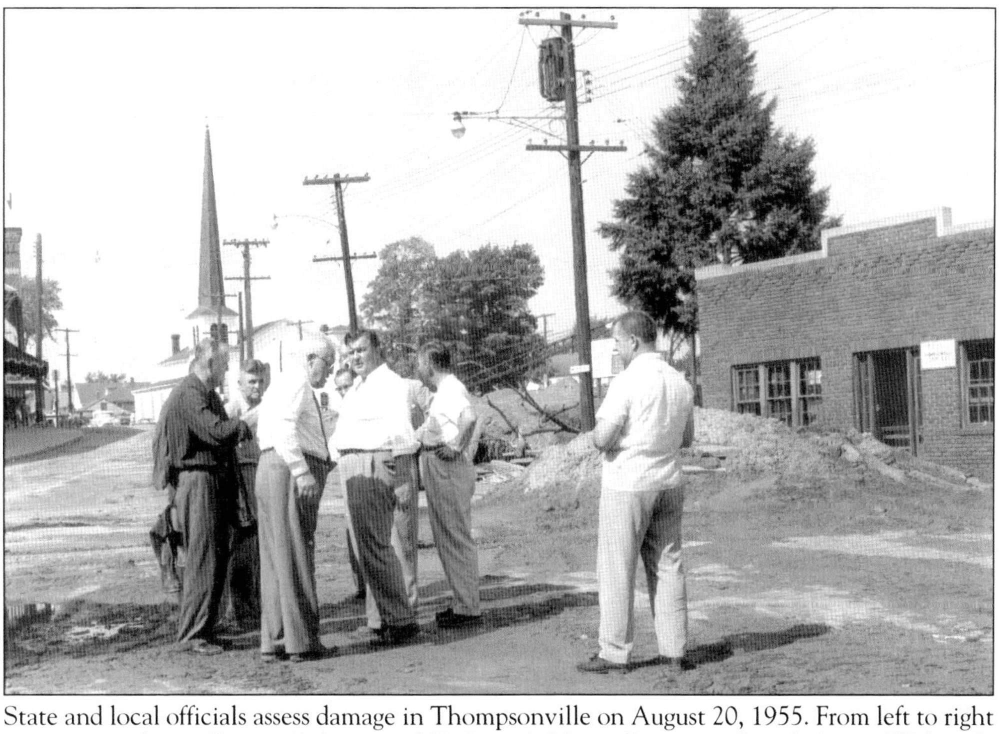

State and local officials assess damage in Thompsonville on August 20, 1955. From left to right are state employees Francis Delaney and Herbert A. Varno Sr., an unidentified man, Walter A. Jekot (deputy sheriff), Norbert D. Senio (selectman), and two unidentified men.

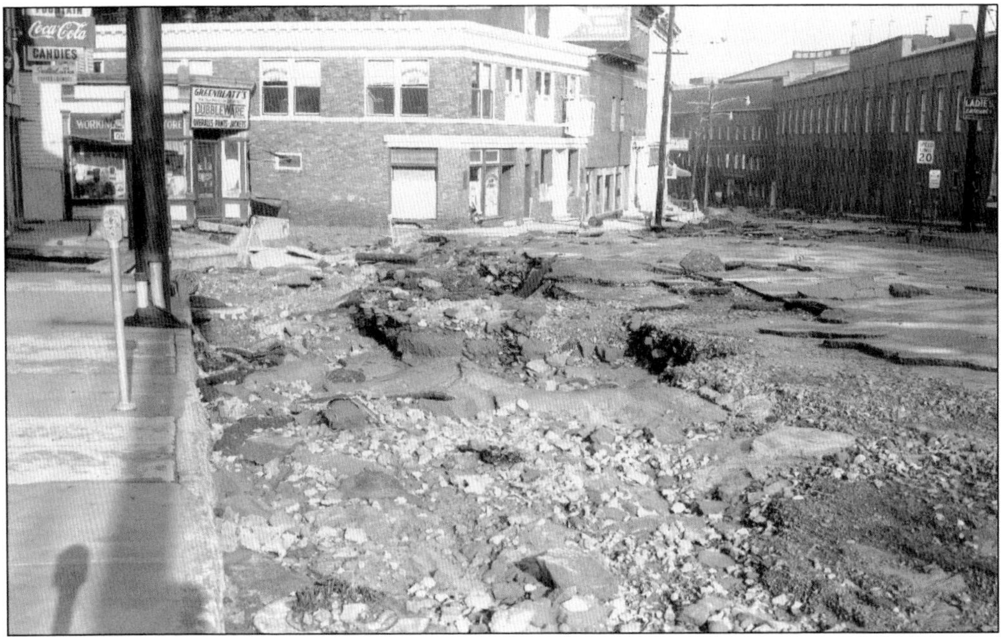

This 1955 view, looking west, shows Main Street ripped apart by raging waters from the day before. The buildings on the left received damage in their cellars from the overflowing waters of Freshwater Brook.

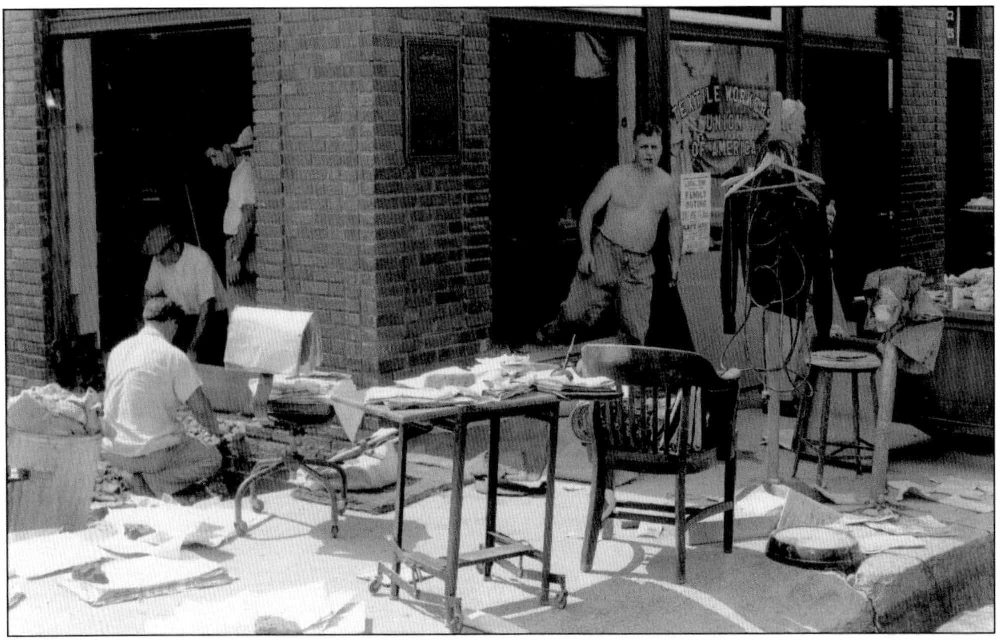

The Textile Workers Union of America office sustained damage to office equipment and to the facade of the building during the flood. Office equipment and ledgers were removed from the building to air-dry on the sidewalk. This view shows employees repairing windows and brickwork on the side of the building, which was one of the few that did not get torn down during the urban renewal project of the 1970s. The building now houses the Yankee Bait and Tackle fishing store.

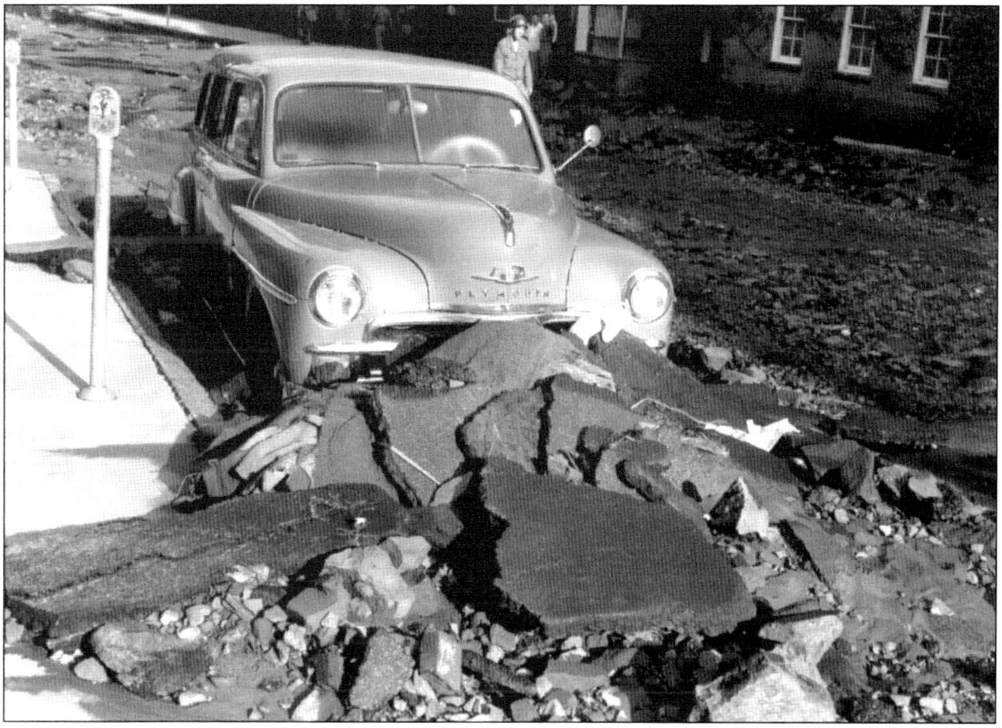

The roadbed piles up on this Plymouth wagon as National Guardsmen patrol Main Street in front of the Bigelow-Sanford Carpet Company.

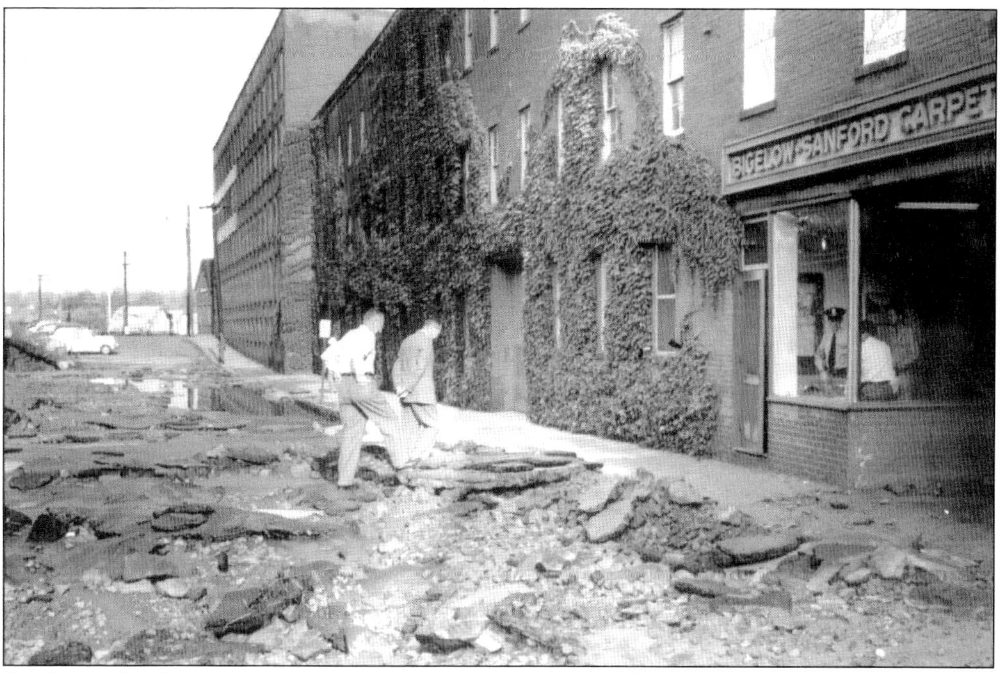

Bigelow officials inspect damage along Main Street near the main entrance of the Bigelow-Sanford Carpet Company. An unidentified man, on the left, and James J. Jackson, plant manager, return back to the mill.

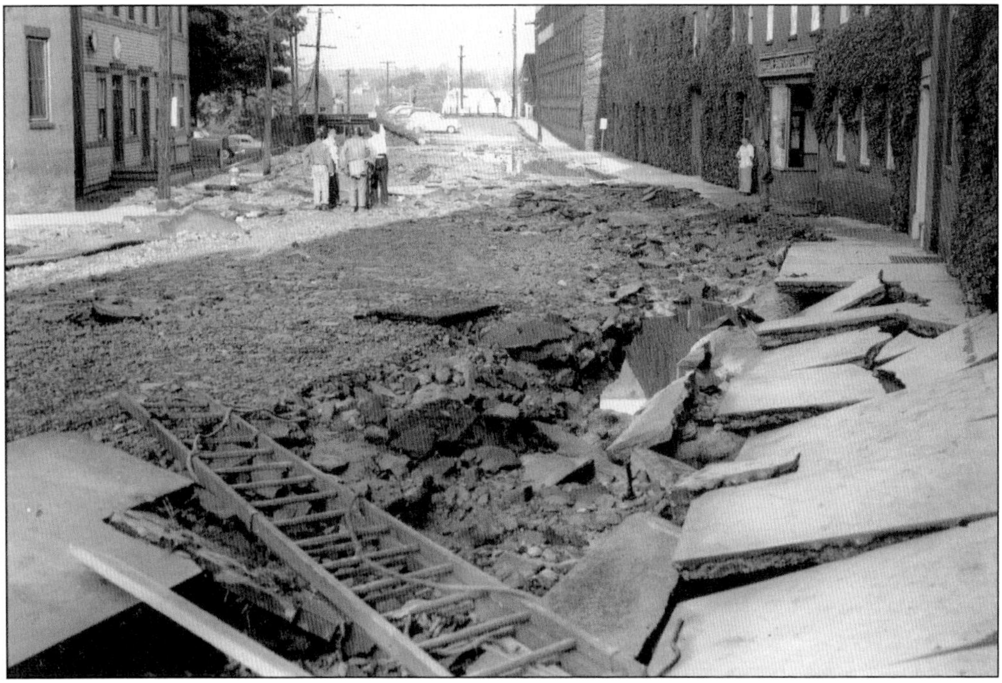

Looking west along Main Street, this view shows the main entrance of the Bigelow plant on the right. Bigelow security officers and National Guardsmen view the damage to Main Street down to the railroad overpass in August 1955.

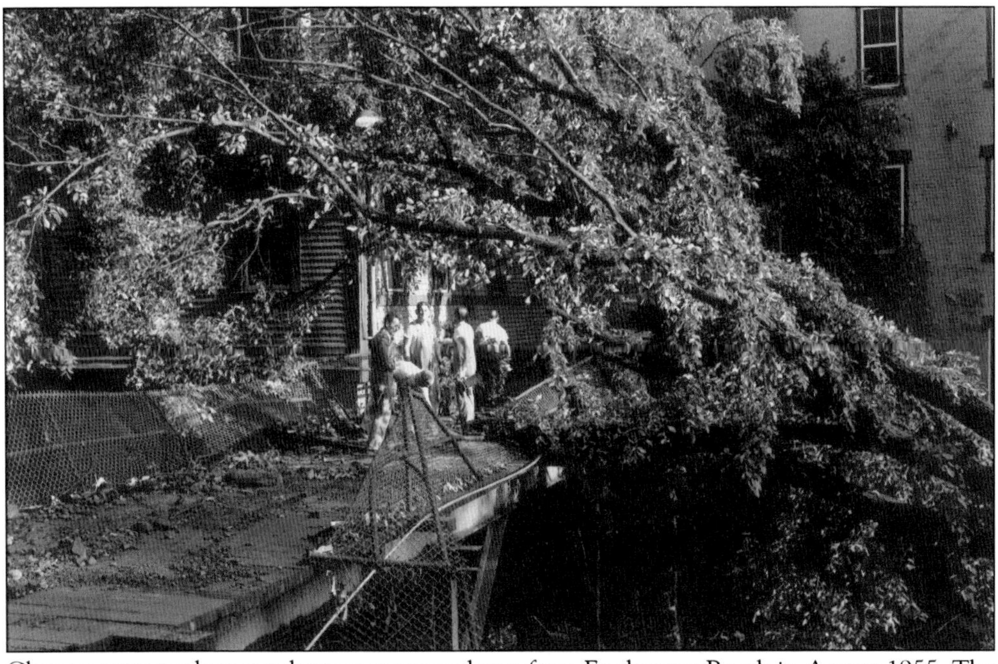

Cleanup crew workers cut down an uprooted tree from Freshwater Brook in August 1955. The "Dye House Bridge" was used as a shortcut by mill workers who lived in the Cottage Green neighborhood. The bridge connected Asnuntuck Street to the main entrance to the carpet mill on Main Street.

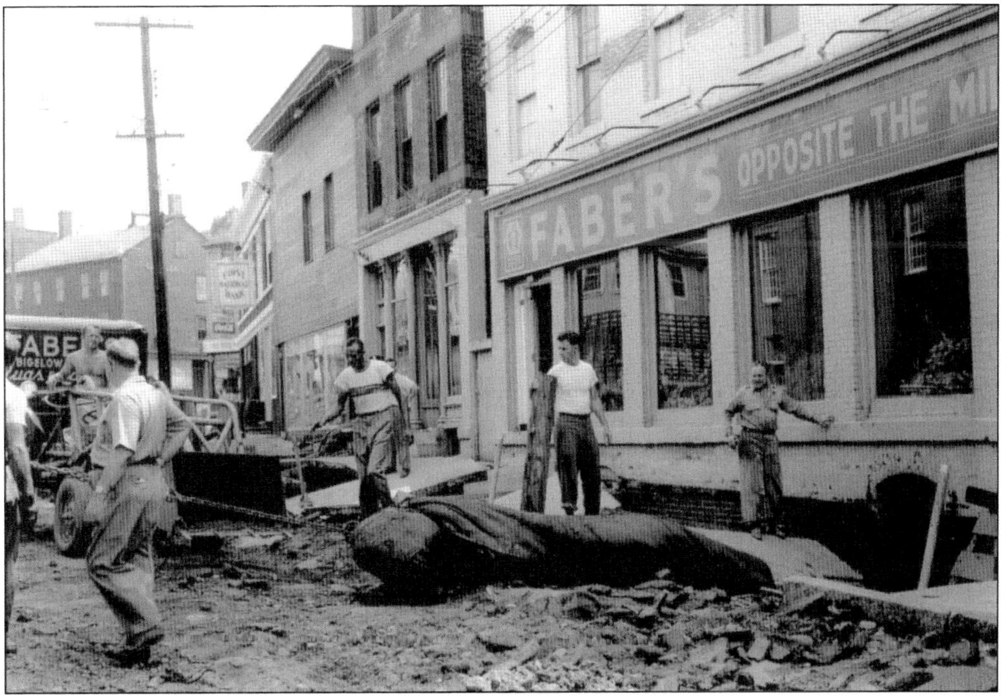

Faber's sustained extensive damage to merchandise in the basement of the store. In this view, employees and cleanup crews remove mud-soaked carpets by crane onto Main Street in August 1955.

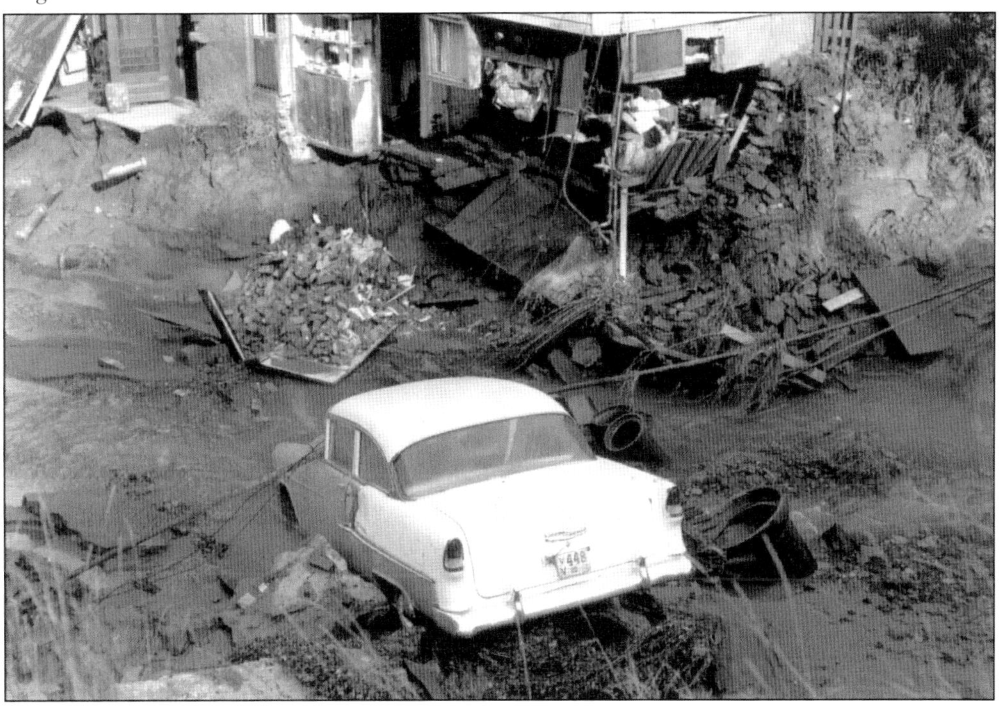

An automobile landed among debris in the backyard of a severely damaged house on South River Street in Thompsonville as a result of the flood.

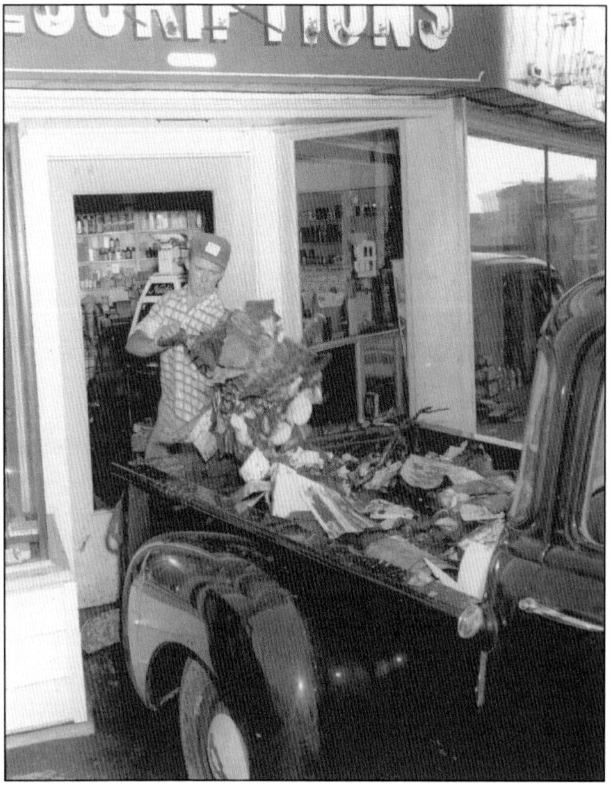

An unidentified man shovels debris into a waiting truck outside the Thompsonville Drug Store, located on Main Street. In the 1950s, the store was operated by Fred A. Mason. In the 1960s, it was operated by Francis A. Padrevita. The store moved across the street to North Main Street in the 1960s.

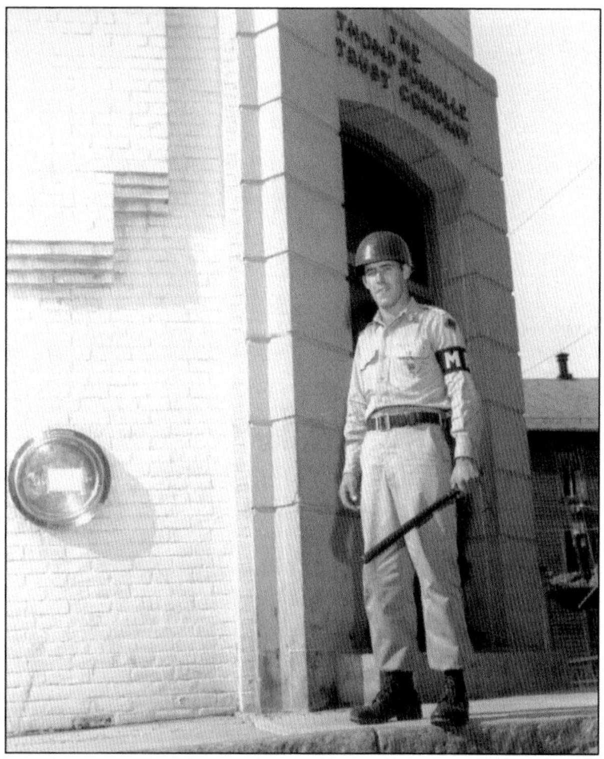

Bob Rookey, an Enfield native and member of the 43rd Connecticut National Guard unit, stood guard outside the Thompsonville Trust Company at the corner of Asnuntuck and Prospect Streets in August 1955. A rear portion of the bank building was damaged by Freshwater Brook, leaving a gaping hole in the building. Rookey stood guard until bank officials reached the building.

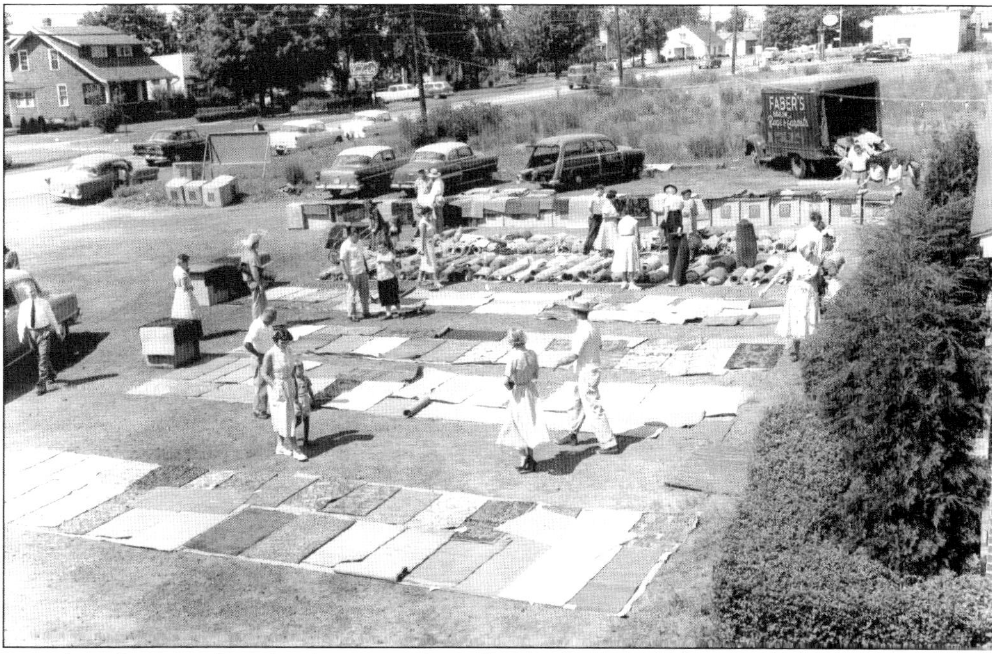

A parking lot served as the showroom for Faber's water-damaged carpets and rugs on Enfield Street, opposite Virginia Avenue. In this view, Enfield residents check out the deals on Bigelow carpets and rugs in August 1955.

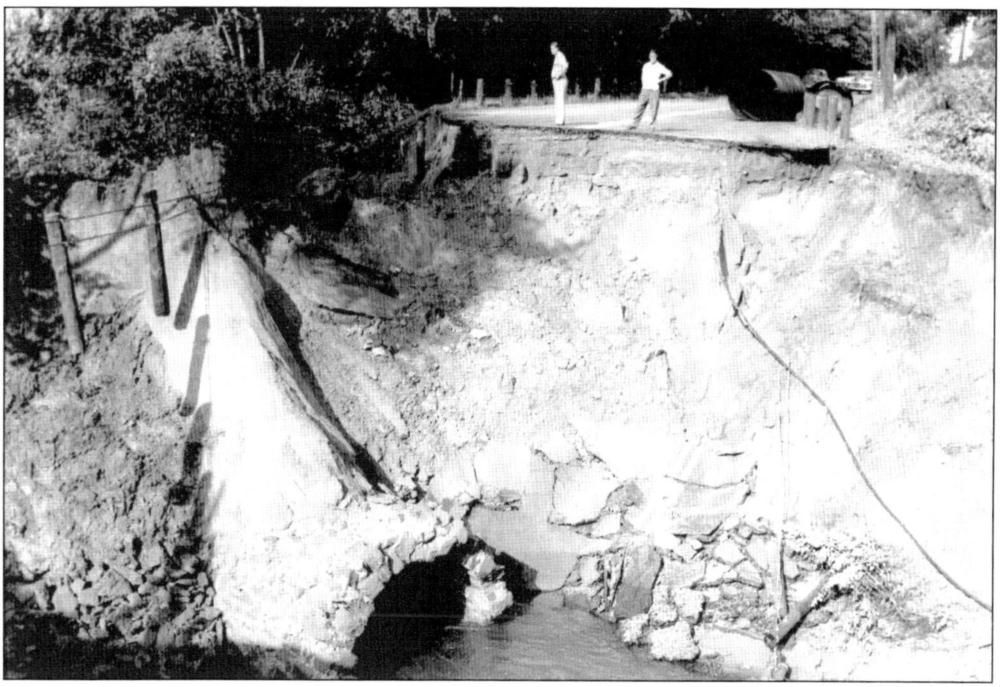

This view, looking east on Main Street (later named Hazard Avenue), shows two unidentified men surveying the erosion and the damaged culvert in Scitico in August 1955. The culvert expanded and ruptured under water pressure from Terry Brook. Road crews restored road traffic to the state road five days after the flood.

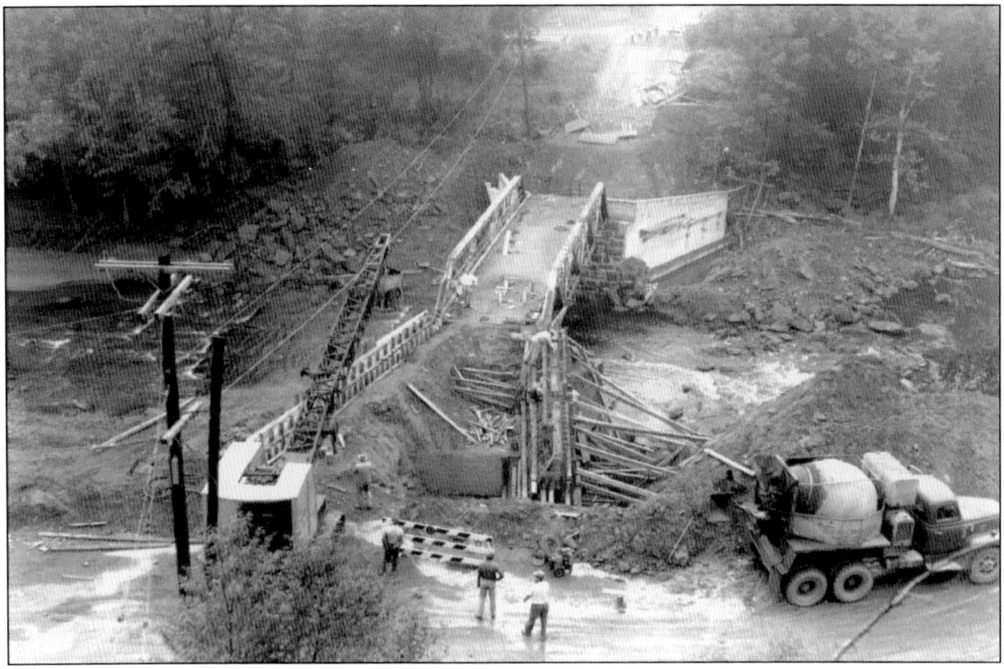

Scantic River floodwaters severely damaged the roadbed near the South Maple Street Bridge in August 1955. The Enfield Road Construction Company was awarded a state contract to reconstruct the bridge and road. This view, looking north on South Maple Street, shows employees of the Enfield Road Construction Company and the Roncari Construction Company repairing the bridge.

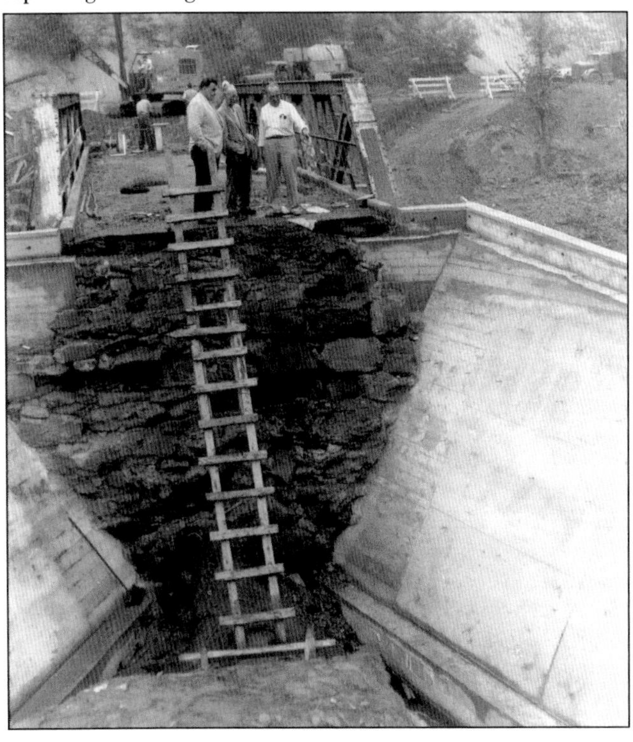

Local and state officials discuss elements of the South Maple Street Bridge reconstruction project in August 1955 as Enfield Road Construction Company employees complete repairs to the bridge and roadbed. First Selectman Norbert D. Senio (left) is shown with two unidentified state employees.

Four

THE CHANGING LANDSCAPE

Enfield has undergone a major transformation from a rural mill-and-farming town of 15,000 to a substantial suburban community of more than 45,000. The town began to change when the carpet industry moved parts of its operation south in the 1950s and the construction of Interstate 91 was completed, bringing new businesses and residents. New housing developments increased rapidly, with homebuilder Leger Starr leading the way. By 1960, the population had risen to 33,000. With a continuing increase in the population, a new school was constructed every year. New businesses moved into Enfield, including U.S. Envelope, Magnani & McCormick, and Olympic Sales (on Moody Road). In the 1970s, the Enfield Memorial Industrial Park opened, including Eli Lilly & Company, Toolkraft, and Dairy Mart, while older businesses in Thompsonville were demolished by the urban renewal project.

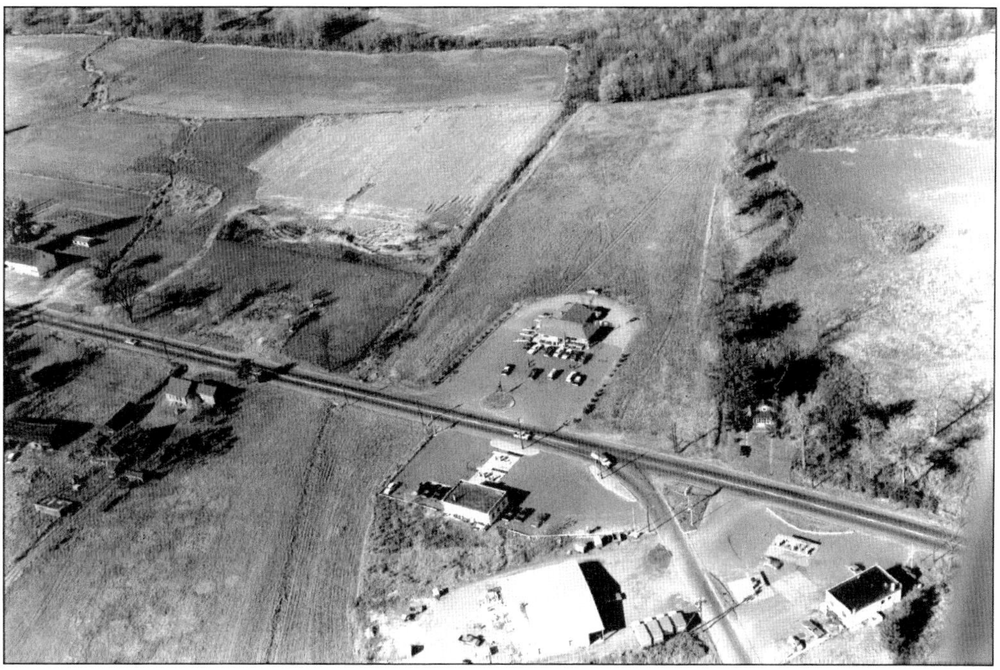

This 1960s view shows Smyth Farm Dairy Bar, owned by Robert Smyth; the Mobil station, operated by Edward Lane; Grondin's Taylor Rental; and Grondin's Texaco gas station (at the intersection of Hazard Avenue and Middle Road), owned by Emile W. Grondin. Open space land surrounding the former Smyth Farm Dairy Bar has since been developed. Enfield Ford was built to the left. Three rows of business and office condominiums were built from behind, and Palomba Drive was constructed to the right.

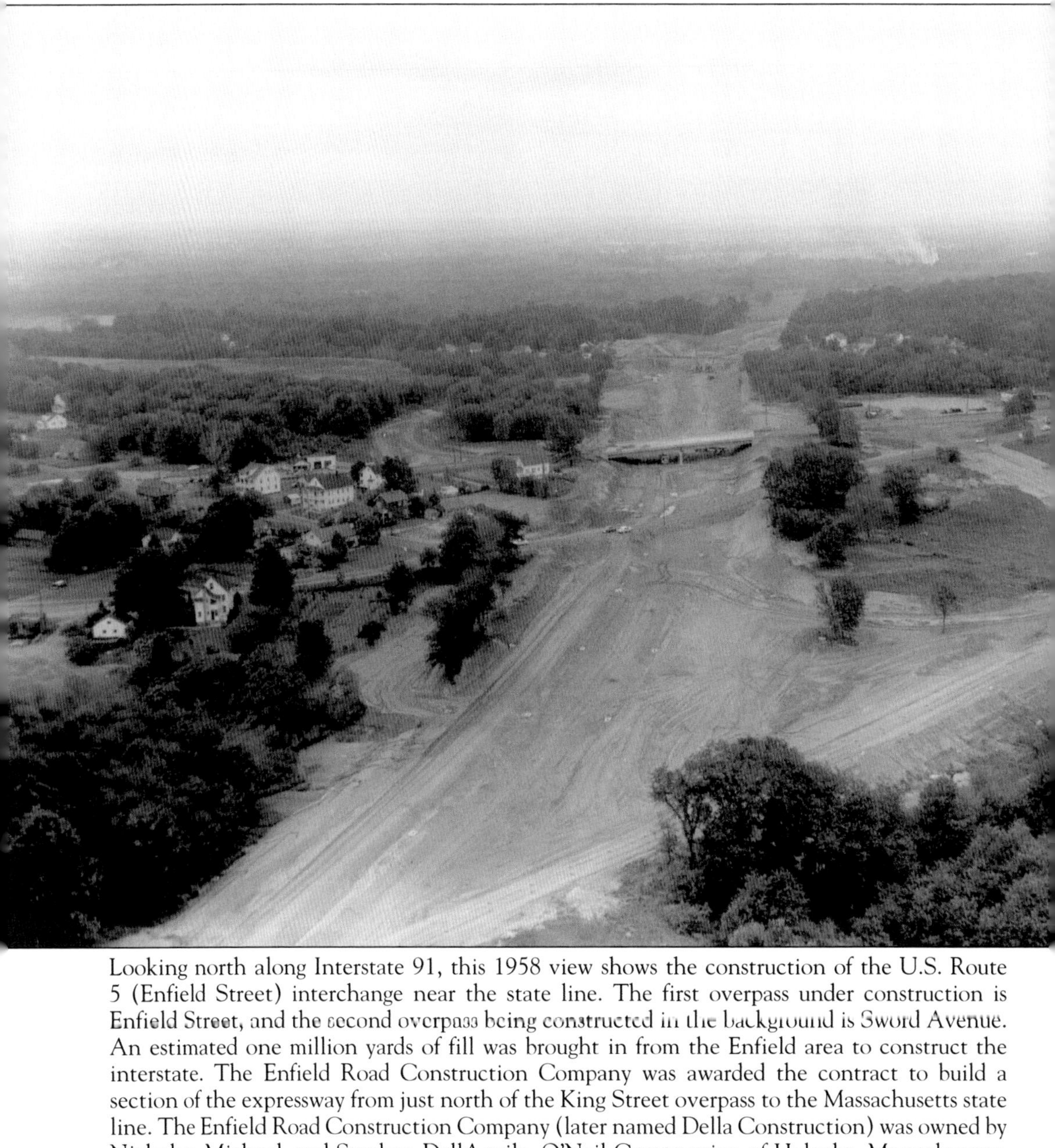

Looking north along Interstate 91, this 1958 view shows the construction of the U.S. Route 5 (Enfield Street) interchange near the state line. The first overpass under construction is Enfield Street, and the second overpass being constructed in the background is Sword Avenue. An estimated one million yards of fill was brought in from the Enfield area to construct the interstate. The Enfield Road Construction Company was awarded the contract to build a section of the expressway from just north of the King Street overpass to the Massachusetts state line. The Enfield Road Construction Company (later named Della Construction) was owned by Nickolas, Michael, and Stephen DellAquila. O'Neil Construction of Holyoke, Massachusetts, was awarded the contract for the bridge overpasses.

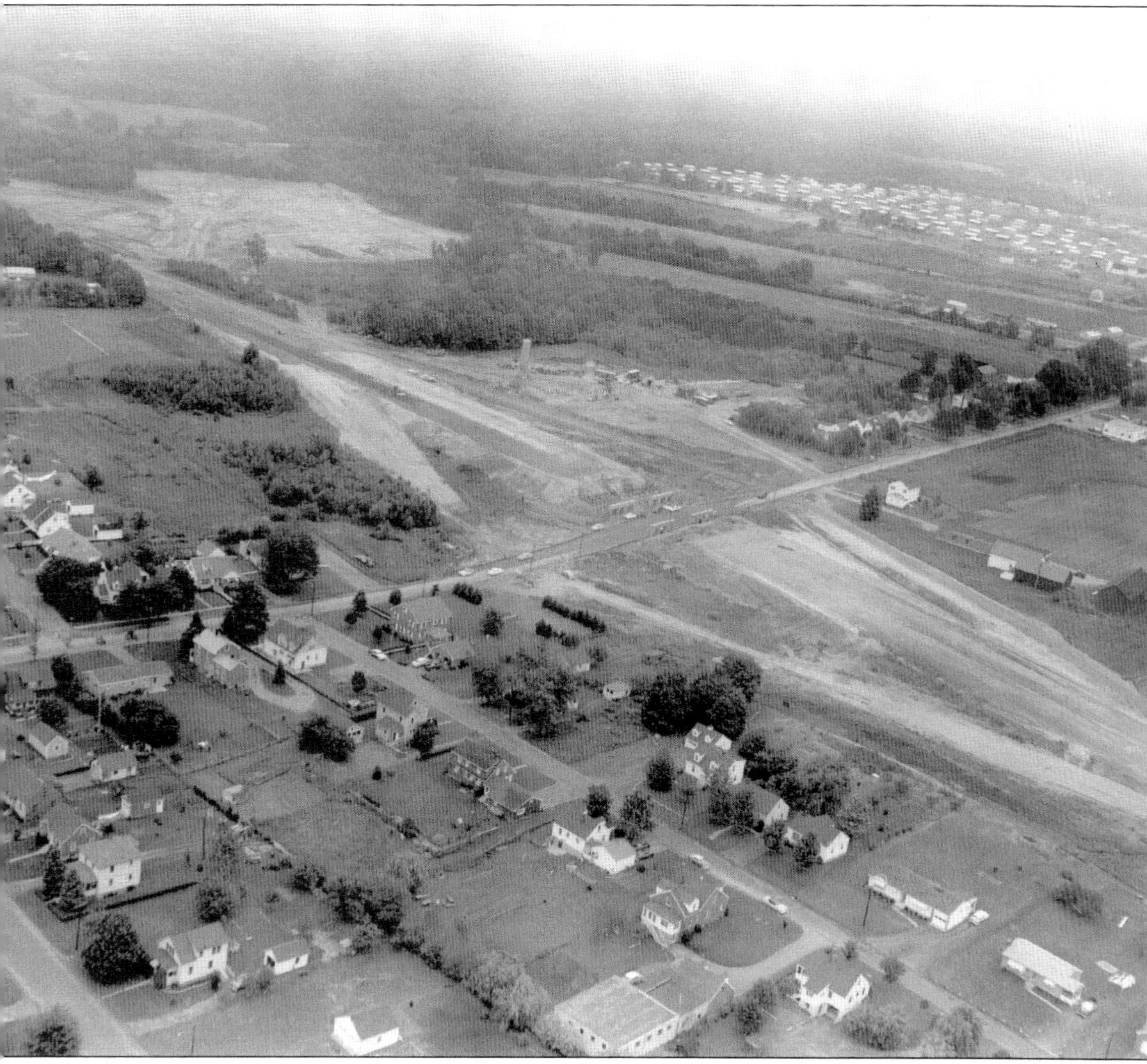

The construction of the Interstate 91 and state Route 220 (Elm Street) interchange is pictured in 1958. The ramps created the shape of a diamond. O'Hear Avenue, Lynch Terrace, and Charles Street are located west of the expressway in the foreground. The land immediately east of the expressway included farmland and single-family homes. Farmers and owners of single-family homes sold their properties to developers, who developed the land in the 1960s and 1970s with shopping plazas and fast-food restaurants along Elm Street.

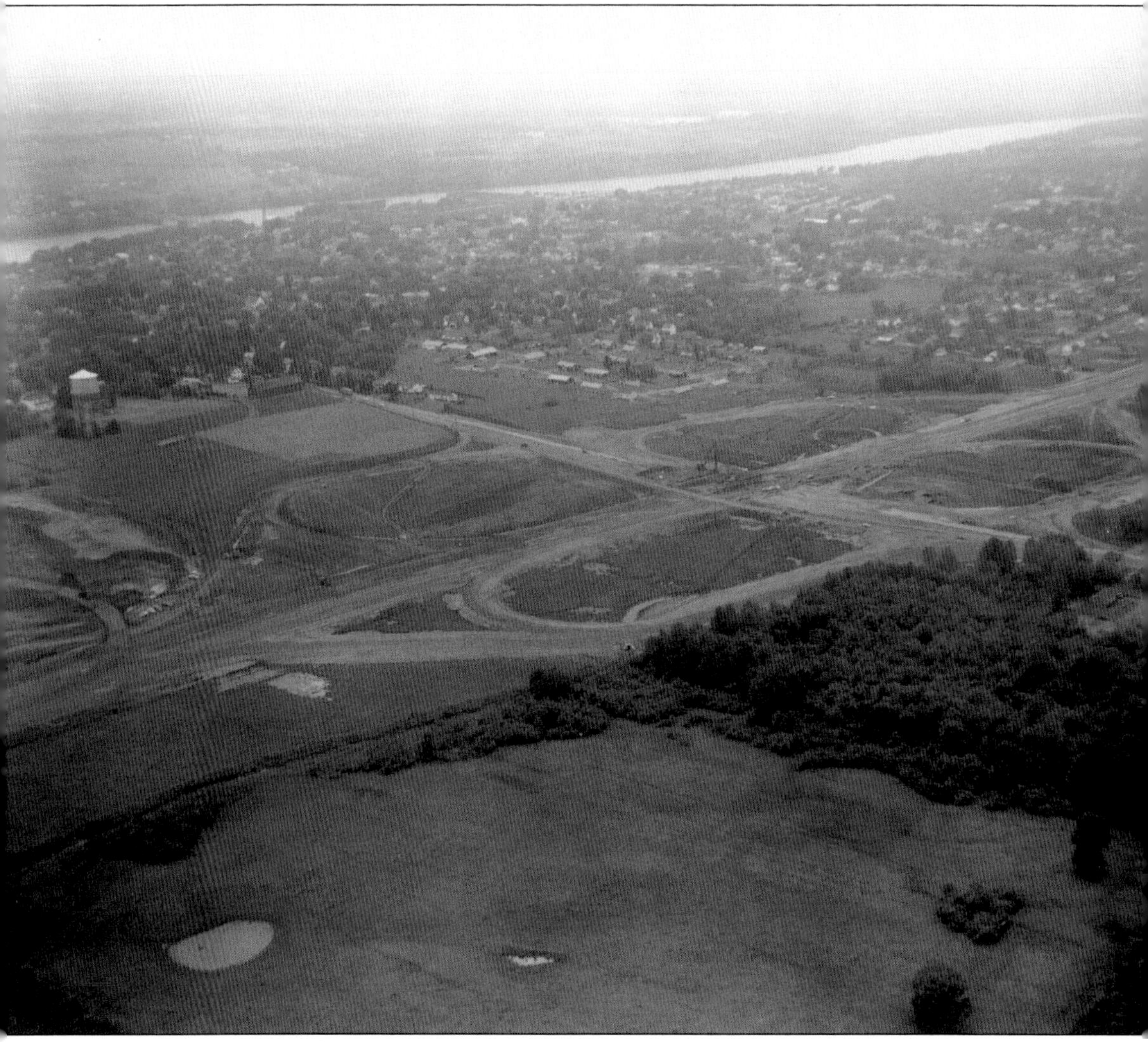

Pictured in a view looking west is the construction of the Interstate 91 and state Route 190 (Hazard Avenue) interchange. The ramps created the shape of a cloverleaf. Undeveloped land was located east of Interstate 91 (foreground). This undeveloped property is currently the last vacant parcel of the Enfield Memorial Industrial Park. The Thompsonville neighborhood, the Connecticut River, and Suffield are west of Interstate 91 (background).

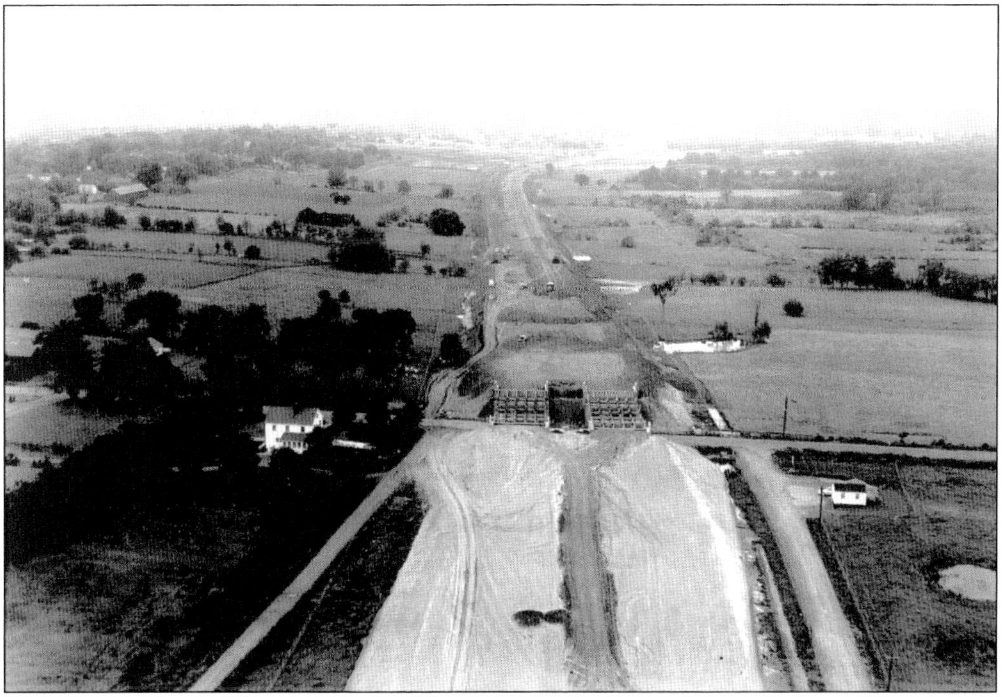

Looking north on Interstate 91 in 1958, this view shows the construction of the South Road overpass in the center of the photograph. The undeveloped land on the right became the home to the Enfield Memorial Industrial Park in the 1970s.

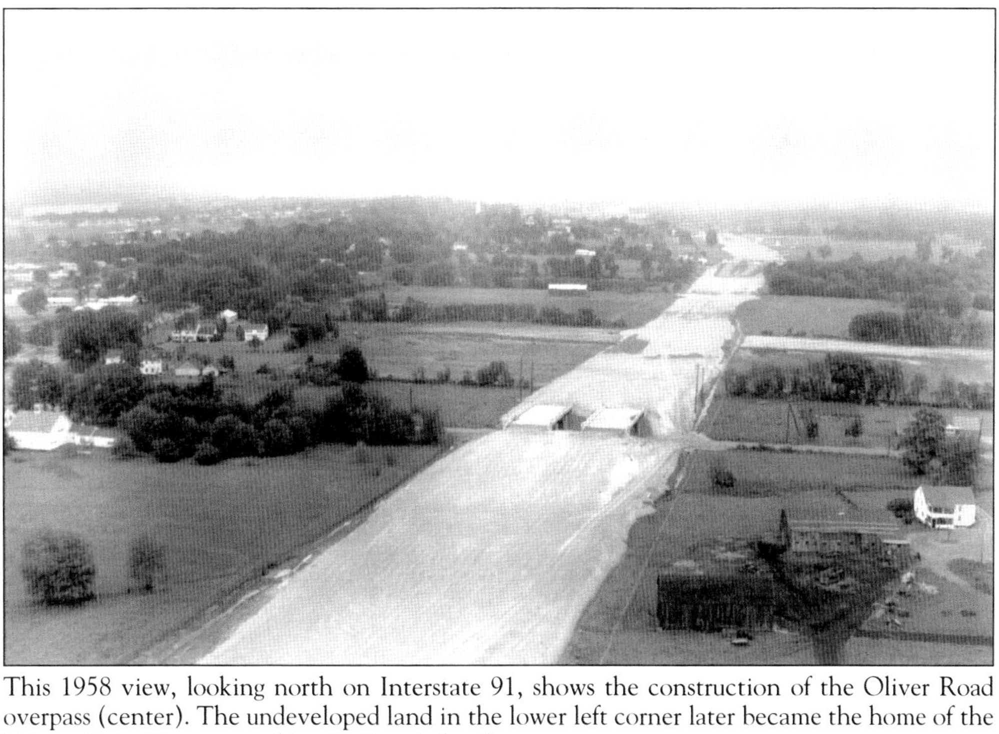

This 1958 view, looking north on Interstate 91, shows the construction of the Oliver Road overpass (center). The undeveloped land in the lower left corner later became the home of the Trinity Dairy Farm, owned by the Smyth family.

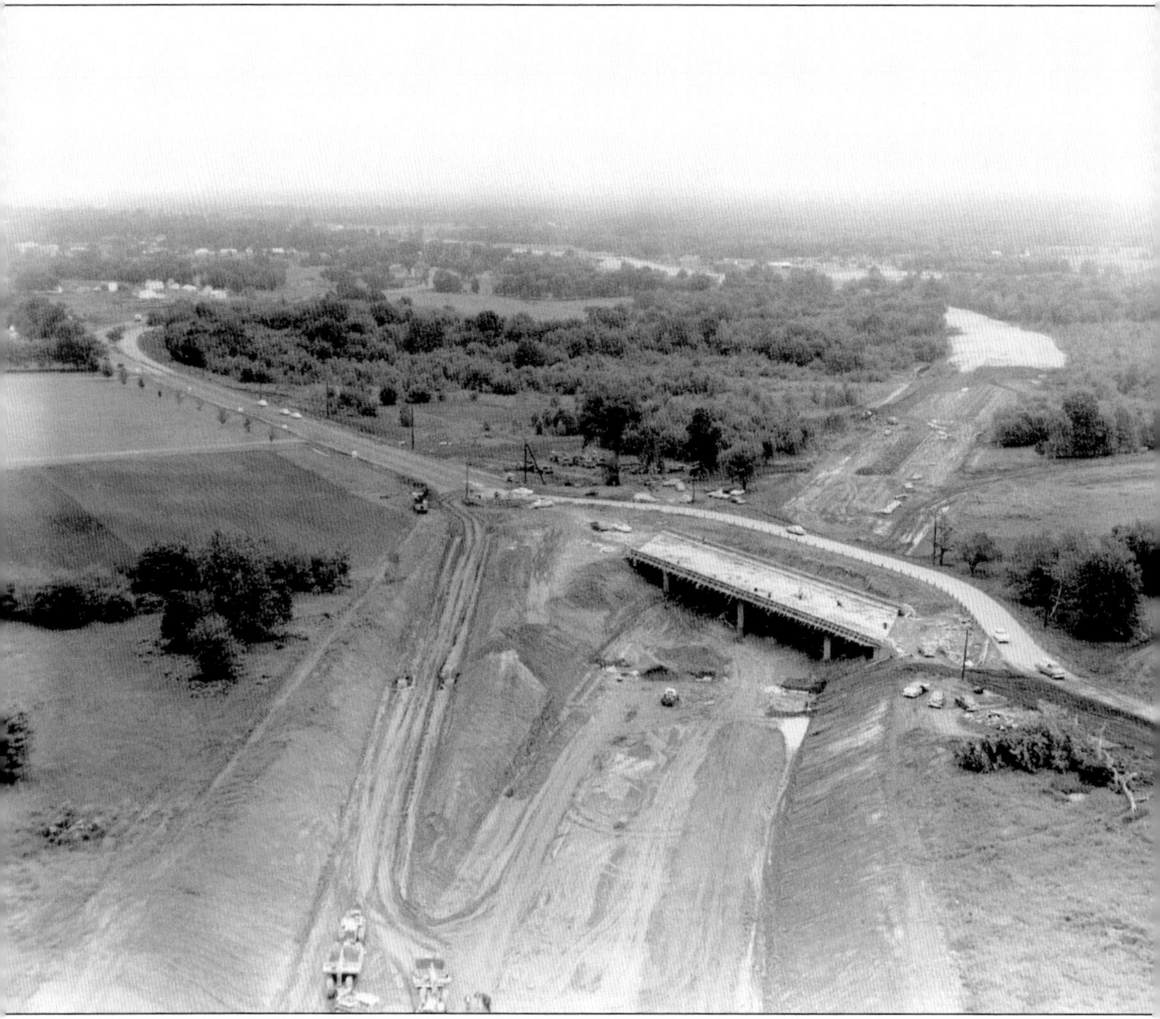

In this photograph of the construction of the U.S. Route 5 (King Street) interchange, the lighter fill north of the overpass is the area completed by the Enfield Road Construction Company. The Arute Brothers construction company from New Britain completed the construction from just north of the King Street interchange to the Dexter Coffin Bridge on the East Windsor side of the Connecticut River. The landscaped property on the left is St. Patrick's Church King Street Cemetery. The property located between King Street and Interstate 91 in the center became the site of Bradlees and Stop and Shop in the 1970s. The property later housed Pace Warehouse and a U.S. Postal Service distribution center. The property in the lower right-hand corner is the home to a Mobil station and King Street Car Wash.

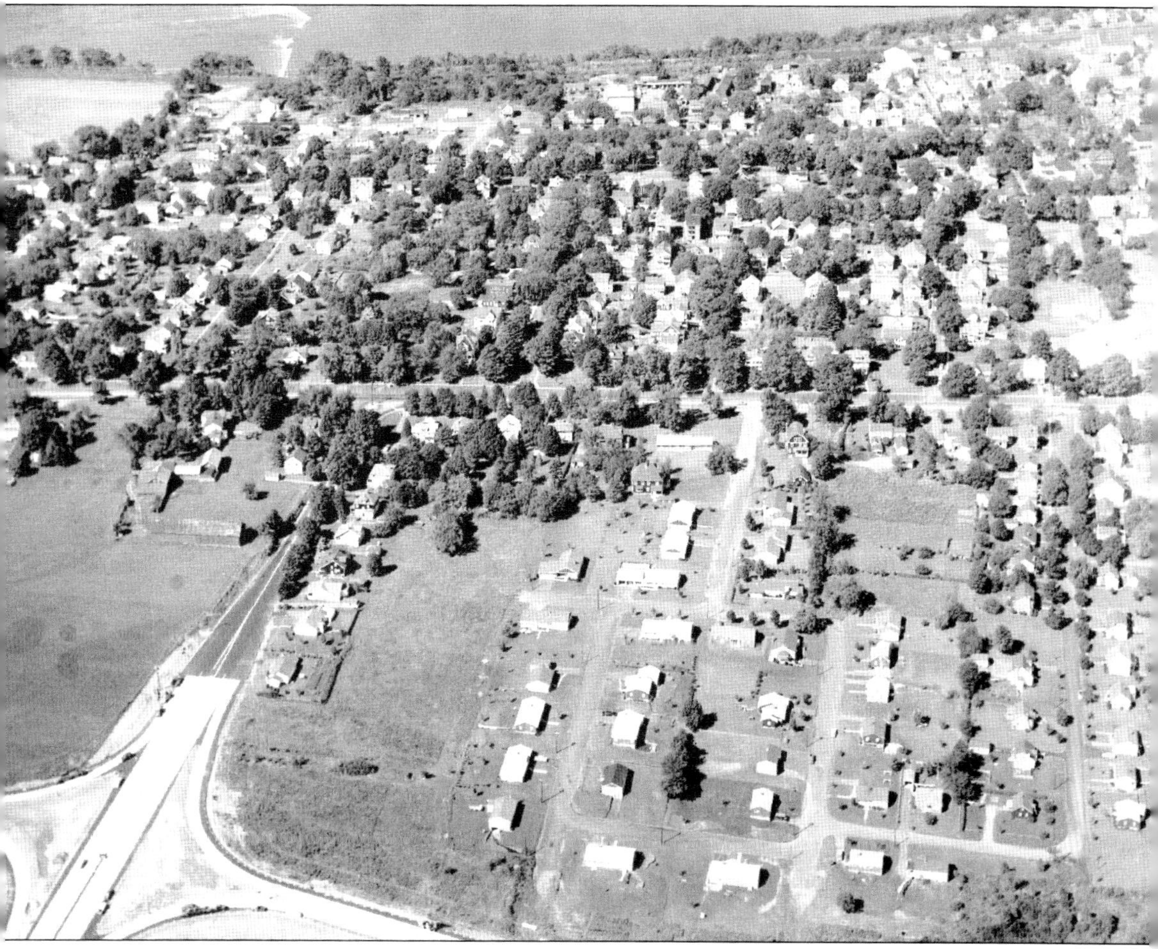

This early-1960s view, looking west from the Interstate 91 and state Route 190 (Hazard Avenue) interchange, shows the southern end of the Thompsonville neighborhood, with the Connecticut River and the Enfield Dam in the background. The state awarded the Enfield Road Construction Company the contract to continue state Route 190 (Hazard Avenue) through this Thompsonville neighborhood to the banks of the Connecticut River in Thompsonville. The 1960s project included razing most of the houses on Enfield Street, Hazard Avenue, Franklin Terrace, Martin Terrace, Pearl Street, Spring Street, and Chestnut Street. Some of these houses were moved to nearby parts of town. The project also included removing over 400,000 yards of shale on the site. The shale was transported to East Windsor for use as fill. Enfield and Pearl Streets bridge overpasses were later constructed to complete the project. The state project also included the construction of a new Enfield–Suffield bridge to replace the old iron bridge in the downtown Thompsonville section. Construction of the new state Route 190 bridge was completed in December 1966.

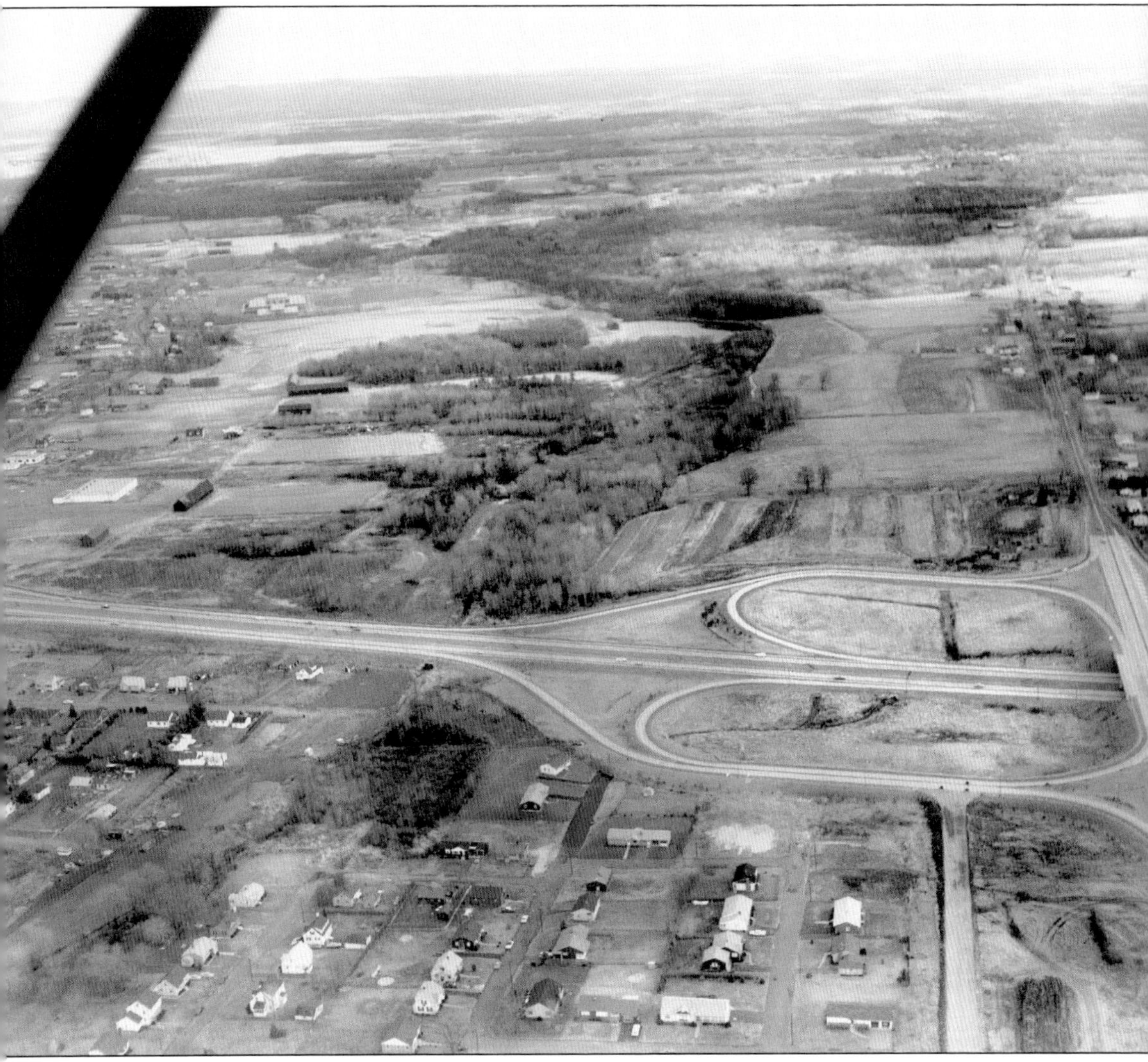

Looking east over the Interstate 91 and state Route 190 (Hazard Avenue) cloverleaf in the mid-1960s, this view shows undeveloped land and the Smyth dairy farm, operated by Richard Smyth, along the north side of Hazard Avenue. These properties became the site of the Enfield Suburban Mall in 1969; the Woolco department store was the first tenant. The Thompsonville Bowling Center (the large building with the white facade on the left) was located on Elm Street, east of Interstate 91. Kosciuszko Jr. High School (now the home to Asnuntuck Community College) and numerous tobacco barns fill up the landscape along Elm Street. The farmland along Elm Street was later occupied by the Enfield Square, State Line Plaza, and car dealerships along Palomba Drive. Residential neighborhoods in the foreground include Lynch Terrace, O'Hear Avenue, John Street, Meadow Street, Claremont Avenue, Roseland Avenue, and Edward Avenue.

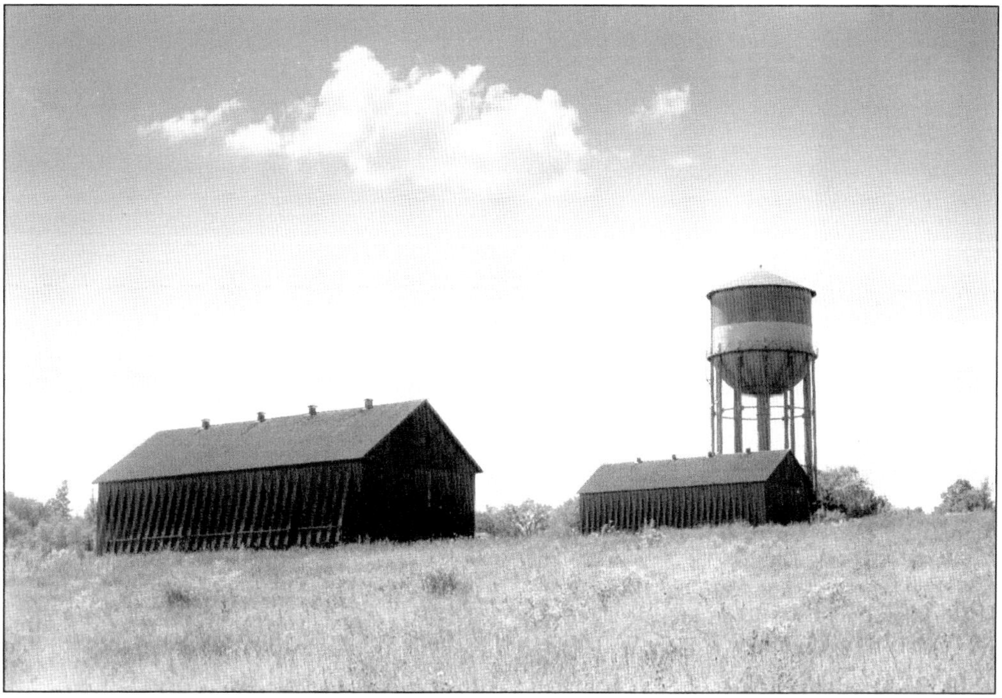

Pictured in the 1950s are the Burgess Farm and the Connecticut Water Company water tower, located at the intersection of Enfield Street (U.S. Route 5) and Hazard Avenue (state Route 190). The Burgess Farm was operated by Jim Burgess. The tobacco barns were torn down, and the Connecticut Water Company added another water tower to the site.

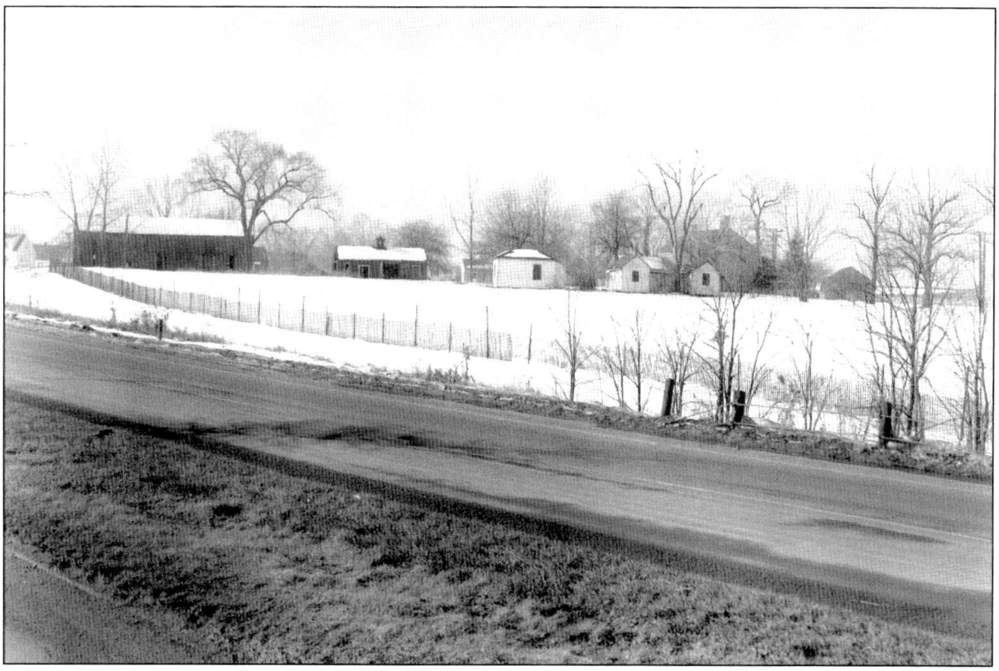

Open space along the west side of King Street (U.S. Route 5) can be seen in this 1960s photograph. The property became the site of the Calvary Presbyterian Church in the 1970s.

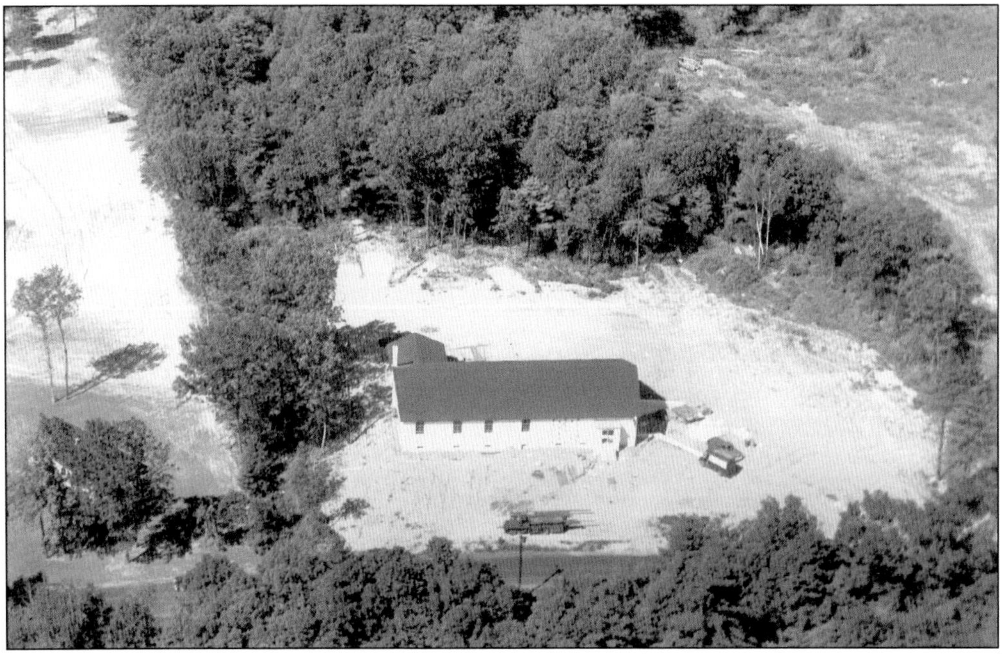

This early-1960s aerial view shows the Washington Road construction site of Knights of Columbus, Washington Irving Council No. 50. On the left, Betty Road site work is under way for future homes to be built.

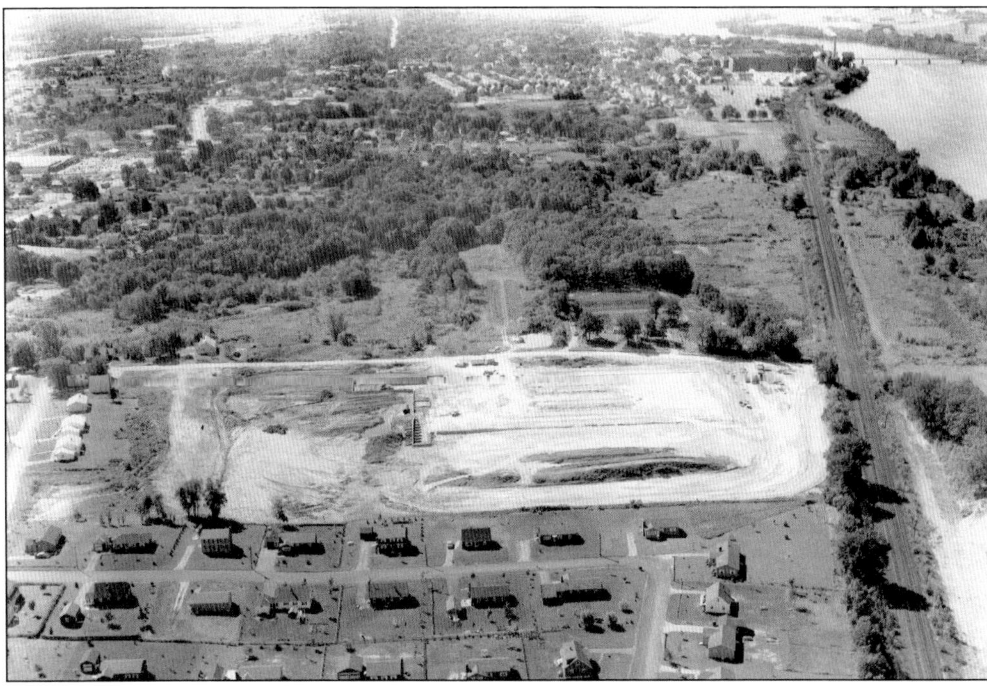

Looking south, this late-1950s aerial view shows the site work completed by the Enfield Road Construction Company for the new Hallmark Cards distribution plant on Manning Road. On the right, railroad tracks and the Connecticut River make their way past the Bigelow-Sanford Carpet Company.

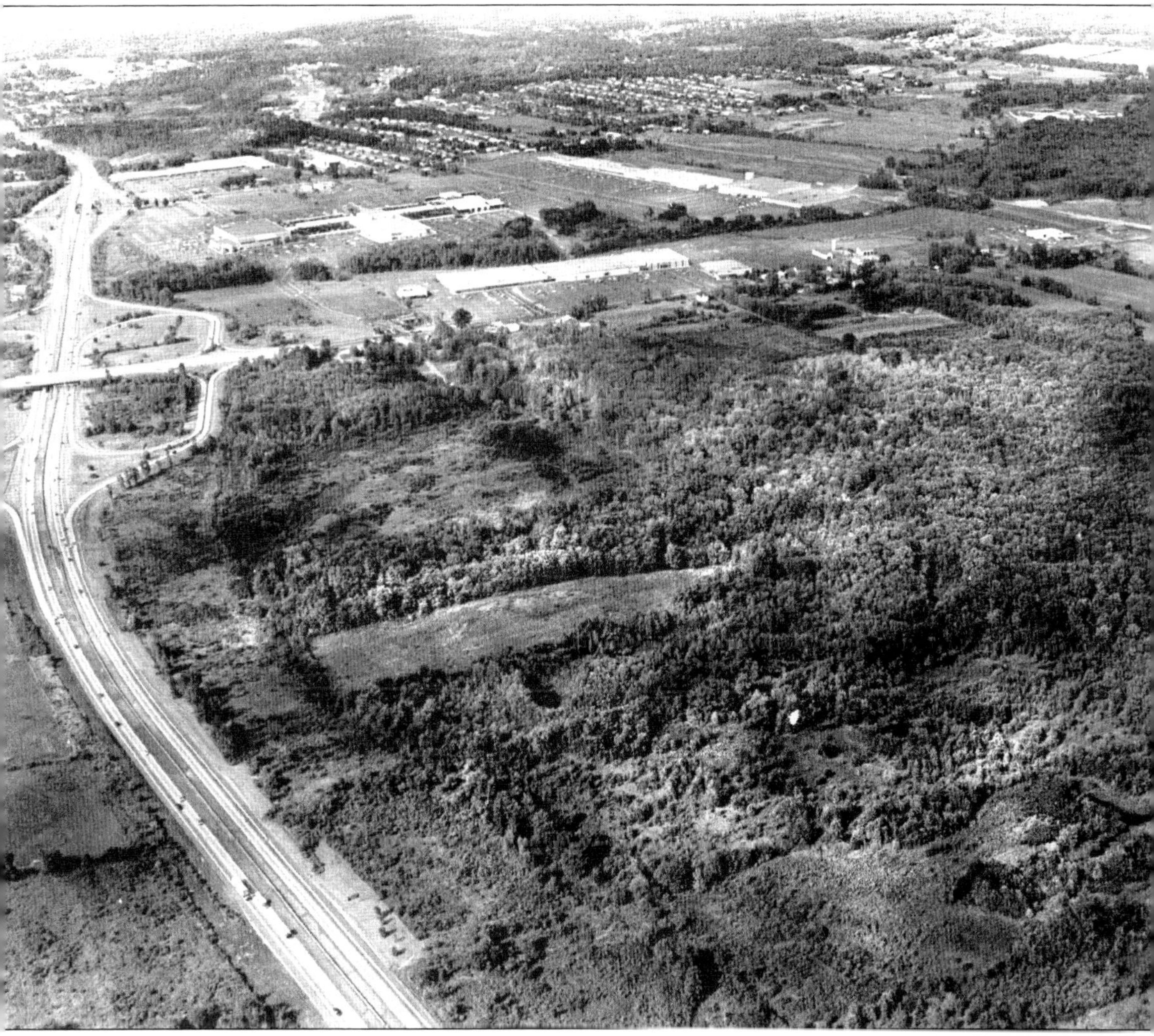

This 1970s view, looking north, shows Interstate 91 (left) and the Enfield Suburban Mall, the Enfield Square, Elm Plaza, and State Line Plaza (center). The undeveloped land to the east of Interstate 91 (foreground) later became the industrial park. In 1971, town residents approved the 550-acre Enfield Memorial Industrial Park. The Town of Enfield purchased more than 100 properties between Hazard Avenue and South Road, 94 of which were located in a mixed residential and business neighborhood south of Hazard Avenue. The homes and businesses were razed, and Tampa, Deland, Orlando, Revere, Beach, and Lafayette Avenues were ripped up and taken off the town street rolls.

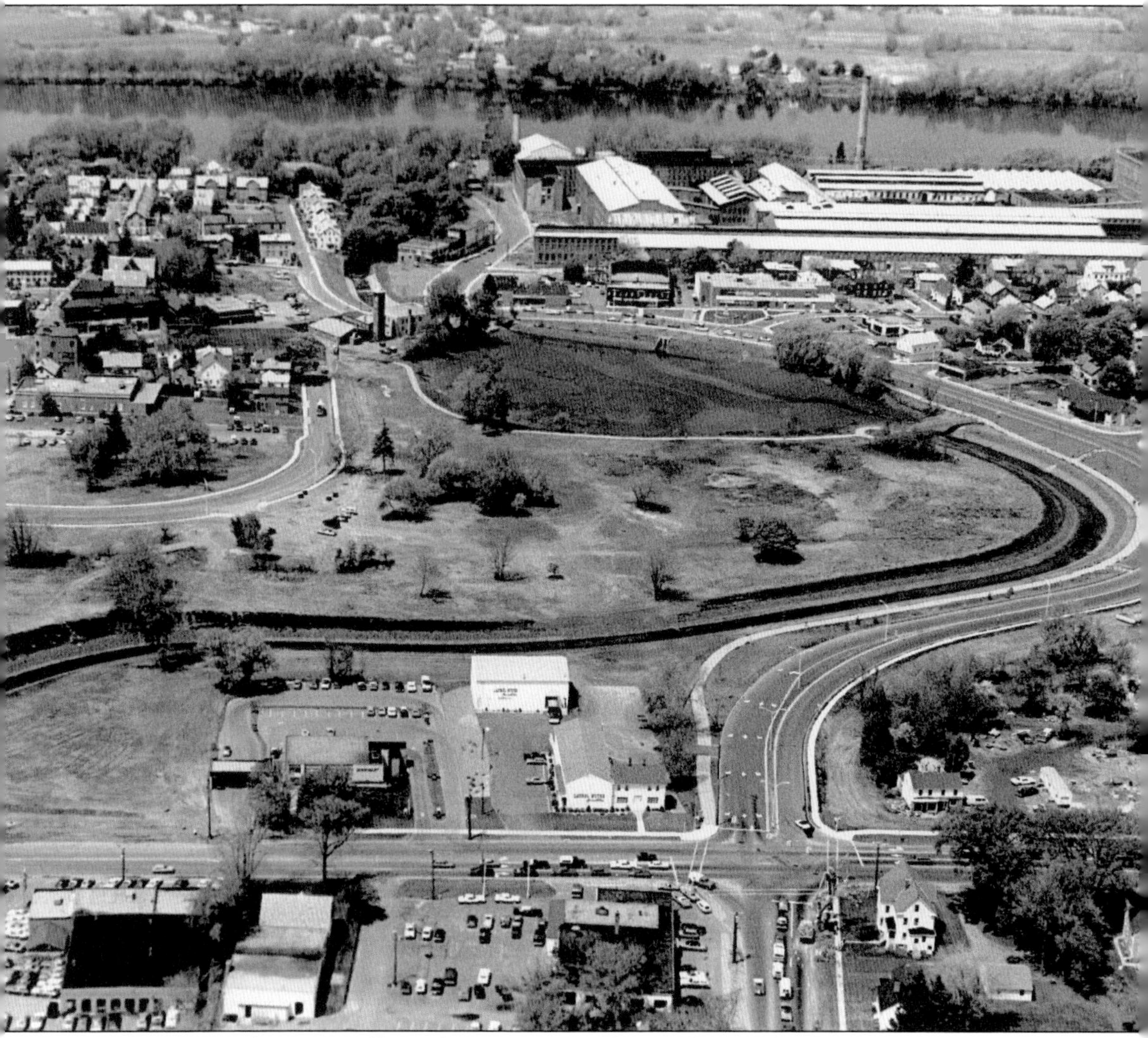

Downtown Thompsonville is shown in 1978 during the final stages of the urban renewal project. A restructured North Main Street wraps around Freshwater Pond, leading to the former Bigelow-Sanford Carpet Company. The Connecticut River and Suffield make up the background scenery. Many businesses and homes were razed along Freshwater Brook and Pond during the project, leaving many vacant land parcels, visible in this photograph. Some streets, including Young and Abbe Avenues, were completely ripped up. In the early 1970s, a scale model was prepared, showing five-story apartment buildings near Freshwater Pond and a five-story office complex right in the middle of the town hall green. The planned apartment and office buildings were never built. The current site adjacent to Freshwater Pond is a combination of the Ella Grasso Manor senior housing complex and Freshwater Pond Apartments. Two shopping plazas were constructed in the 1980s—one at the intersection of Central and High Streets opposite the Enfield Senior Center and another on Enfield Street across the street from the Enfield Chrysler Plymouth dealership.

Five

PEOPLE, PLACES, AND EVENTS

The Enfield community was made up of many special people, places, and events between 1950 and 1980. Enfield residents were accustomed to see Angelo Lamagna at the youth center, Harry Tatoian at high school events, the Spanswick brothers on the baseball diamond, and Leger Starr conducting construction business from his Lincoln Continental. Local children played at the youth center, and they fished and skated on Freshwater Pond. A local hangout for teenagers was the Mid-Nite Spa, on North Main Street. Young adults listened to musical acts at Shaker Park, and older adults dined at the Mountain Laurel Restaurant. Families ate at Terwilliger's hamburger stand, the Smyth Farm Dairy Bar, and the Enfield Dairy Bar. Many building dedications took place in the 1950s—the Felician Sisters Motherhouse, St. Bernard's Church, and St. Joseph's and St. Adalbert's Schools. The Thompsonville Mount Carmel Society and Auxiliary held its annual celebration at Mount Carmel Park on Park Avenue. In 1960, Sen. John F. Kennedy's motorcade stopped for a brief campaign stop on the expressway.

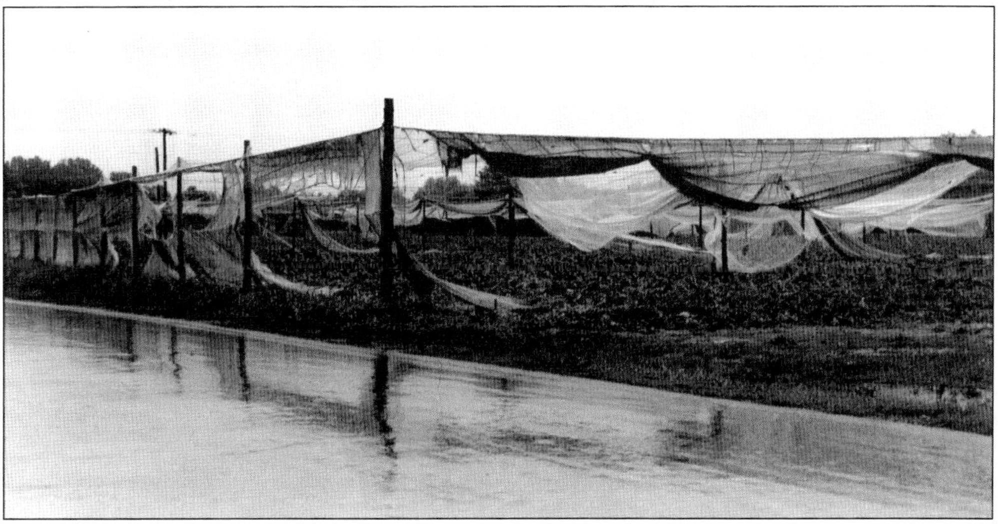

This 1954 view shows the damaged tobacco plants and ripped cheesecloth netting of an Enfield farm after Hurricane Carol. Tobacco has played an important role in the history of Enfield, located in the middle of Tobacco Valley. The region stretches from Middletown, Connecticut, to Deerfield, Massachusetts. Enfield has had many tobacco growers, including the Jarmoc family, George Raffia and Sons, John R. Polek, the Consolidated Cigar Corporation, the L.B. Hass Corporation, Patrick Maxellon, Edward Rapacki, and the Woodworth Farm. Tobacco farmers employed hundreds of teenagers each summer from Enfield and surrounding communities. The popularity of cigars has increased in recent years, adding to the amount of acreage farmed, construction of new tobacco barns, and cigar shops.

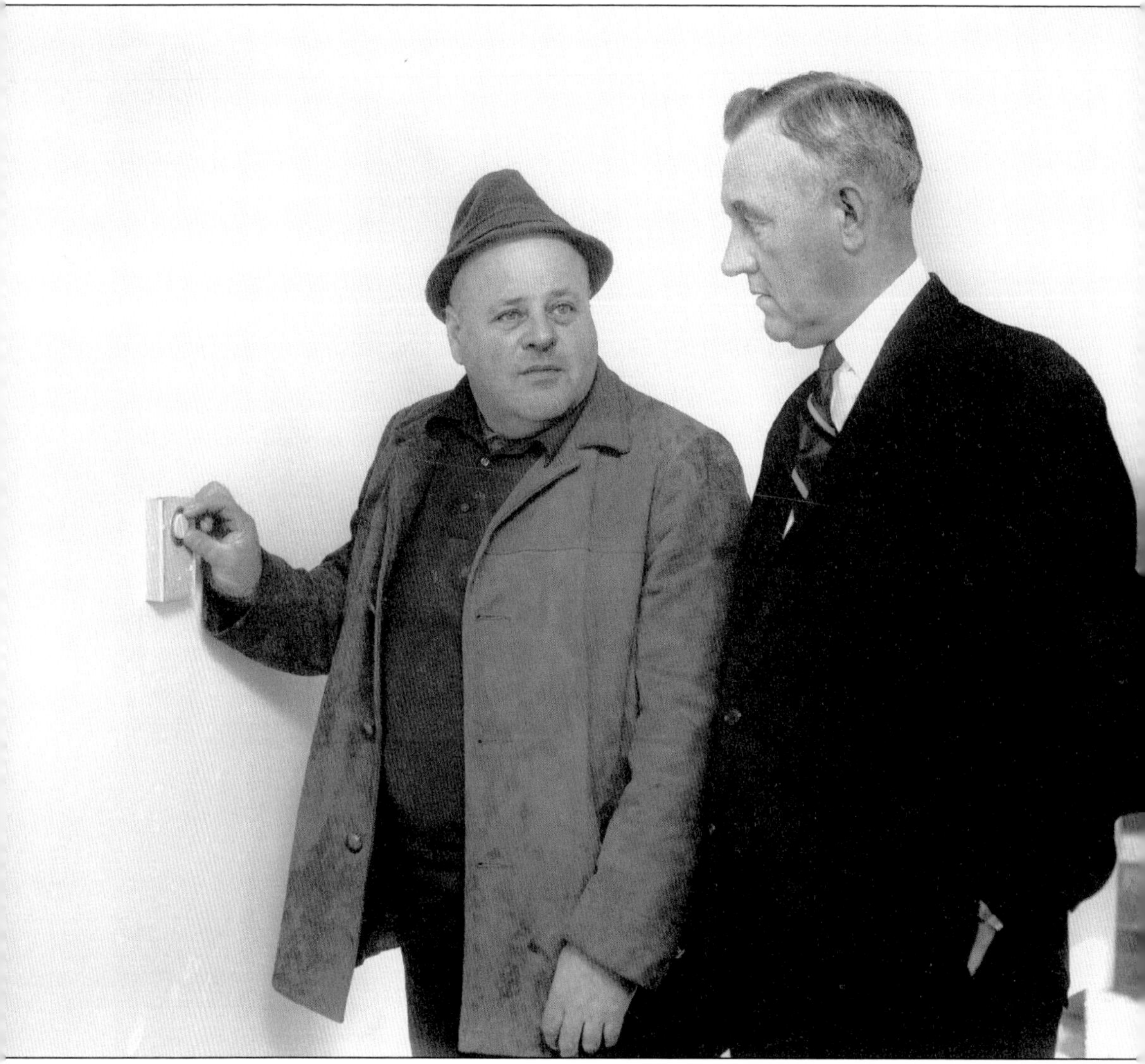

S. Leger Starr (left) controls the electric heat in the first Gold Medallion home as Connecticut Light and Power official John Moran looks on in 1967. Starr became the owner of the family construction company after his father passed away in 1948. For the next 28 years, Starr dramatically changed the landscape of Enfield. He built thousands of single-family homes, a majority of them in Enfield. The Town of Enfield built one school per year in the 1960s to keep pace with hundreds of children coming from Starr subdivisions. Starr and his employees worked hard over the years to build quality homes. Starr passed away at the age of 54 on February 20, 1976.

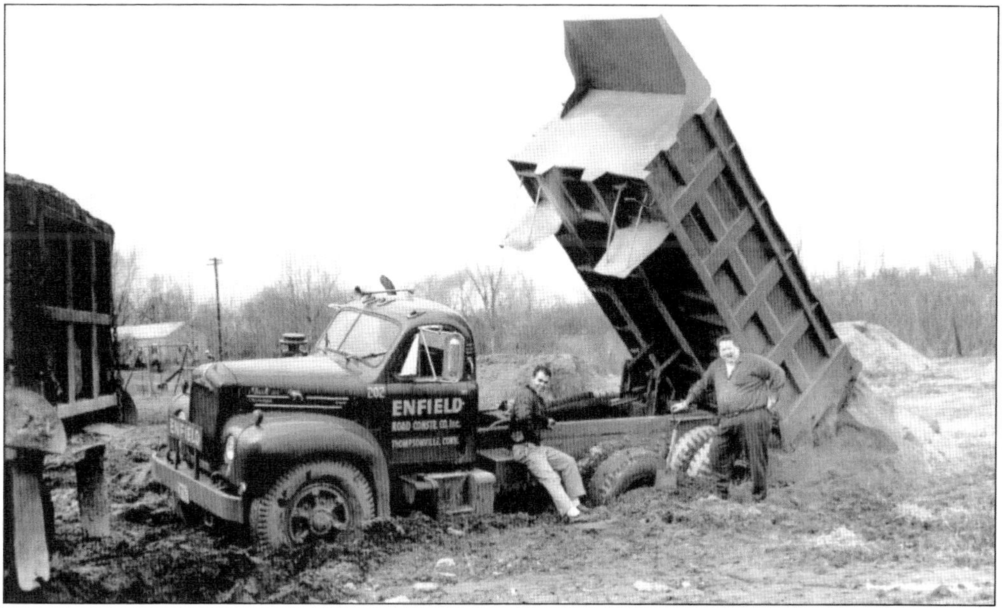

Enfield Construction Company employees Richard LaVallee (left) and John Conley take a break from shoveling out their dump truck at the end of Claremont Avenue in the 1960s. The company was owned by the DellAquila family of Thompsonville.

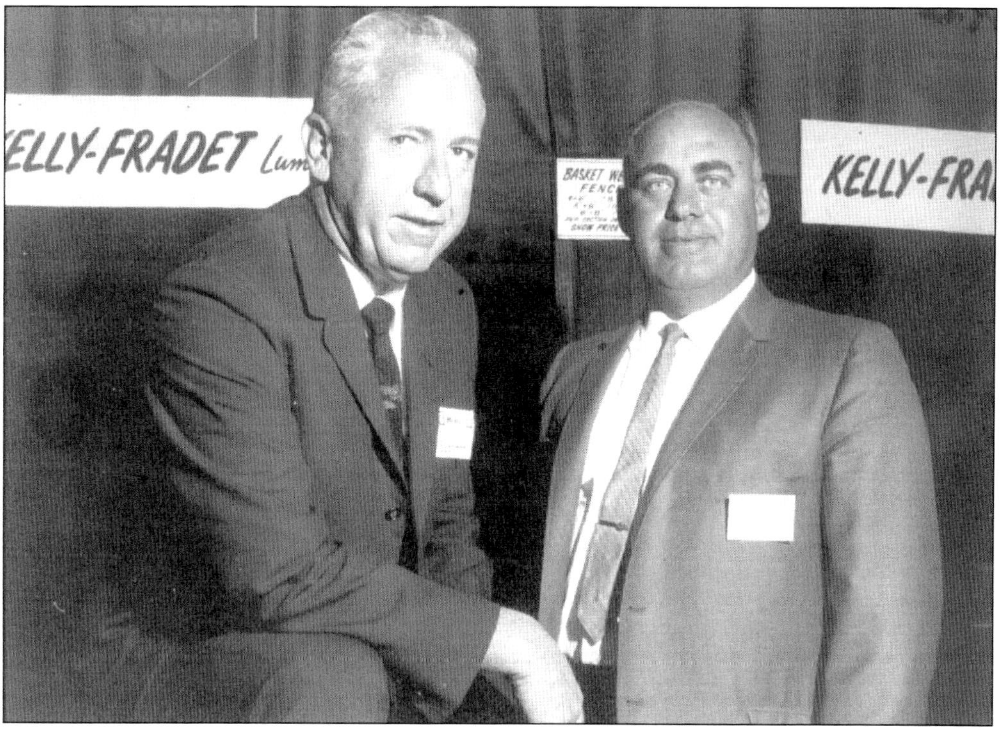

Treasurer Clarence "Red" Weeks (left) and manager Fred P. Bomely (right) represent Kelly-Fradet Lumber Marts at the North Central Chamber of Commerce Home Show in Thompsonville in the 1960s. In the 1970s, Weeks became the owner of Kelly-Fradet Lumber Marts.

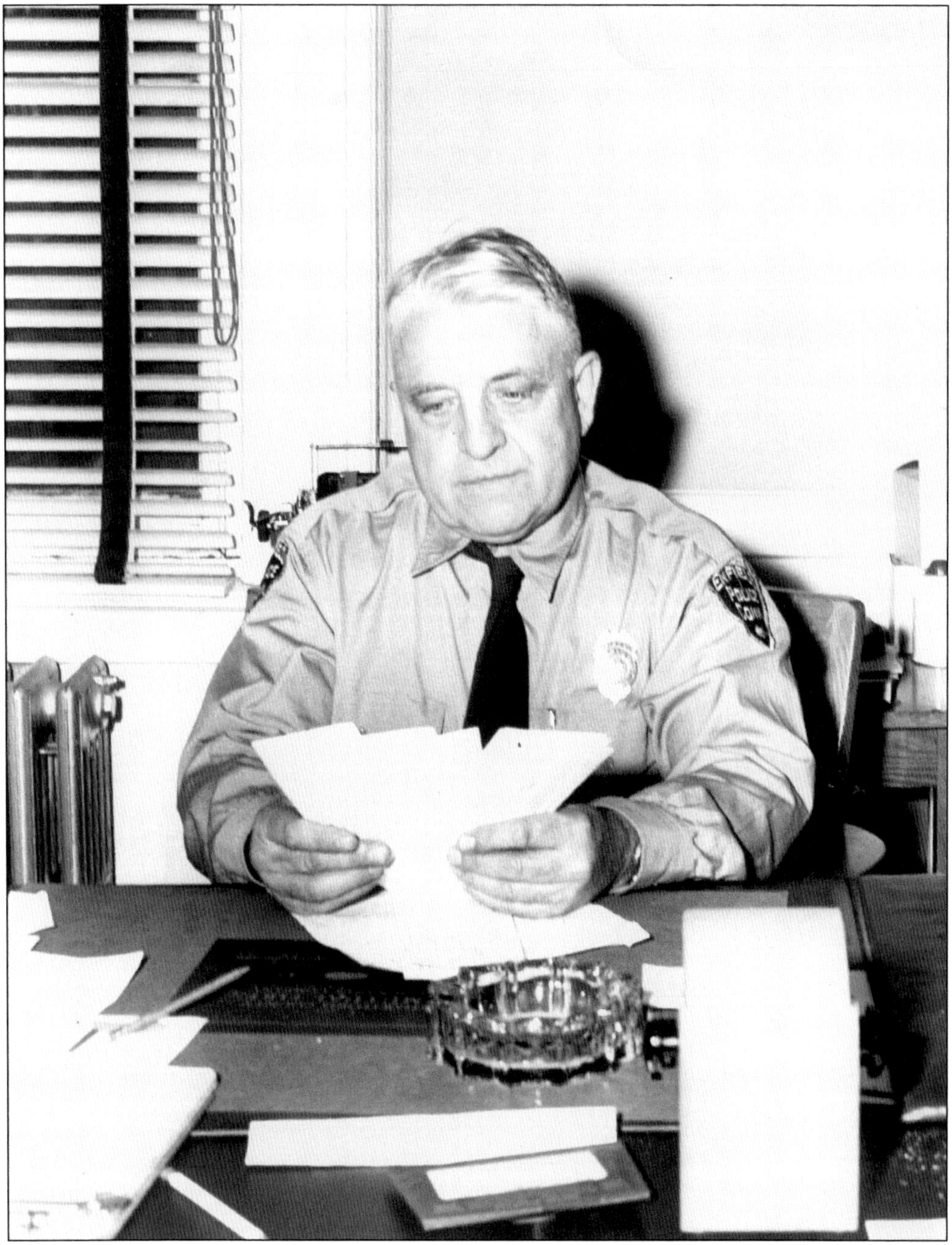

Police chief Earl Reynolds is seated at his desk in the old police station on North Main Street in the 1950s. His career spanned more than 35 years. He served as a patrolman from 1922 to 1950, as sergeant from 1950 to 1952, as deputy chief in 1952, and as the ninth chief of police from 1952 to 1958. He retired from the police force in March 1958. He passed away on January 17, 1983.

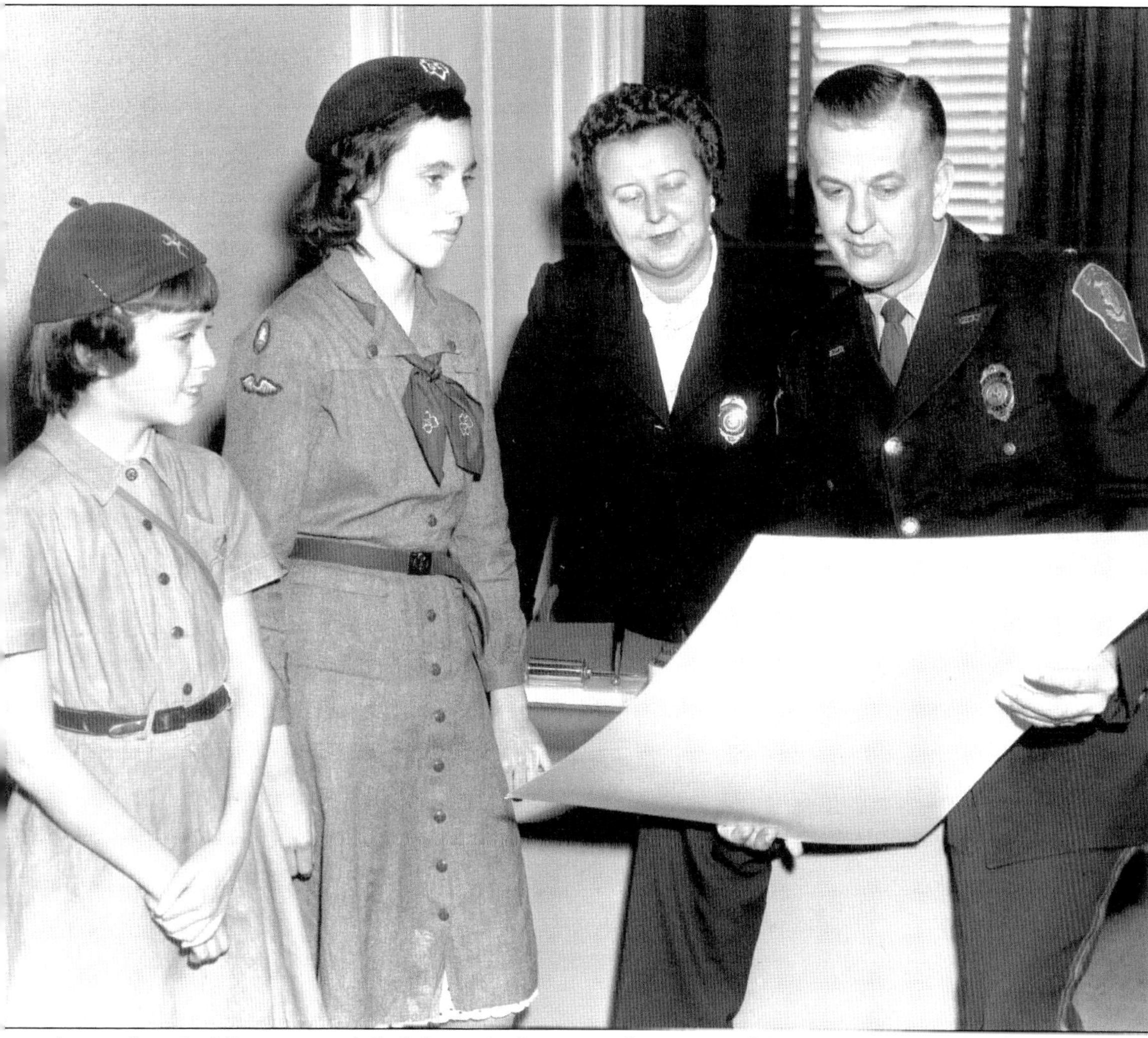

An unidentified Brownie and Girl Scout look on as policewoman Margaret Arietti and police chief Walter J. Skower view a proclamation in the late 1950s. Skower's career spanned more than 43 years. He served as a supernumerary appointment from 1947 to 1949, as patrolman from 1949 to 1955, as sergeant from 1955 to 1958, and as the tenth chief of police from 1958 to 1990. He retired from the police force in August 1990 and passed away on March 27, 1992.

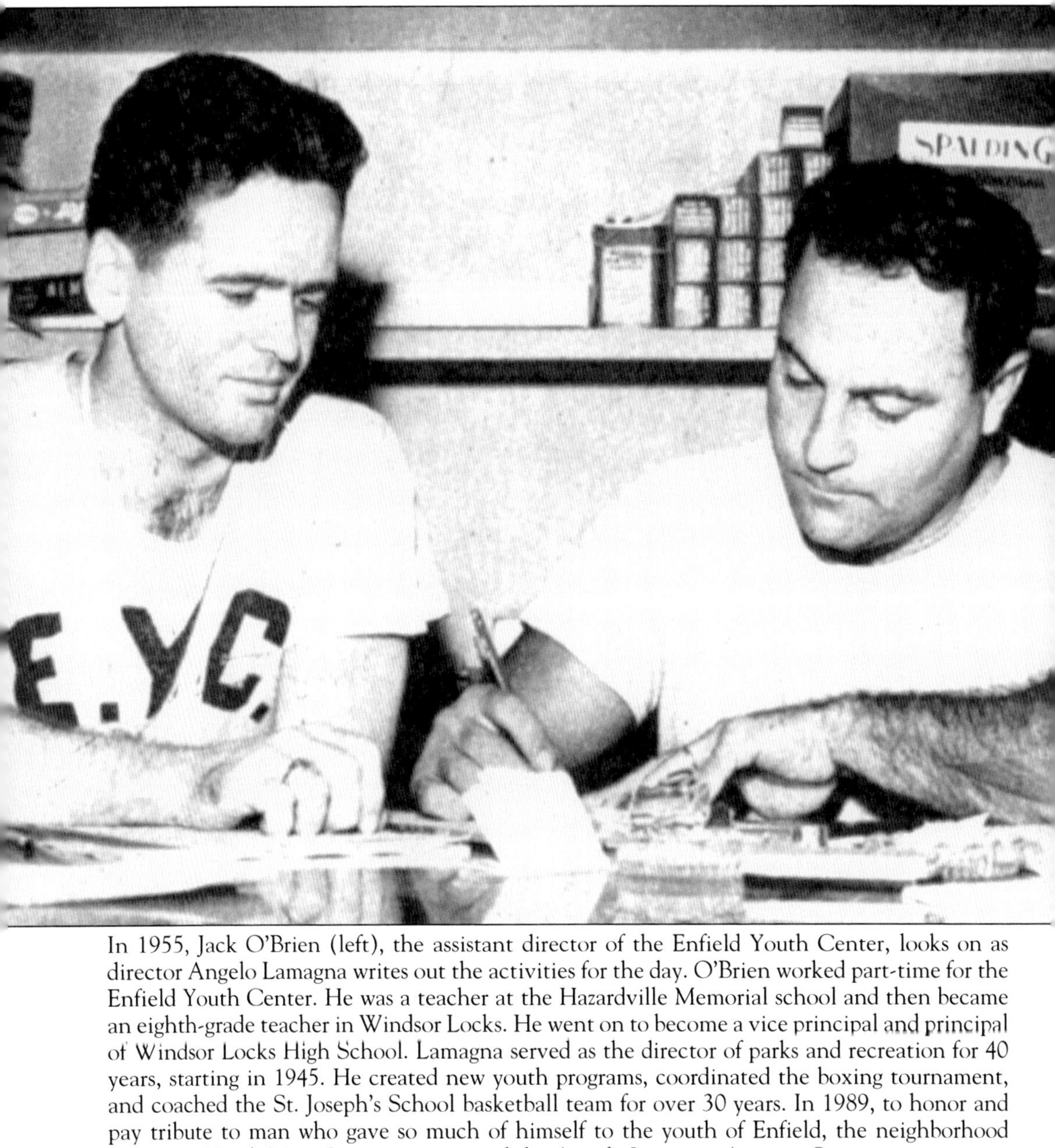

In 1955, Jack O'Brien (left), the assistant director of the Enfield Youth Center, looks on as director Angelo Lamagna writes out the activities for the day. O'Brien worked part-time for the Enfield Youth Center. He was a teacher at the Hazardville Memorial school and then became an eighth-grade teacher in Windsor Locks. He went on to become a vice principal and principal of Windsor Locks High School. Lamagna served as the director of parks and recreation for 40 years, starting in 1945. He created new youth programs, coordinated the boxing tournament, and coached the St. Joseph's School basketball team for over 30 years. In 1989, to honor and pay tribute to man who gave so much of himself to the youth of Enfield, the neighborhood center on North Main Street was renamed the Angelo Lamagna Activity Center.

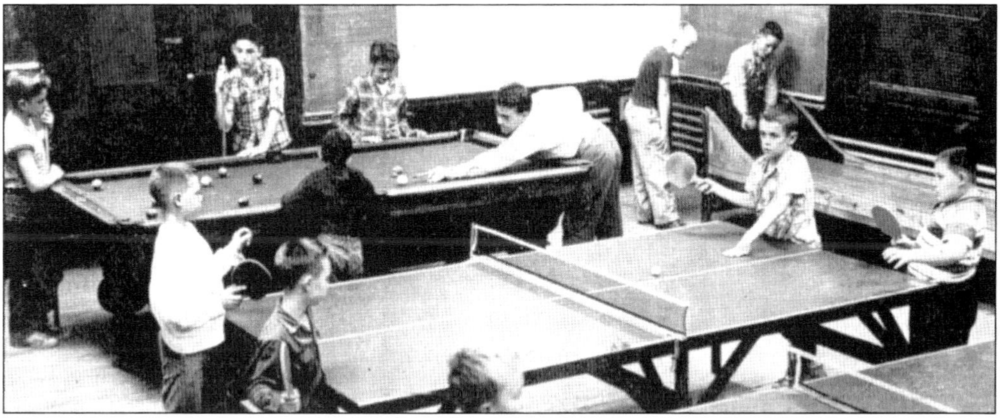

The Enfield Youth Center was located on the second floor over the courthouse on North Main Street. The photograph shows Enfield youths playing table tennis, billiards, and bowling in the game room in 1955.

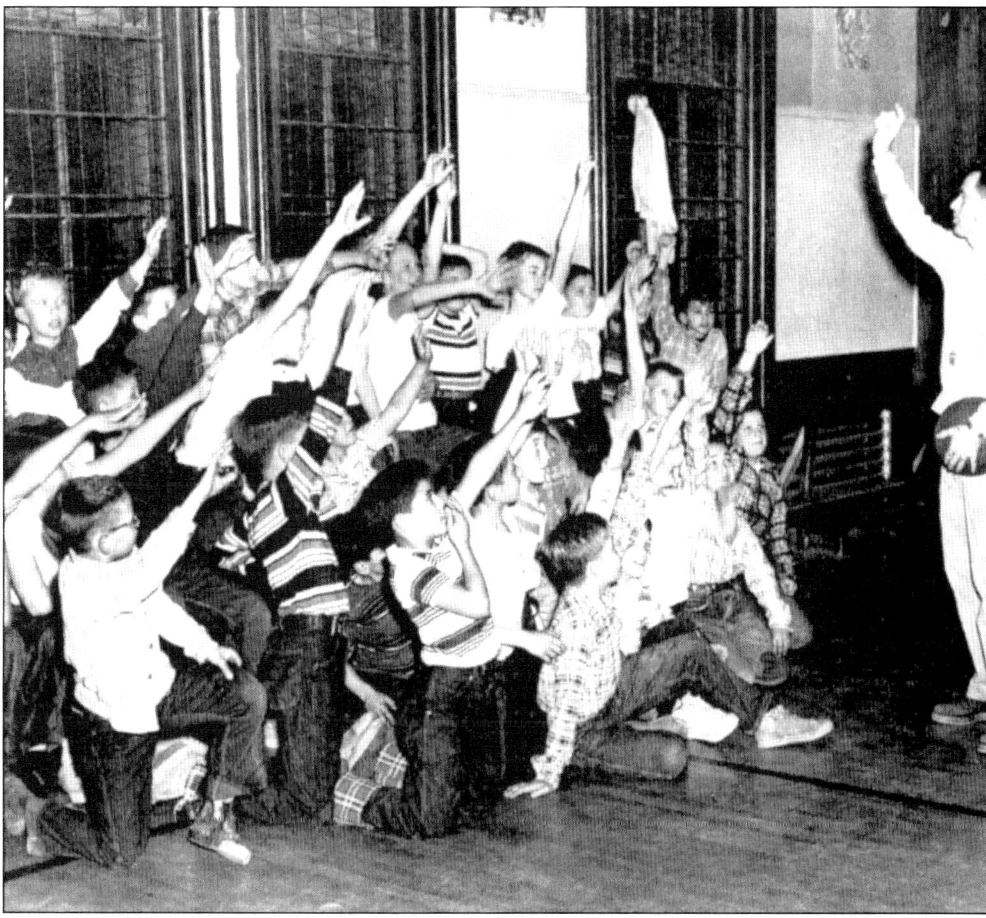

Assistant director Jack O'Brien picks teams for a basketball game at the Enfield Youth Center in 1955. The ceiling on the second floor was lower than in most gymnasiums. High-arcing shots would constantly hit the ceiling, forcing players to take line drive shots at the basketball hoop.

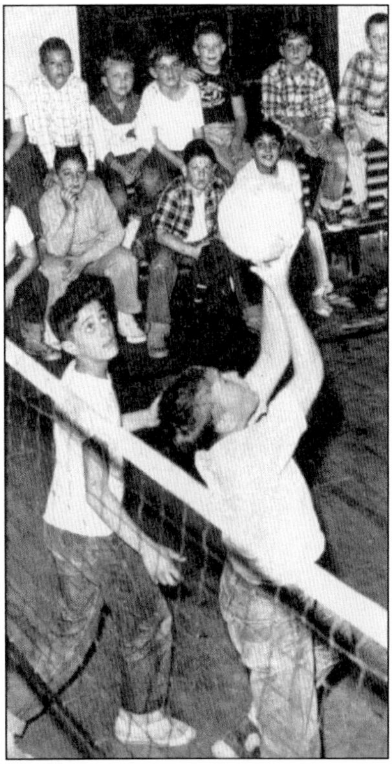

Ronald Landry returns the ball over the net in a volleyball game at the Enfield Youth Center in 1955.

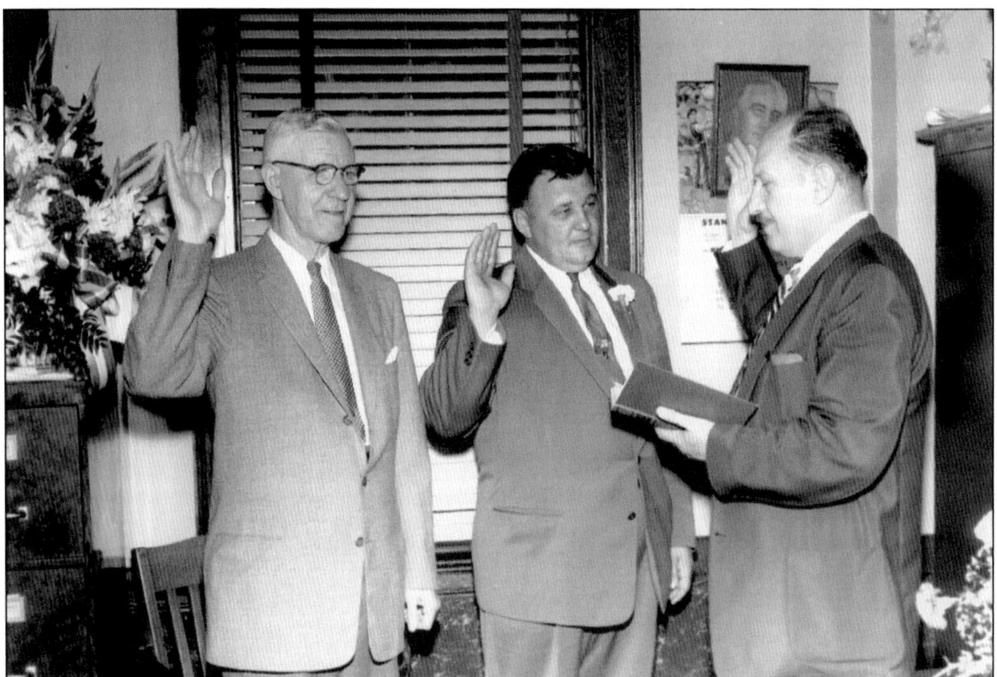

This 1955 view shows town selectmen getting sworn into office. From left to right are Cornelius F. Sullivan (selectman), Norbert D. Senio (first selectman), sworn in by Joseph T. Glista (Probate Court of Enfield judge).

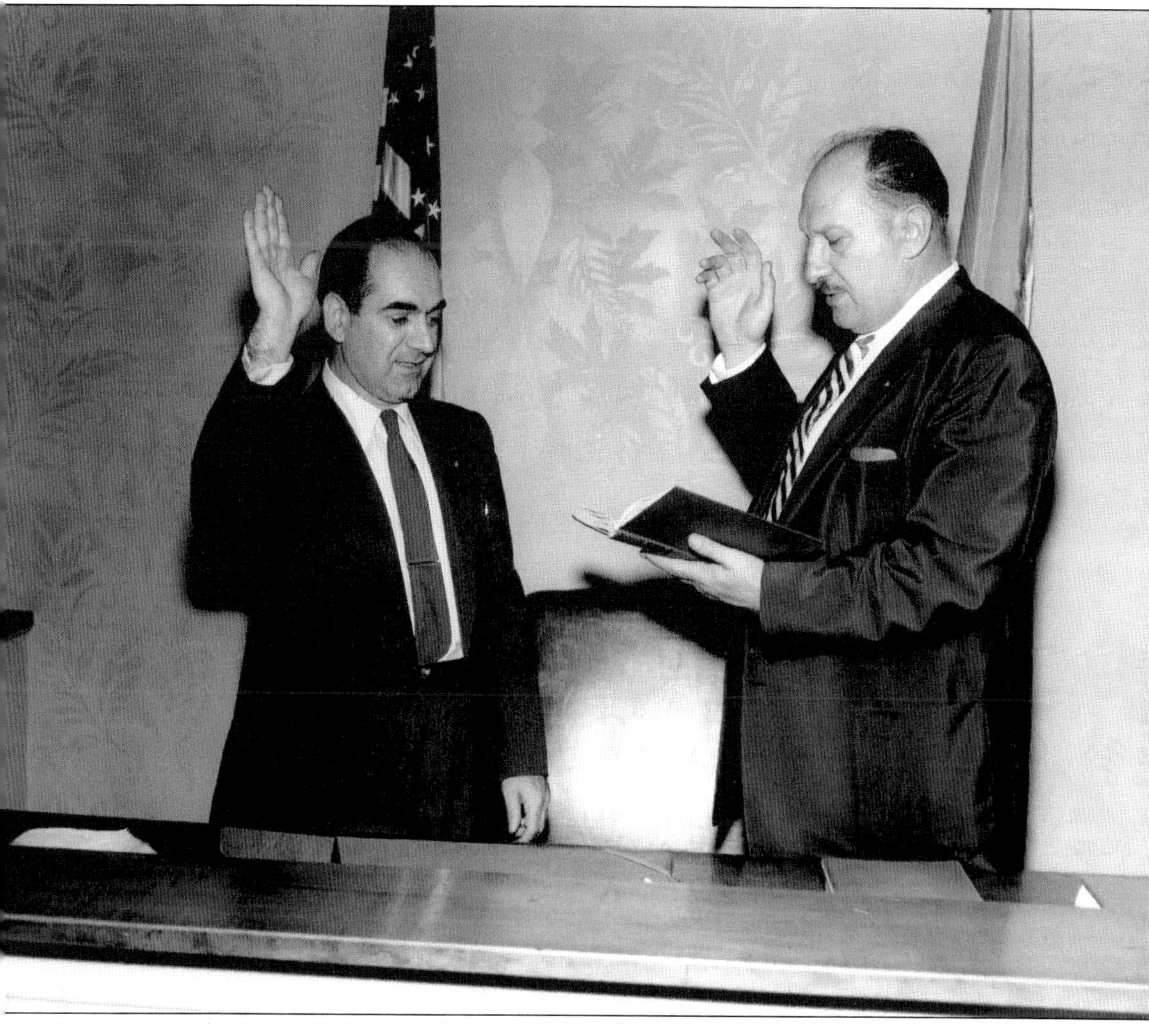

Town court judge James C. Parakilas (left) is sworn in by Probate Court of Enfield judge Joseph T. Glista in 1955. Parakilas operated his own law practice for over 53 years. He served as prosecuting attorney in Thompsonville Court from 1941 to 1942, as judge of the Thompsonville Municipal Court from 1955 to 1957, as chairman of the Enfield Democratic Town Committee, and as president of the Hartford County Bar Association. Judge Joseph T. Glista's career spanned over 32 years; he served from 1941 to 1973 as probate judge of Enfield. He was involved in many community clubs, including the Kiwanis Club and the Enfield Historical Society, and was a member of the Greys football team.

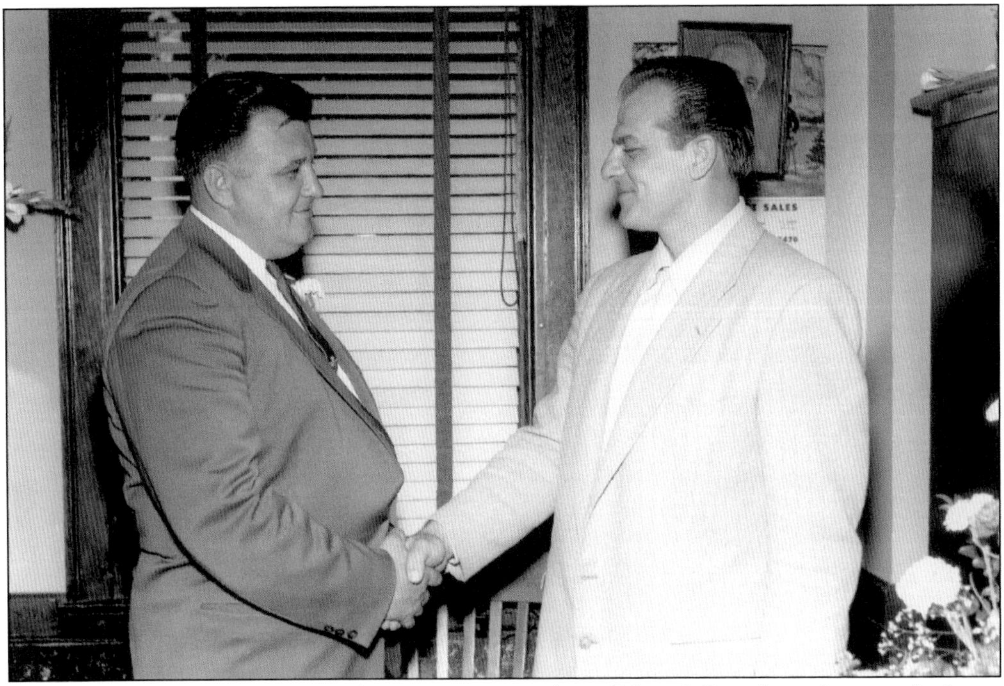

Norbert D. Senio (left), first selectman, congratulates Edward Piepul as the new highway superintendent for Enfield in 1955.

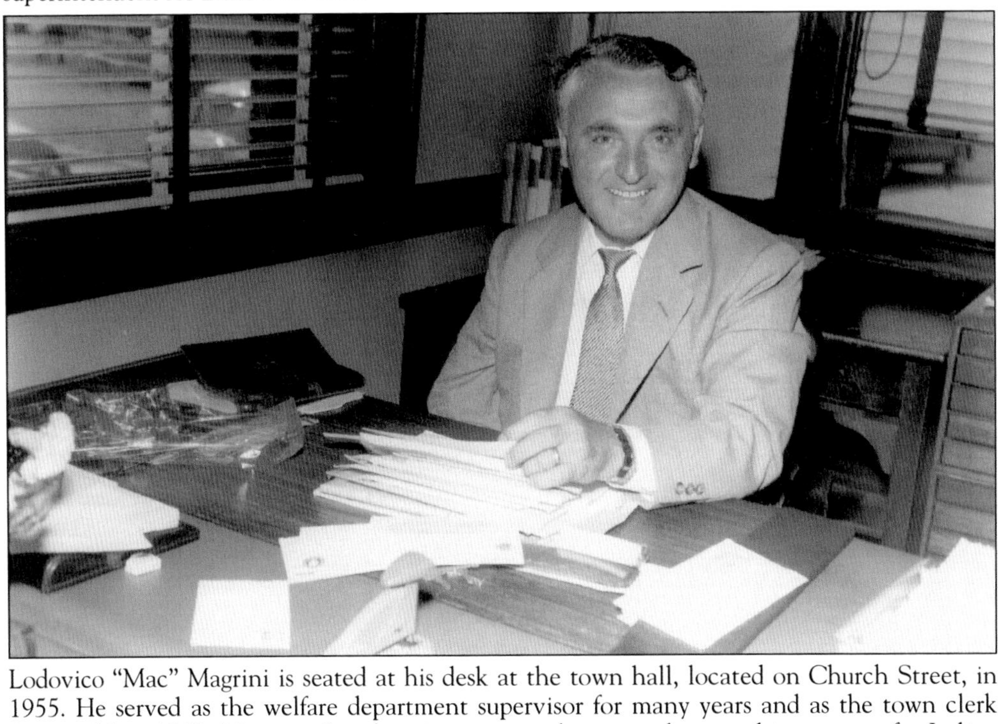

Lodovico "Mac" Magrini is seated at his desk at the town hall, located on Church Street, in 1955. He served as the welfare department supervisor for many years and as the town clerk from 1955 to 1965. Magrini played an important role as translator and interpreter for Italian immigrants in Enfield in the 1930s. He also taught the Italian language to first-generation Americans of Italian descent.

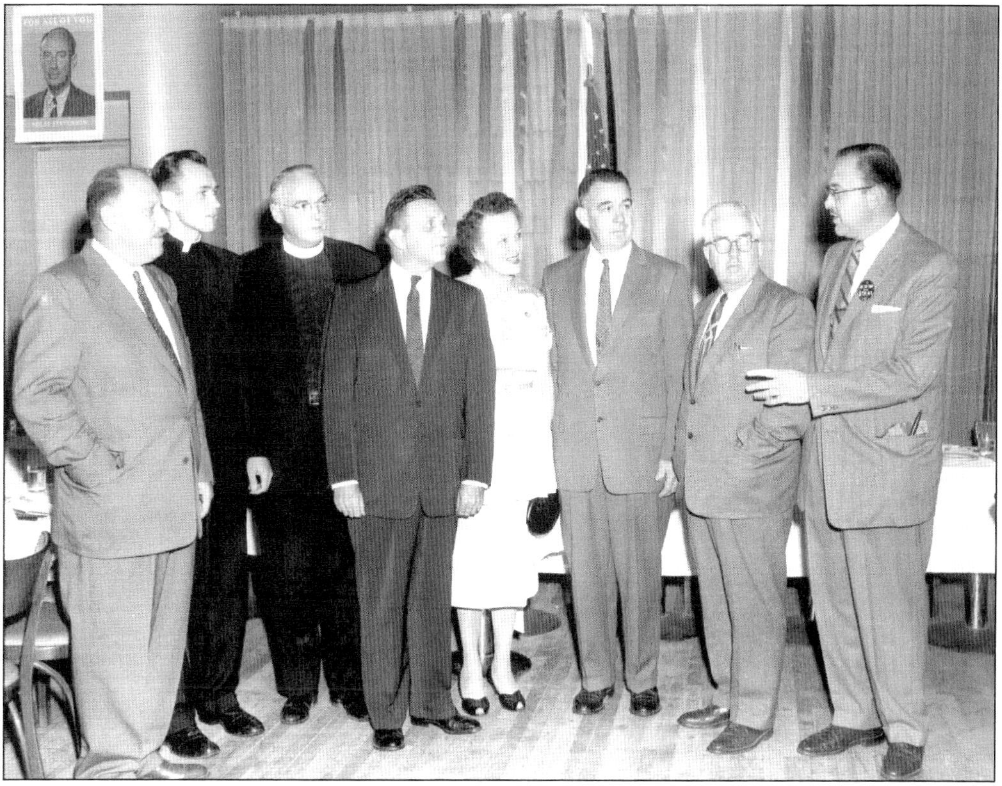

This photograph was taken during a Democratic party gathering at the Silhouette Club and Restaurant, on Enfield Street near the state line, in 1956. From left to right are Judge Joseph T. Glista; Rev. Edward Jaksina, St. Adalbert's Church; Rev. Edward J. Reardon, St. Bernard's Church; an unidentified man; Helen Javorski; Peter Crombie; an unidentified man; and Dominic Cimino. Notice the Democratic presidential candidate poster of Adlai Stevenson on the wall in the background.

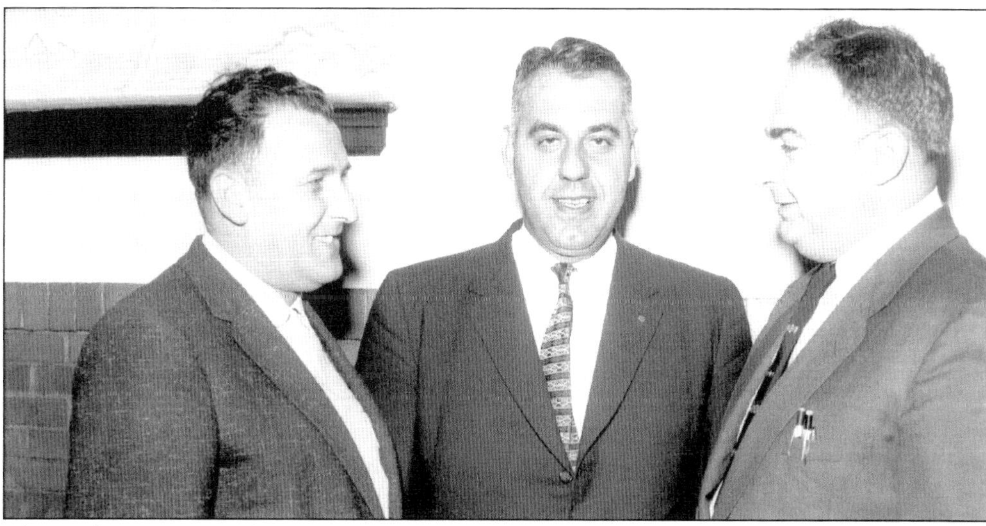

This mid-1950s view shows a gathering of Republican party leaders. From left to right are Charles Maggio, Phillip E. Tatoian Jr., and Nickolas J. DellAquila.

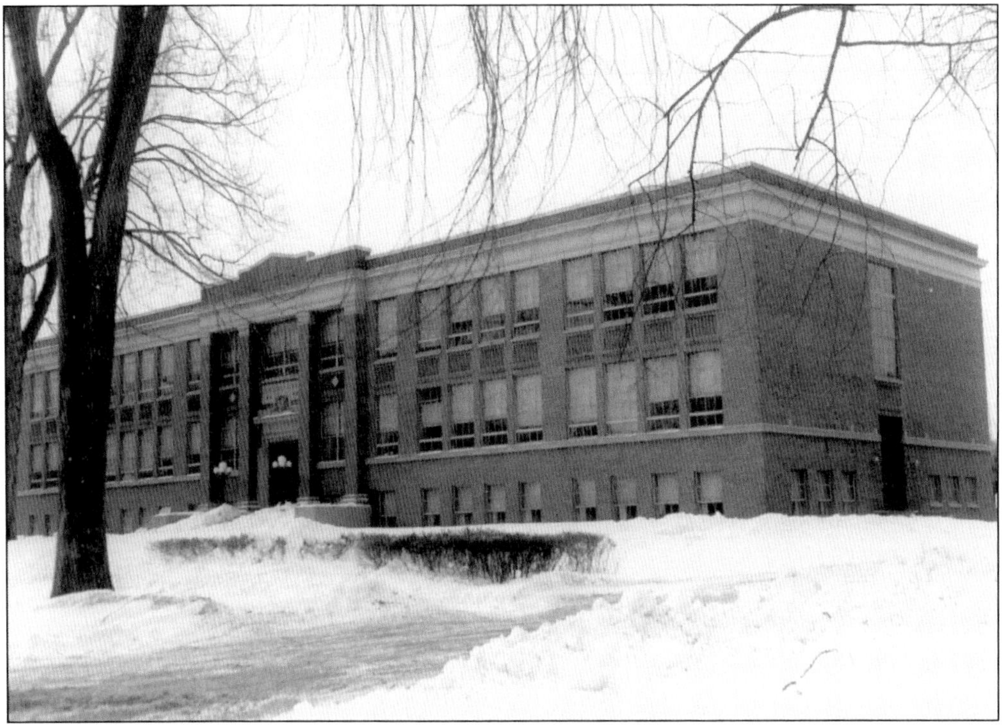

In the early 1900s, discussions were held to build a new high school, but the proposal was turned down by town officials. In the early 1920s, Dr. Thomas Grant Alcorn served as chairman of the high school building committee and worked very hard to make his vision come true. The second Enfield High School, located on Enfield Street, opened in 1925 and served as the high school until 1962. It later served as the intermediate school and, in 1977, was rededicated as the Alcorn Elementary School. It was refurbished in 1994 at the cost of approximately $6 million.

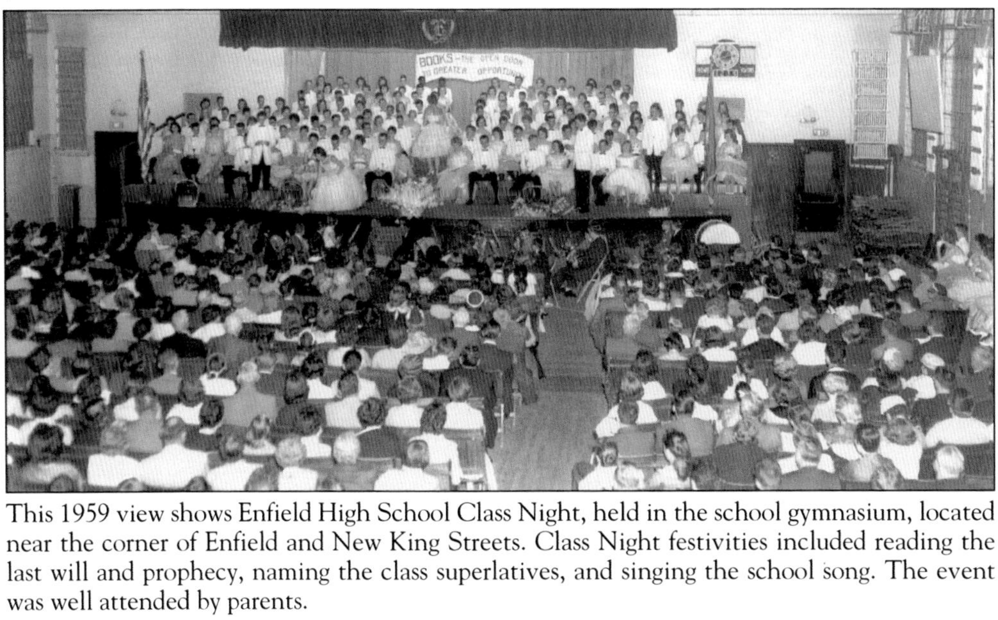

This 1959 view shows Enfield High School Class Night, held in the school gymnasium, located near the corner of Enfield and New King Streets. Class Night festivities included reading the last will and prophecy, naming the class superlatives, and singing the school song. The event was well attended by parents.

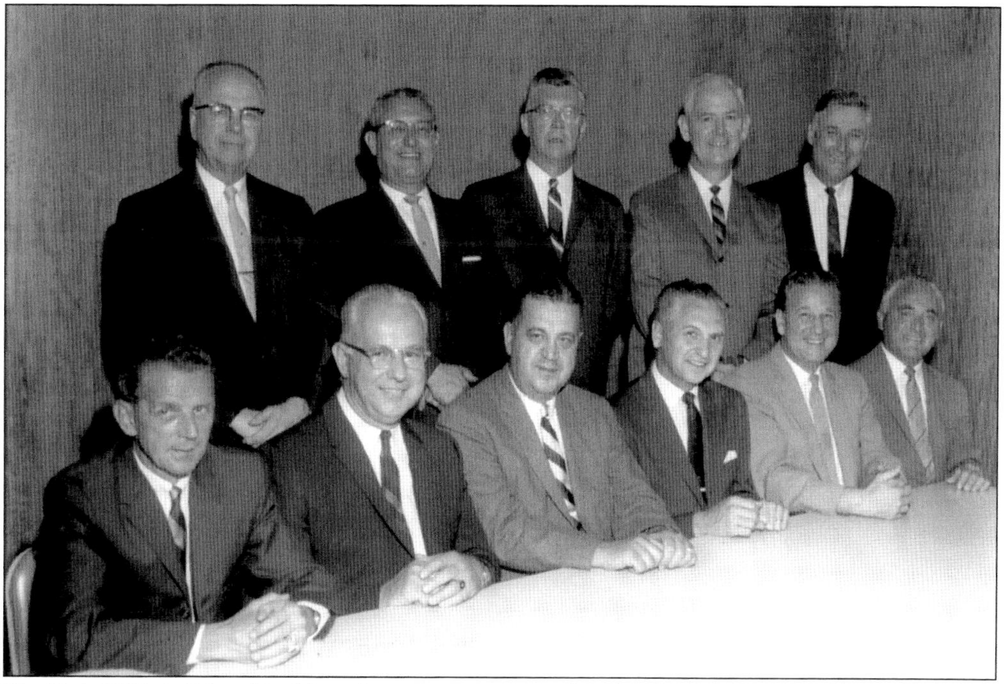

The Enfield High School Building Committee is pictured in the new conference room in 1962. The committee members are, from left to right, as follows: (front row) Stanley A. Bigos, vice chairman; Fred Stroiney; Harry E. Tatoian, principal; Francis J. Pilch, secretary; Dr. Carl Scavotto, chairman; and Lodovico Magrini; (back row) Karl D. Lee, superintendent emeritus; Pellegrino Reveruzzi; Howard M. Bromage; Arthur B. FitzGibbons, and Maurice F. Smith, superintendent.

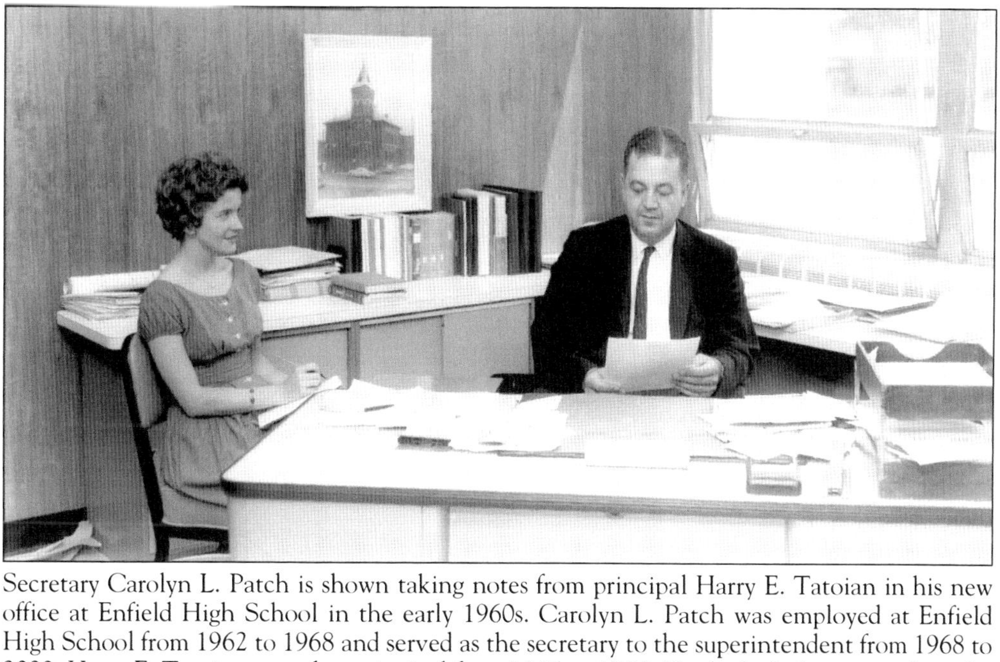

Secretary Carolyn L. Patch is shown taking notes from principal Harry E. Tatoian in his new office at Enfield High School in the early 1960s. Carolyn L. Patch was employed at Enfield High School from 1962 to 1968 and served as the secretary to the superintendent from 1968 to 2000. Harry E. Tatoian served as principal from 1946 to 1966. He died of a heart attack at the age of 54 a few days before classes opened in 1966.

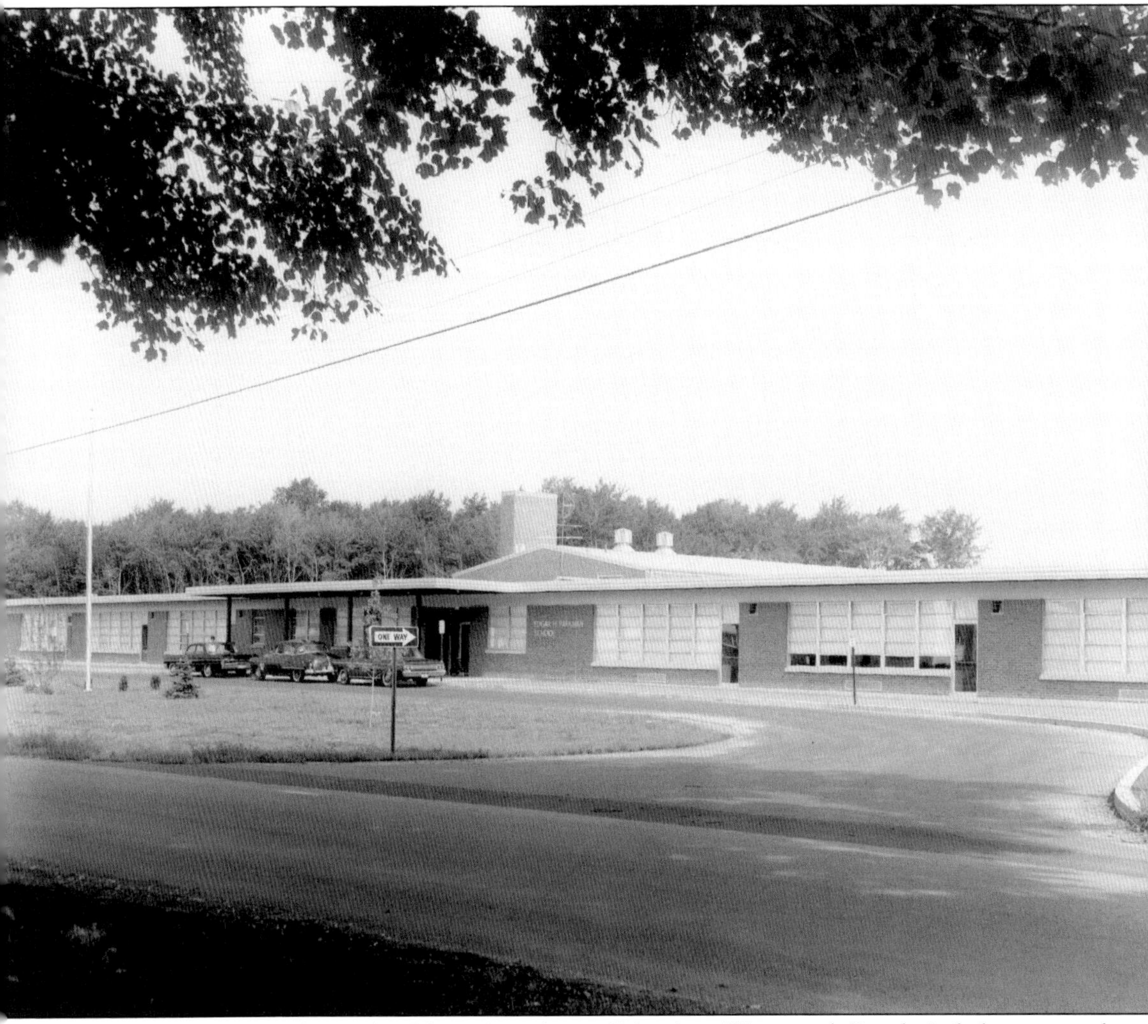

This 1960s view shows the Edgar H. Parkman School on Weymouth Road. A dedication and open house at the elementary school building took place on November 7, 1965. The Enfield Elementary Building and Site Committee included Kenneth W. Goodsell, chairman; William E. Wehrle, secretary; Edward Arrowsmith; Robert E. Blomstrann, Peter A. Crombie; Karl D. Lee; John R. Nasto; Richard E. Stevens; Stanley J. Swiatownski; Charles A. Szuberla, superintendent of schools; and Leo E. Garrepy, assistant superintendent of schools. The architect was Walter R. Furey, A.I.A., of Thompsonville, and the general contractor was the John Romano Construction Company of Suffield. The school was named after Edgar H. Parkman, who served as a teacher and principal at Enfield High School and was the superintendent of schools in Enfield.

THOMPSONVILLE FESTIVAL

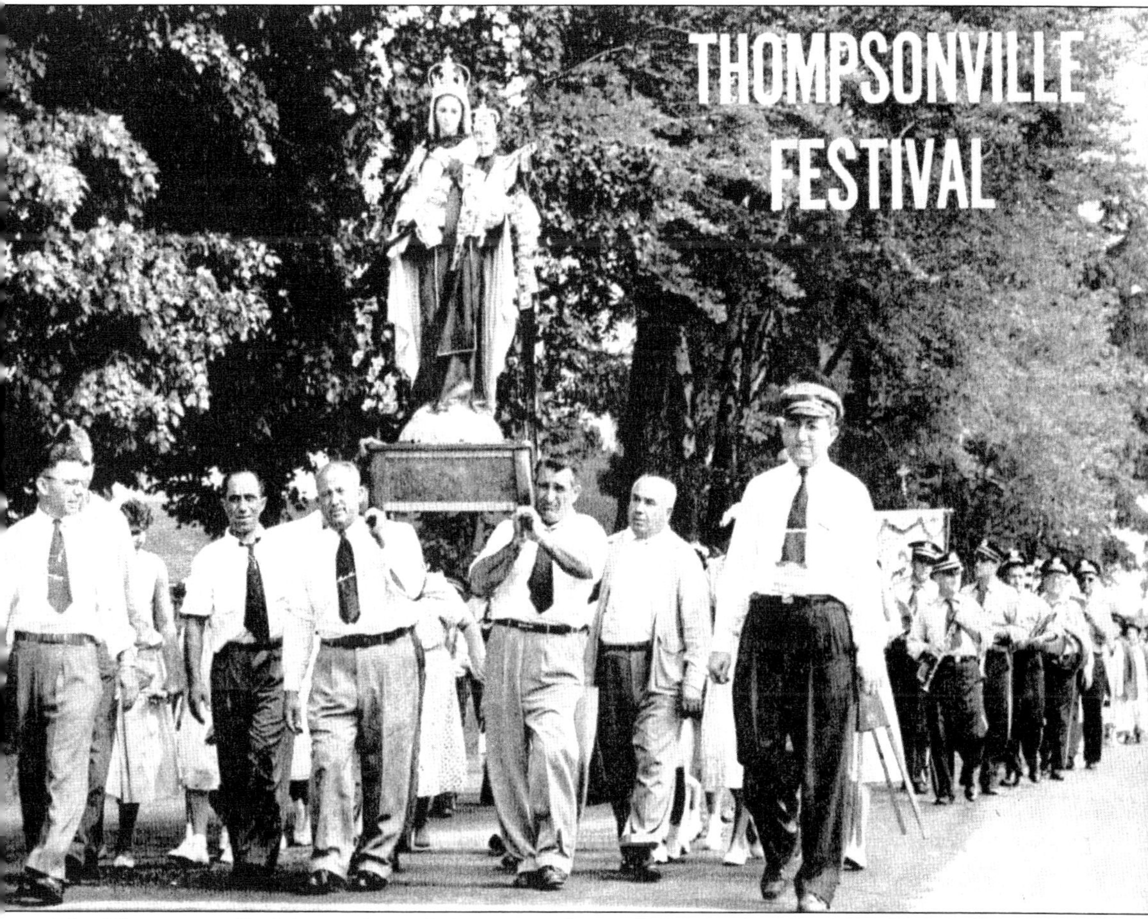

The Thompsonville Mount Carmel Society and Auxiliary, at Mount Carmel Park on Park Avenue, inaugurated the celebration of the Feast of Our Lady of Mount Carmel in 1920s. The celebration has grown over the years from a two-day event in the 1950s to a four-day event today. The celebration begins with a parade through the streets of Thompsonville. The statue of Our Lady of Mount Carmel was carried by society members and stopped along the parade route for the band to play as people pinned money to the statue. Pictured in 1955, these Thompsonville Mount Carmel Society members are, from left to right, Charles Renna, Felice Russo, Anthony Troiano Sr., Frank Tamero, Albert Vesce, and Anthony Porto.

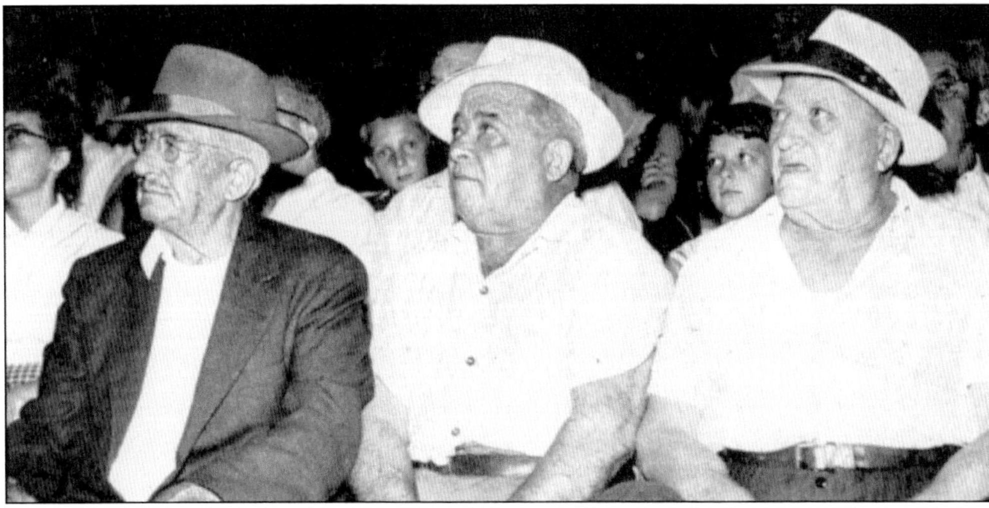

Longtime Mount Carmel Society members listen to band music in August 1955. From left to right are Lucien Albano, founder of the society; Vincent Sarno, charter member; and Anthony Romano, original celebration organizer.

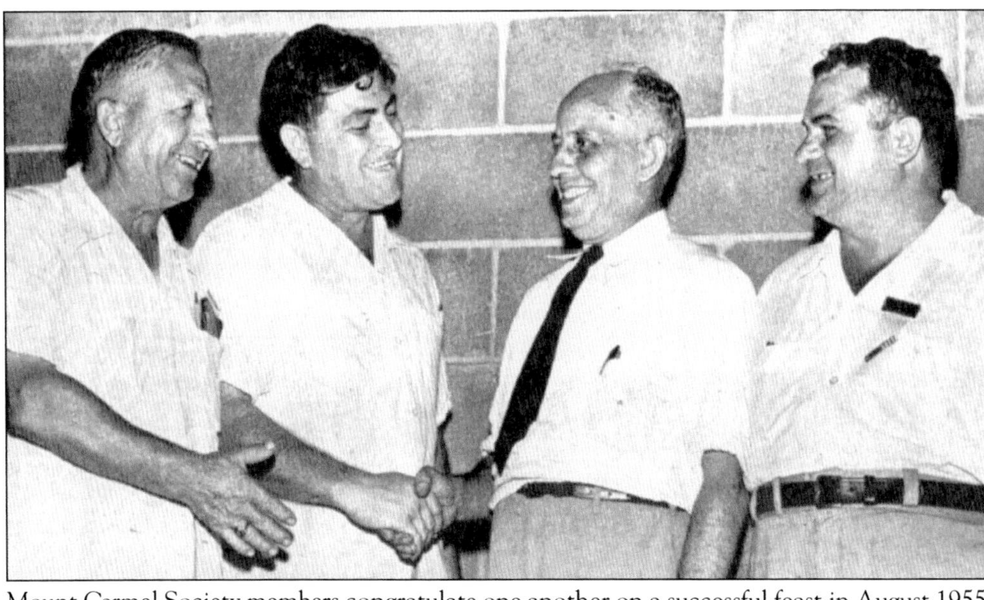

Mount Carmel Society members congratulate one another on a successful feast in August 1955. From left to right are John Reveruzzi, co-chairman; Joseph DiMaso, president; John Albano, co-chairman; and Jack Carenza, vice chairman.

The Mount Carmel feast is well known for its Italian delicacies. Michael Fasano is ready to eat a slice of pizza and an Italian ice in August 1955.

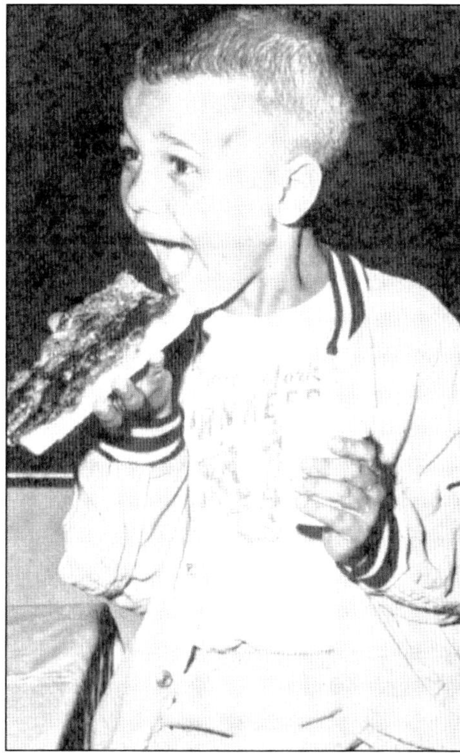

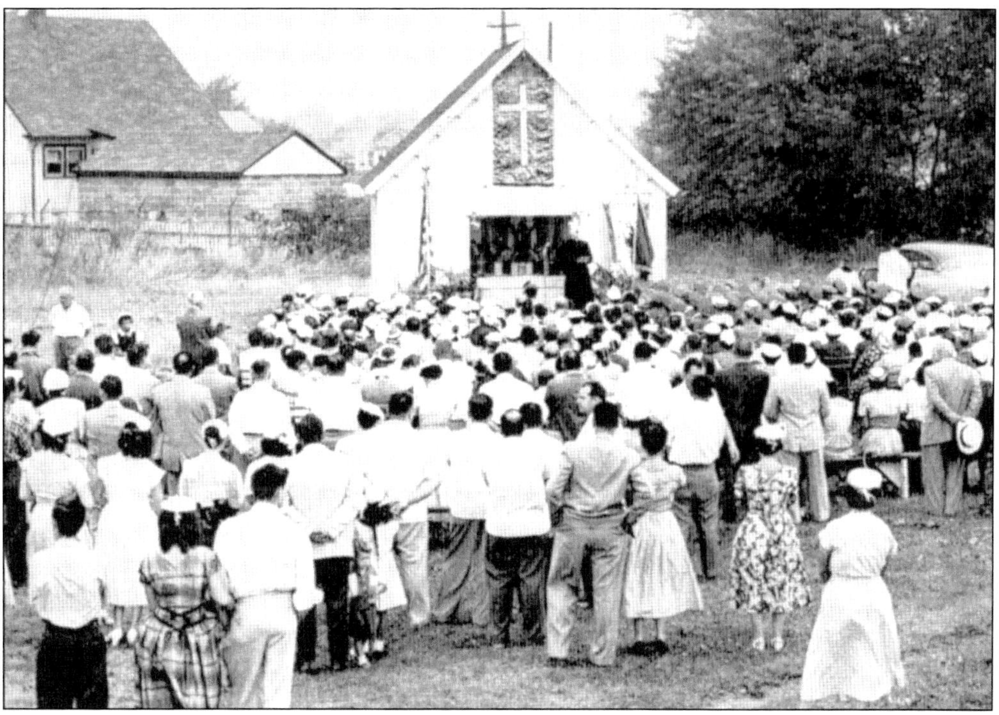

Rev. Dario Wegher celebrates an outdoor Sunday mass on park grounds before hundreds of society members in August 1955.

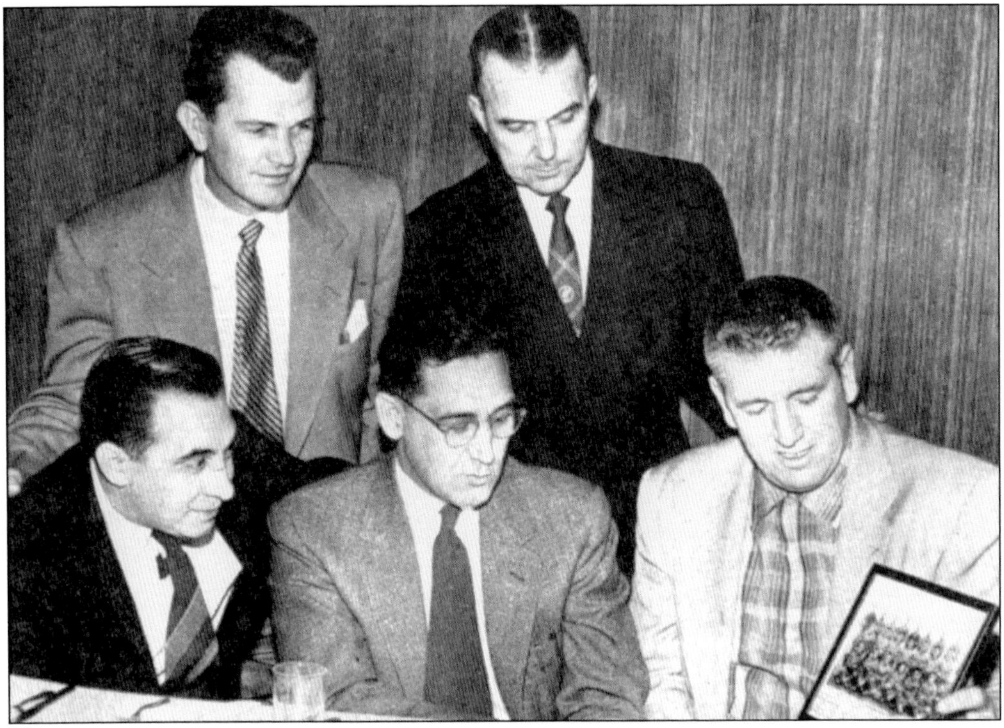

The Thompsonville Greys Club football team was organized in 1924. Some 100 former team members gathered for a reunion dinner in 1956. A team photograph of the 1924 team is viewed by former football stars. The team members are, from left to right, as follows: (front row) Pete Frangiamore, Carl Angelica, and Charles "Chick" Reilly; (back row) Ed Kukulka and Dave Luke.

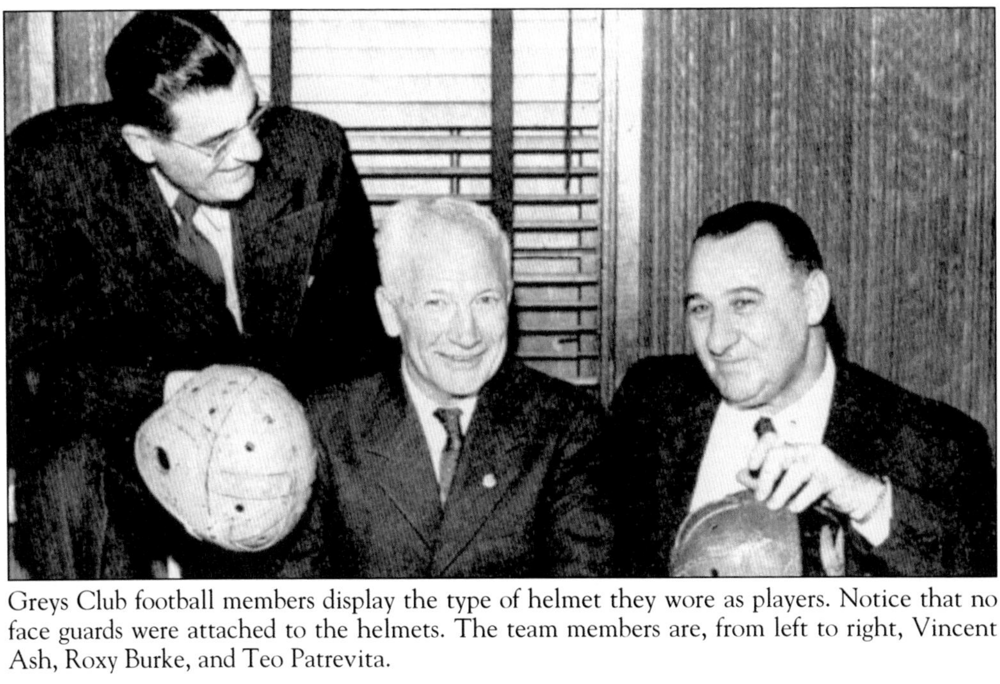

Greys Club football members display the type of helmet they wore as players. Notice that no face guards were attached to the helmets. The team members are, from left to right, Vincent Ash, Roxy Burke, and Teo Patrevita.

Former Greys football stars sing while accompanied by the piano in 1956. Sitting at the keyboard is team member Larry Lamont. The others are, from left to right, Dan Reader, Sam Gannuscio, and Pete Crombie.

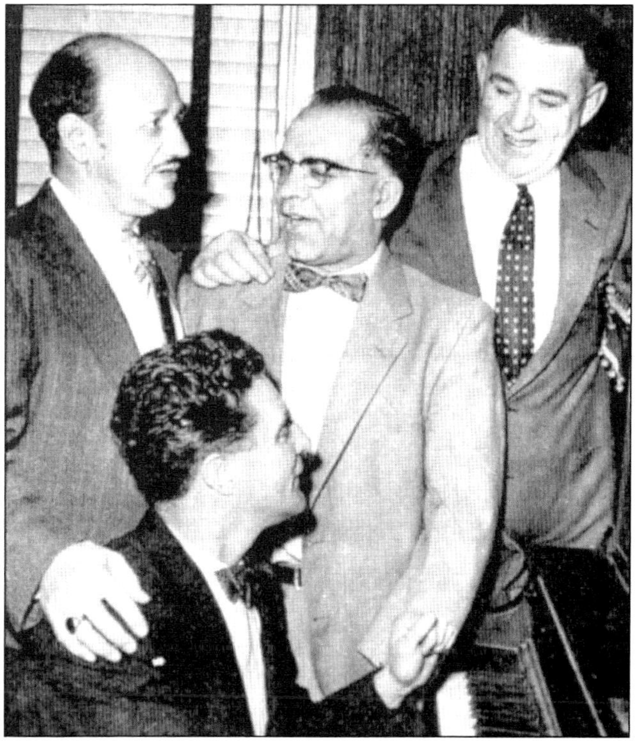

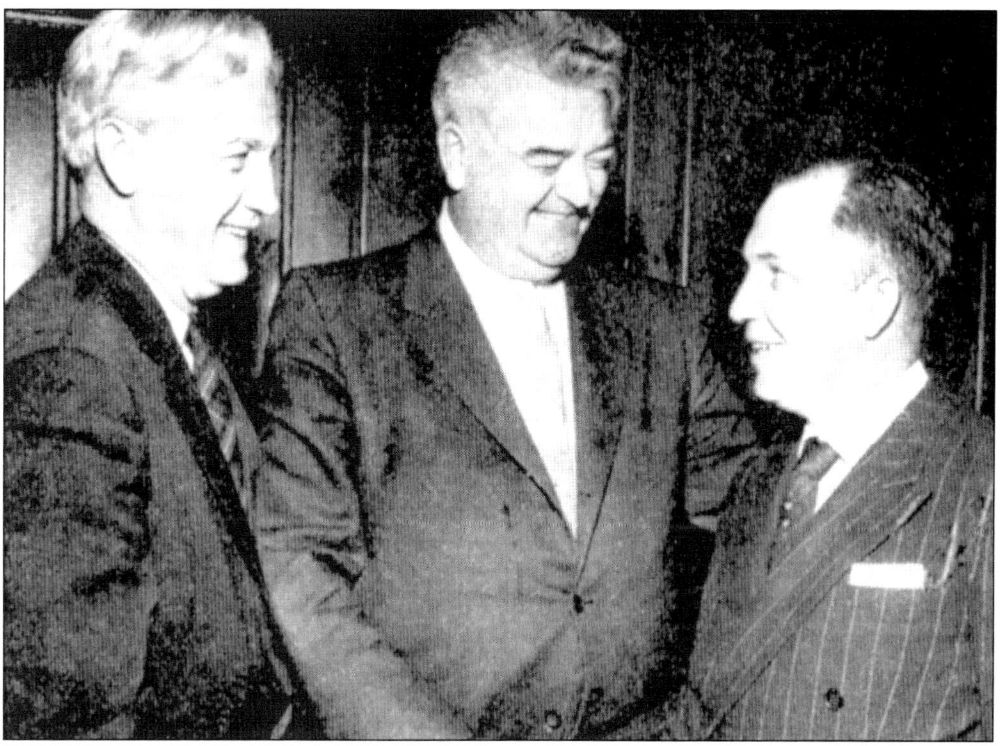

Former Greys stars share a light moment at the reunion dinner in 1956. From left to right are Charles H. Kegley, Austin Reilly, and Grover "Kiddo" Luke.

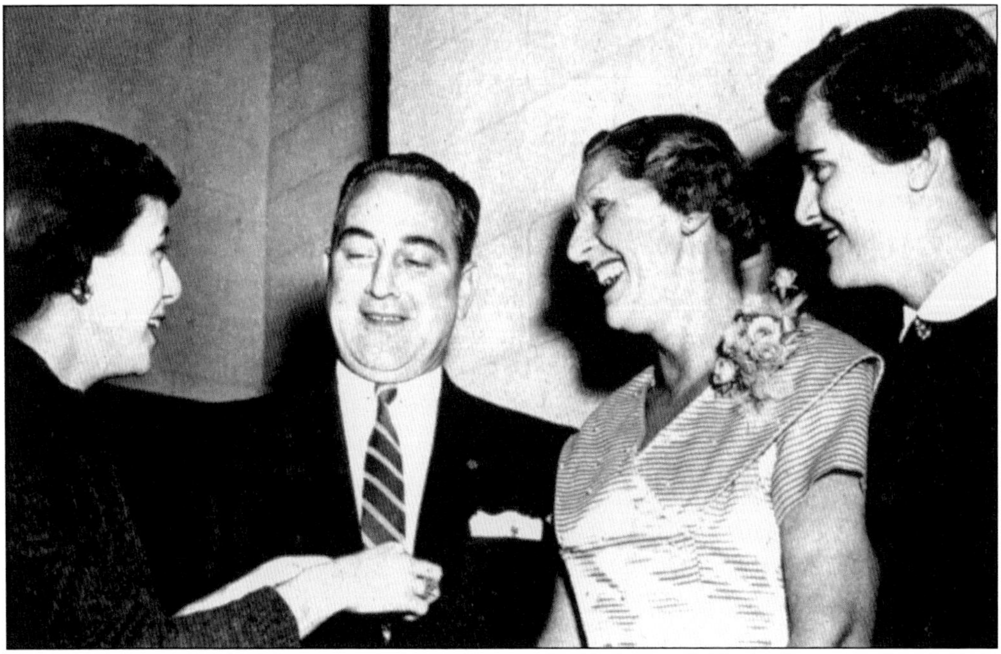

In 1956, a testimonial dinner was held at St. Joseph's hall on Cross Street in honor of Francis D. Charette for his support of youth sports and religious programs at St. Patrick's Church. Family members are, from left to right, Joyce Charette, daughter; Francis D. Charette; Lorraine "Rene" Charette, wife; and Joan Charette, daughter.

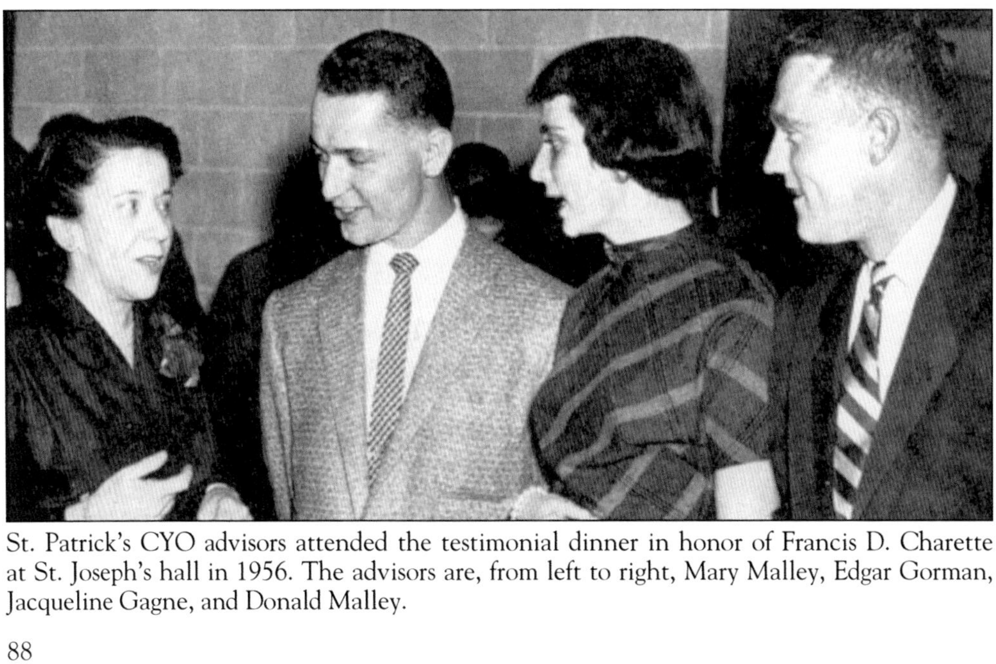

St. Patrick's CYO advisors attended the testimonial dinner in honor of Francis D. Charette at St. Joseph's hall in 1956. The advisors are, from left to right, Mary Malley, Edgar Gorman, Jacqueline Gagne, and Donald Malley.

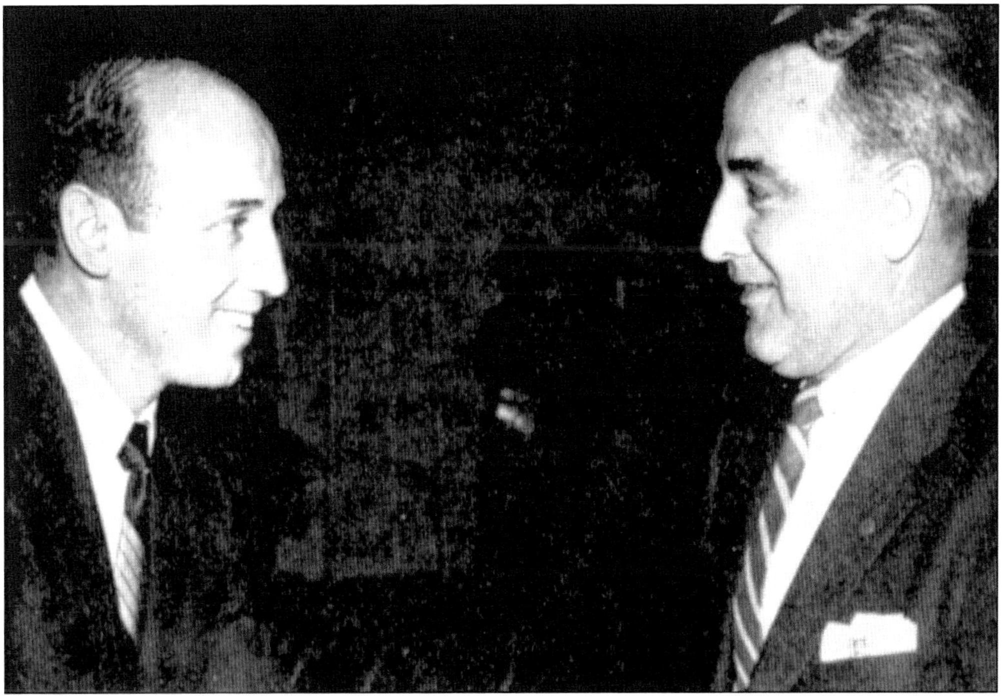

St. Patrick's CYO basketball coach Nick "Coco" Gaetani (left) congratulates Francis D. Charette on his achievements in youth sports and religious programs at St. Patrick's Church for a testimonial dinner at St. Joseph's hall in 1956.

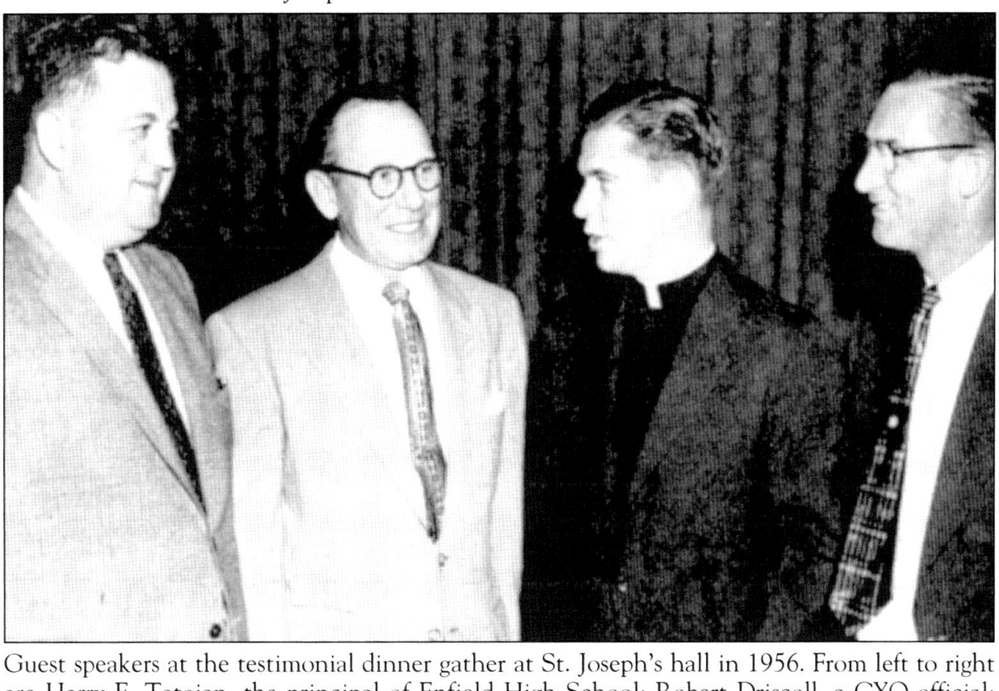

Guest speakers at the testimonial dinner gather at St. Joseph's hall in 1956. From left to right are Harry E. Tatoian, the principal of Enfield High School; Robert Driscoll, a CYO official; Rev. Vincent E. Lyddy, a St. Patrick's CYO spiritual leader; and William Gray, the president of the Thompsonville Little League.

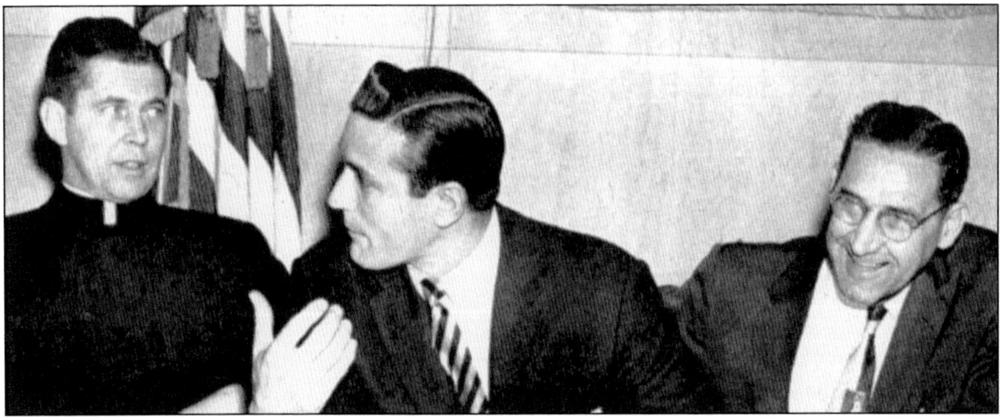

Knights of Columbus, Washington Irving Council No. 50 had Jimmy Piersall, outfielder of the Boston Red Sox, as the guest speaker at the father-son banquet at the American Legion hall on Enfield Street in 1957. Piersall leads a discussion at the head table. From left to right are Rev. Vincent E. Lyddy, council chaplin; Jimmy Piersall; and Carl Angelica, master of ceremonies.

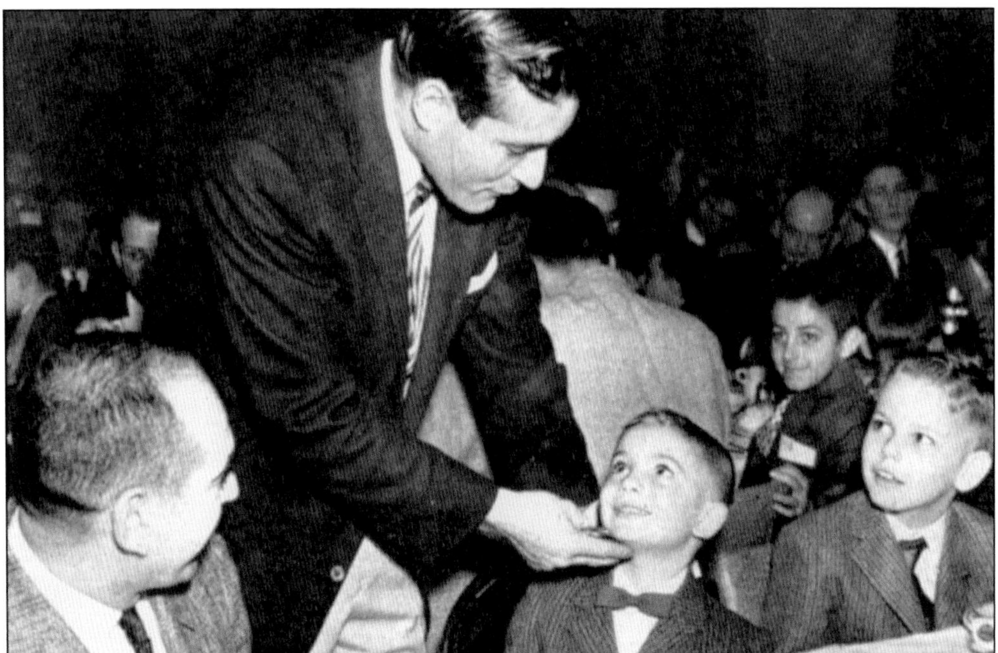

Jimmy Piersall makes his way around the American Legion hall to chat with young baseball fans in 1957. From left to right are Judge James C. Parakilas, Jimmy Piersall, James Parakilas, and Tommy Sullivan Jr.

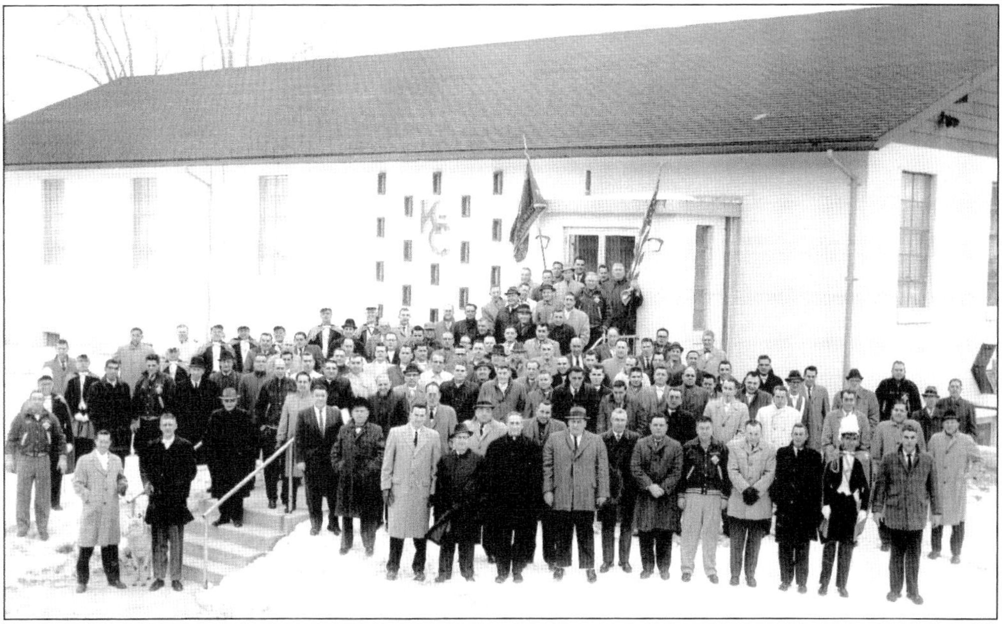

This 1964 view shows Knights of Columbus members in front of their brand-new hall on Washington Road. Edward J. Malley Jr. captured the shot from the front end of a bucket loader at the edge of the parking lot.

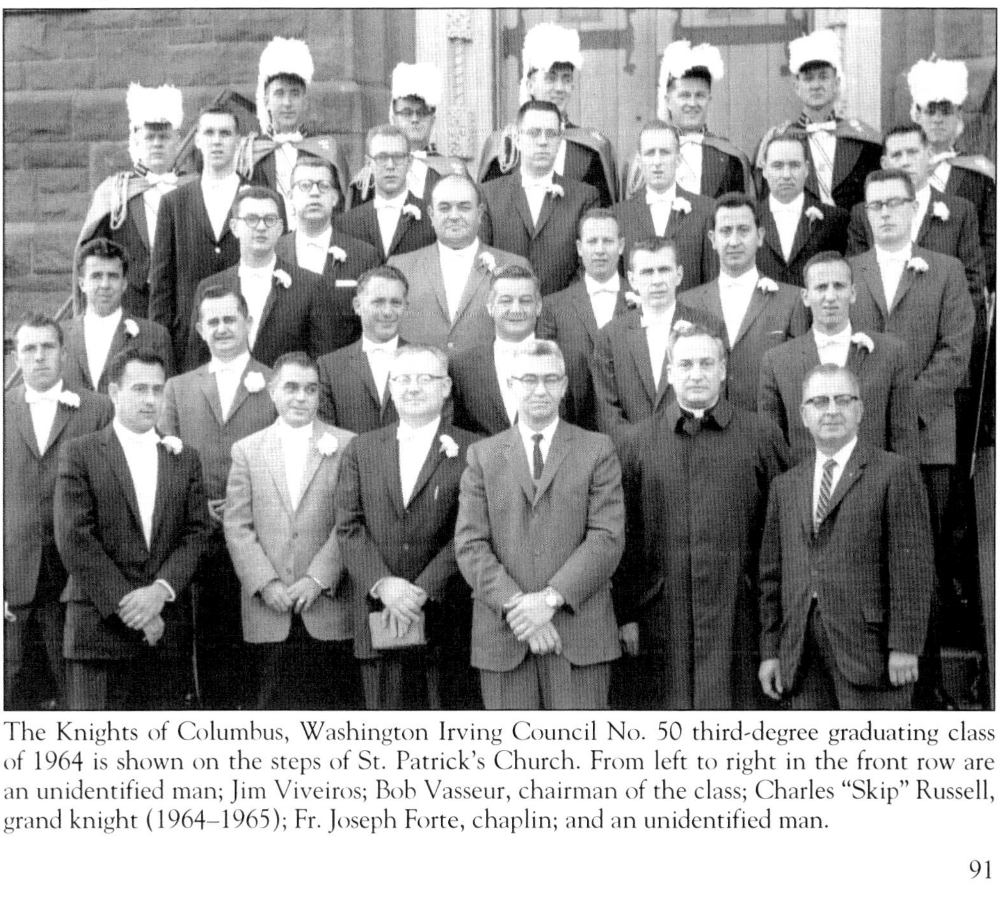

The Knights of Columbus, Washington Irving Council No. 50 third-degree graduating class of 1964 is shown on the steps of St. Patrick's Church. From left to right in the front row are an unidentified man; Jim Viveiros; Bob Vasseur, chairman of the class; Charles "Skip" Russell, grand knight (1964–1965); Fr. Joseph Forte, chaplin; and an unidentified man.

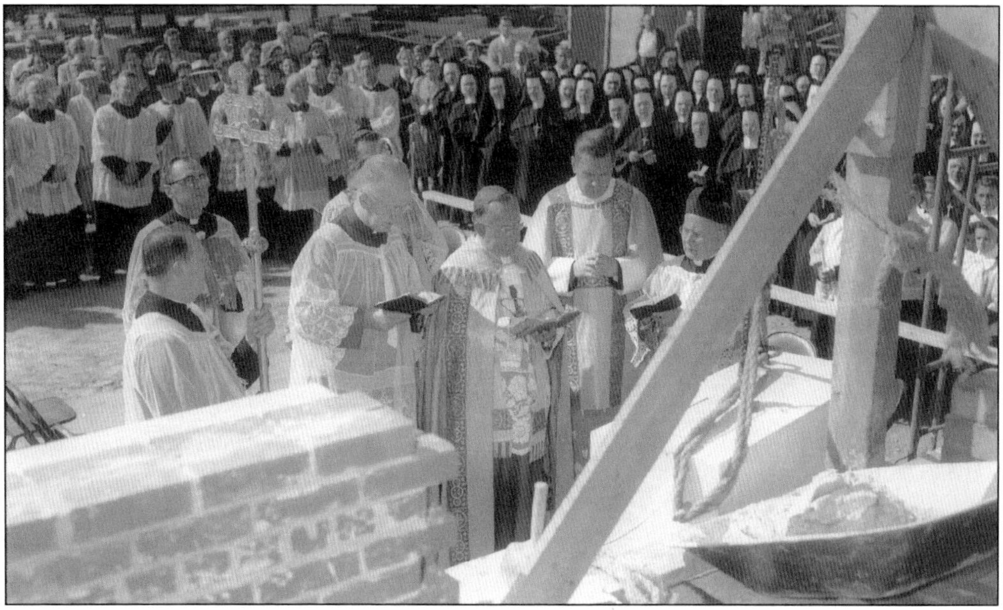

Shown in 1955 is the cornerstone ceremony for the new Felician Sisters Motherhouse, located at the intersection of Enfield Street and South Road. The ceremony was officiated by the Most Reverend Henry J. O'Brien. From left to right are two unidentified priests, Rev. Stanley Musiel of Hartford, the Most Reverend Henry J. O'Brien, Rev. Eugene Solega of Middletown, and Rev. Michael Grygiak. Area priests, Felician Sisters of St. Francis, and local residents are shown in the background.

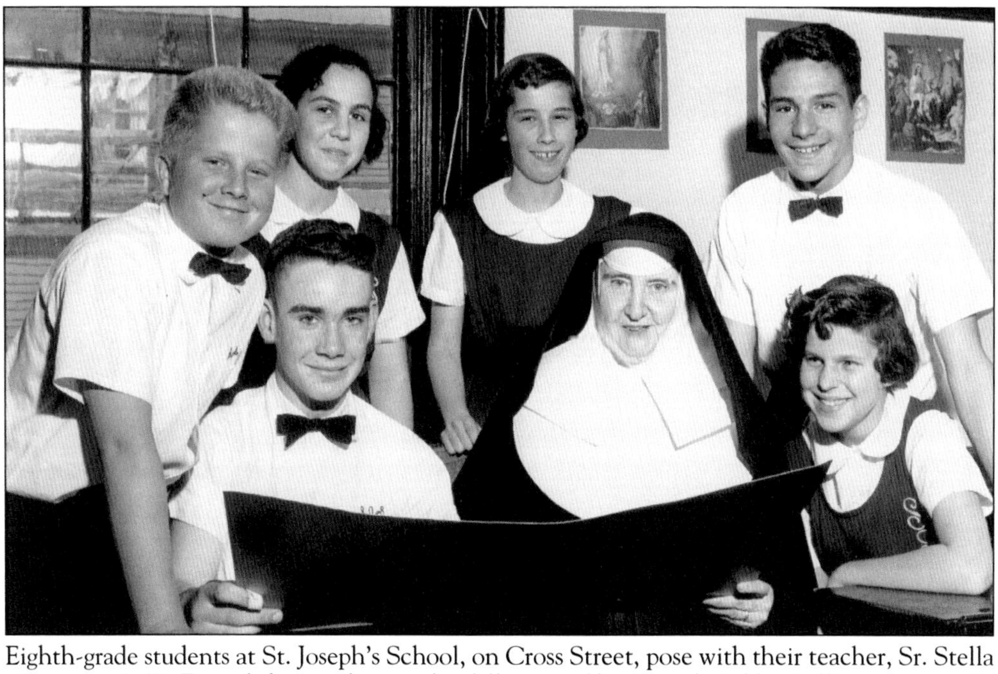

Eighth-grade students at St. Joseph's School, on Cross Street, pose with their teacher, Sr. Stella Marie, in 1957. From left to right are the following: (front row) Bobby Sullivan, Sr. Stella Marie, and Rose Marie LeBlanc; (back row) Drew Miller, Mary Lou Mistretta, Mary Ellen Malley, and Bernie Russotto.

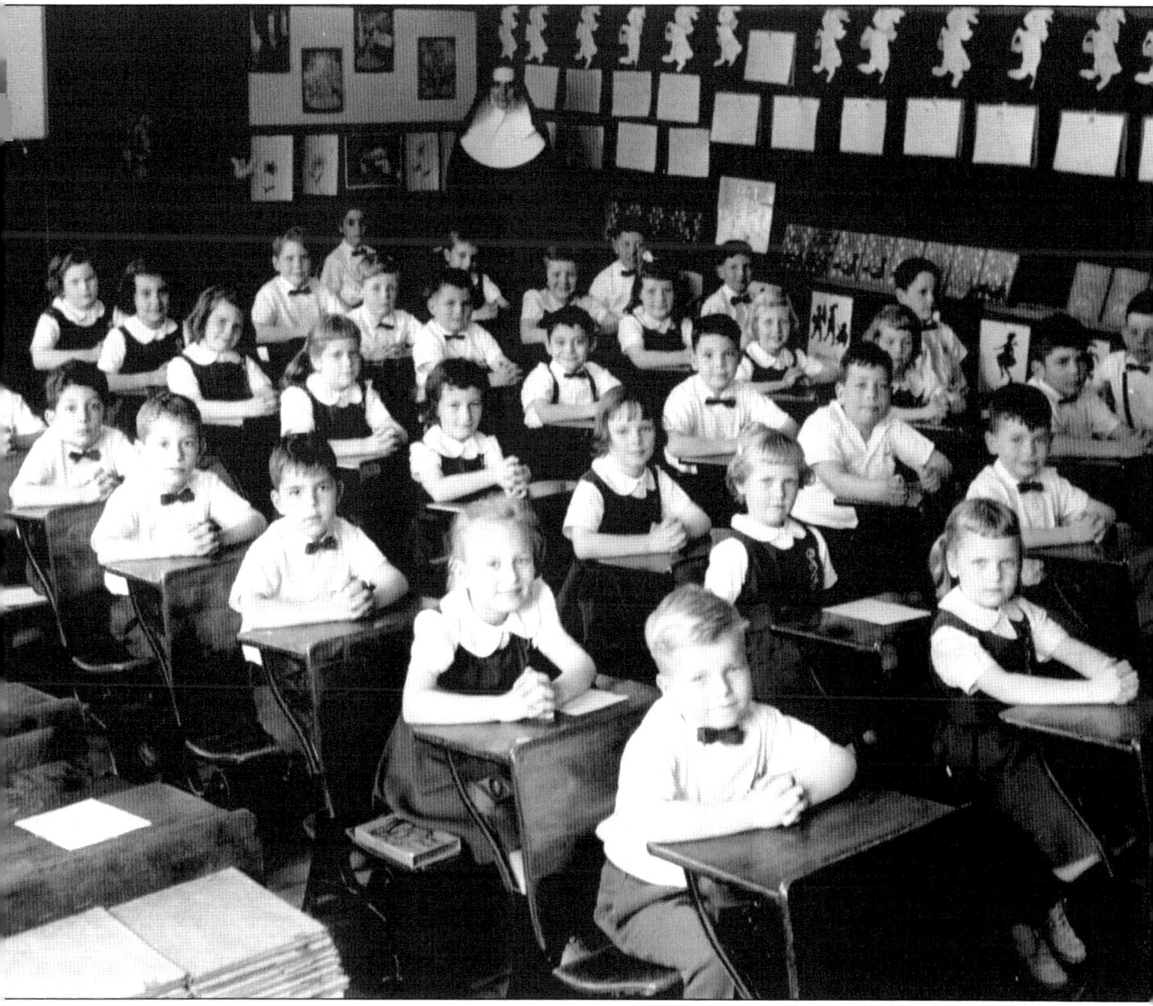

Second-grade students pose at the St Joseph's School annex building on Cross Street during the 1957–1958 school year. From front to back are the following: (first row) Gregory Miller, Virginia Browne, Allen St. John, Gregory Casinghino, Michael Casinghino, and Chuck Lauria; (second row) Cheryl Lynch, Linda Clarkin, Eileen McAdore, Mary Olko, Jan Jatkevicius, Leighton Perry, Mary Yacovone, and Andrea Krochalis; (third row) Edward Wakelee, Michael Petraska, Joe Vesce, Jim Reveruzzi, Mark Hines, John McKinstry, and John Crombie; (fourth row) John Rago, an unidentified person, Linda McIntosh, Sue Terni, Barbara Scavotto, Cathleen O'Donnell, and Ben Kakluskas; (against the wall) Billy Mills, Bill Reilly, Richard Lempitsky, Vito Tallarita, and Sr Mary Arthur.

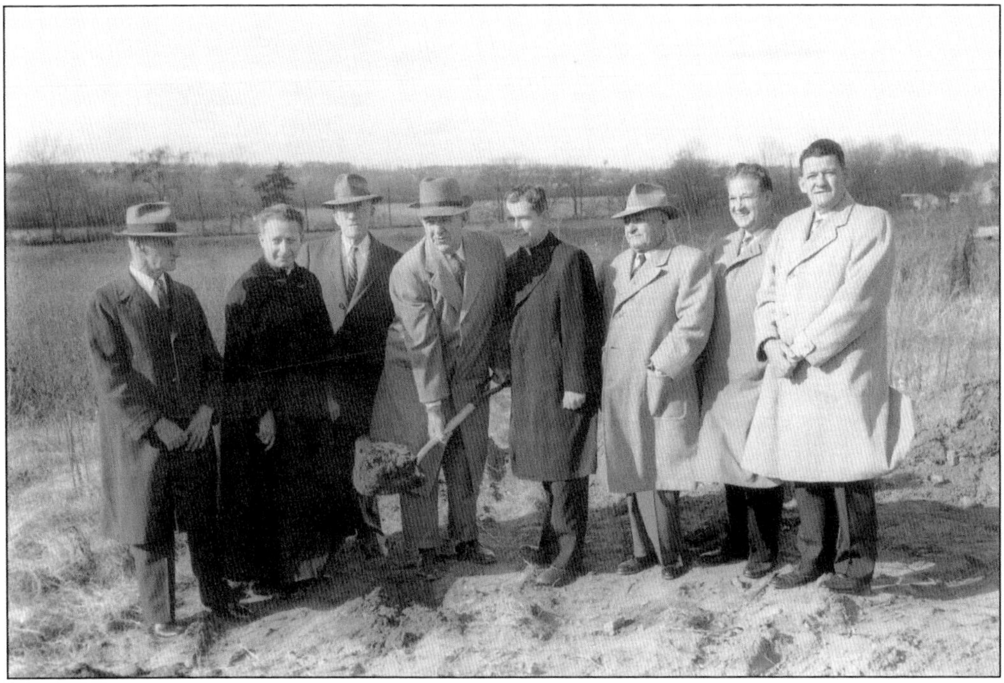

The groundbreaking for St. Joseph's School, at the intersection of Pearl Street and Hathaway Avenue, is shown in the mid-1950s. From left to right are Arthur Starr, Rev. John DeZinno, an unidentified person, Peter Crombie, Rev. Vincent E. Lyddy, Anthony Gannuscio, Dr. Carl Scavotto, and Eddie Cunningham.

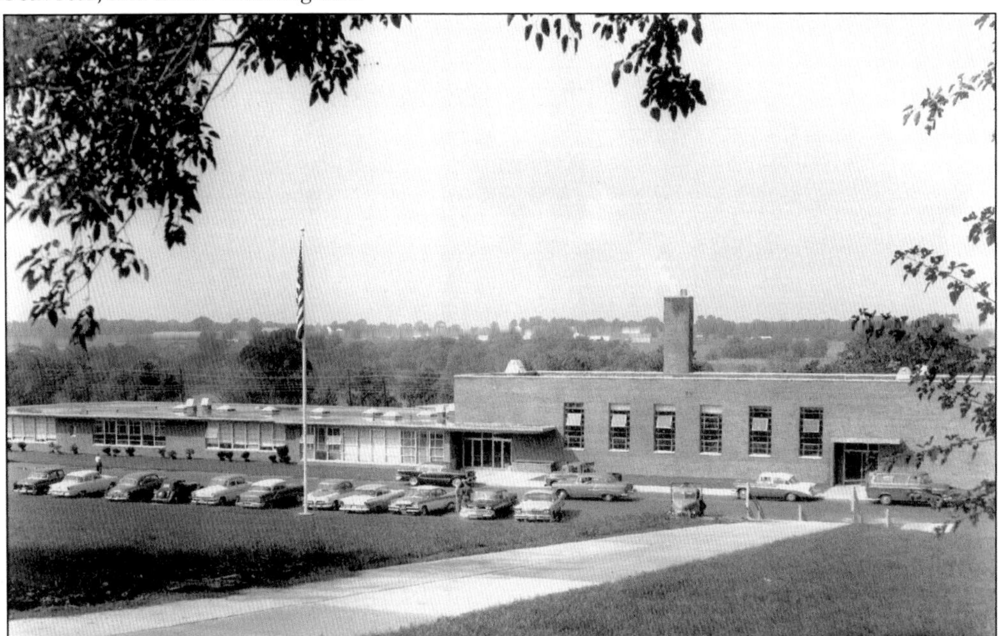

This 1958 view shows the new St. Joseph's School building on Pearl Street. The dedication took place in September 1958. The school was organized in 1872 and closed its doors in 1996. The doors of the school building remained open as a part of St. Bernard's Church and School.

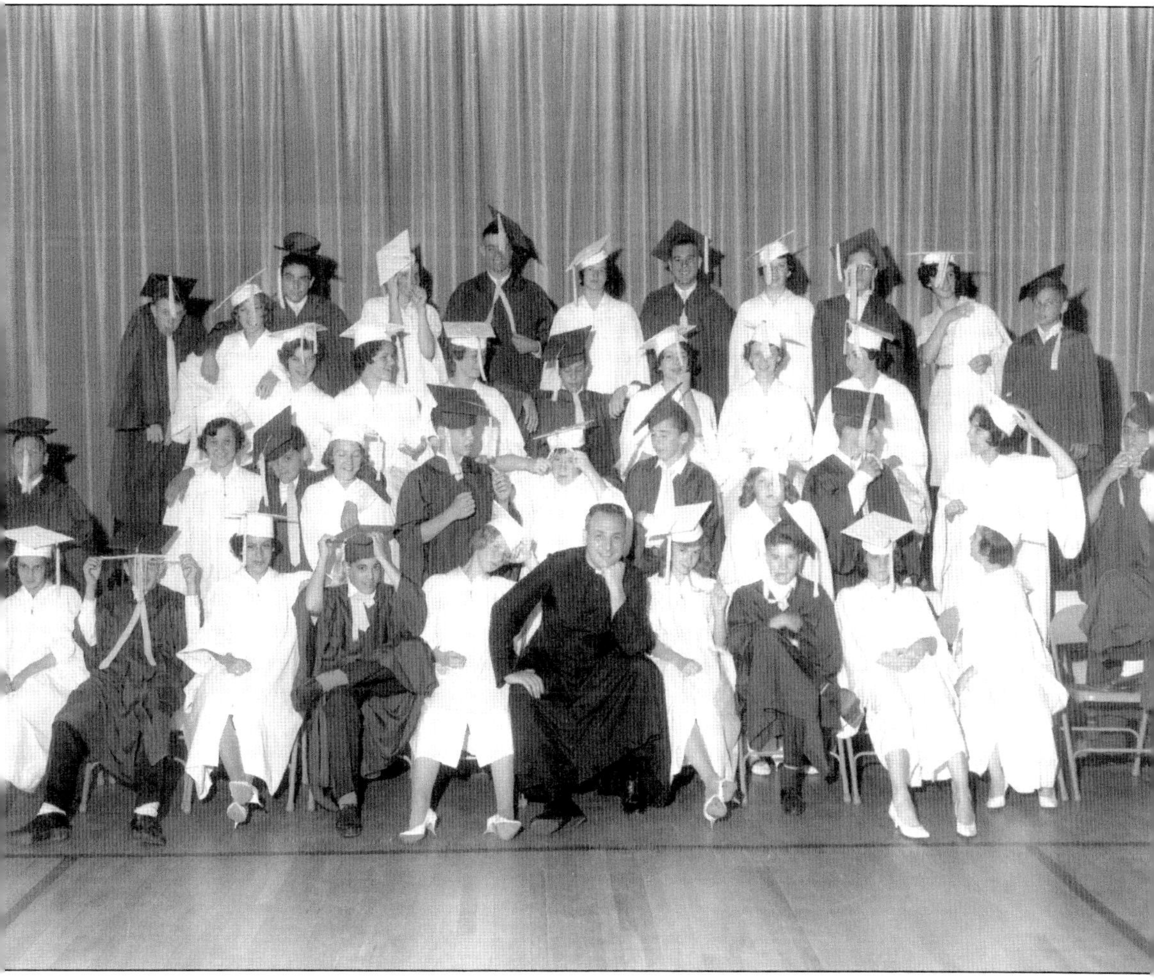

Members of the 1962 eighth-grade graduating class of St. Joseph's School ham it up for photographer Edward J. Malley Jr. From left to right are the following: (first row) Elaine Mahalski, Vinny Petrone, Patty Daddabo, Chris Harlambakis, Lynn Conley, Fr. Joseph Forte, Maureen "Mo" Mercik, Paul Panosky, Alice Marinaccio, and Kathy Colton; (second row) Mike Angelica, Betty Sarno, Eddie Yacovone, Susan Gaudet, Phil Brown, Ellen FitzGibbons, Pat Reilly, Jeannie Olschafskie, Jack Whiteley, Ann Marie Liucci, and John Parisi; (third row) Ann Nadeau, Karen Cusimano, Lynne Bartlett, Michael Marinaccio, Kathy Liucci, Marilyn Cherry, and Ann DiLorenzo; (fourth row) Joey Wallace, Cathy Malley, Zane Pumiglia, Carol Cuscovitch, Rick LaFleur, Colleen Schneider, Bob Goss, Theresa Hines, John Trappe, Diane Wakelee, and Louie Tallarita.

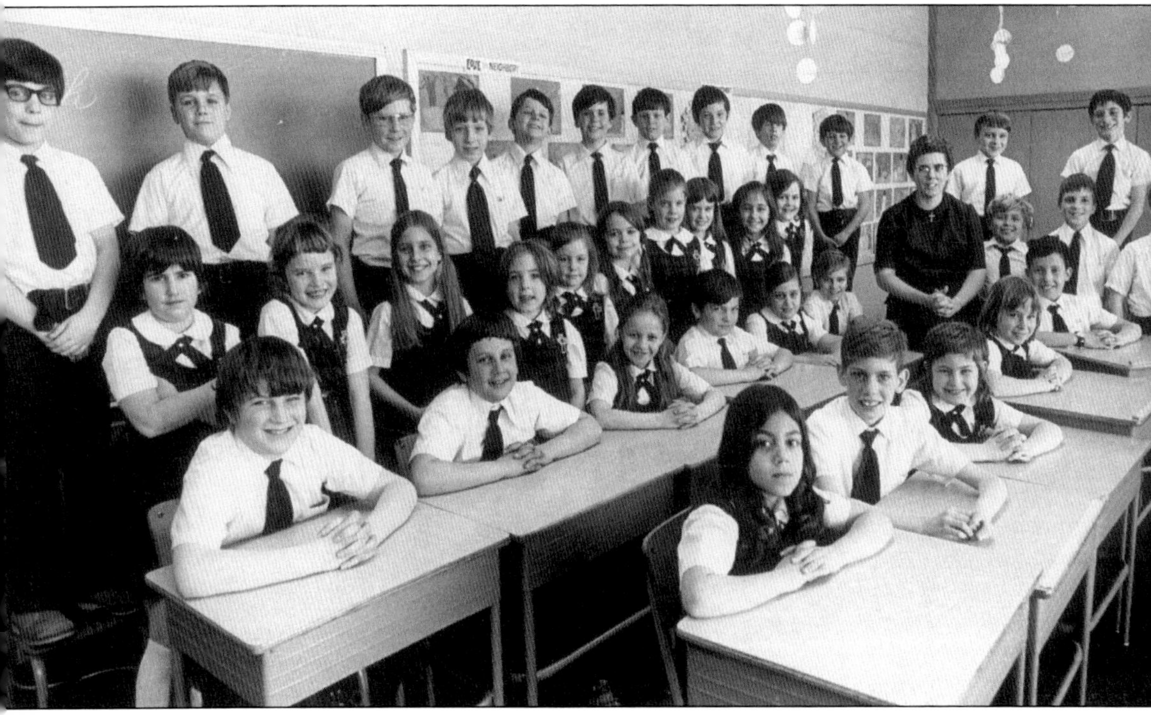

Third-grade students at St. Joseph's School pose in 1973. From left to right are the following: (first row) Marie Troiano, Sean Leahy, Jodi DeGray, Heather Dee, and Leonard Guerriero; (second row) Christopher French, Anthony Caronna, Karen Muller, Anthony Ziter, Laura Sferrazza, and Kurt Glende; (third row) Jean Orefice, Deirdre Butler, Mariann Caronna, Lisa Desrosiers, Susan Ayers, Mary O'Brien, Patricia Wyrostek, Eileen Sullivan, Celine Landry, Kathleen Garvey, Sr. Dorothy O' Dywer, Marc Michaud, Daniel Wells, and Edward Carroll; (fourth row) Joseph Organ, James Wegrzyn, Dennis Keller, Randy Larsen, Victor Petrone, Patrick McGuire, Patrick Tallarita, Peter Wakelin, Robert McGovern, James Malley, Thomas Boucher, and Christopher Scarfo.

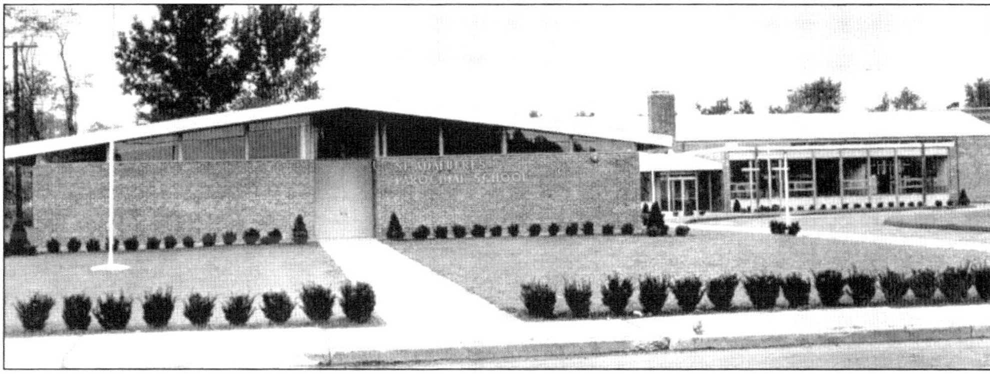

This 1959 view shows the St. Adalbert's School, located on Alden Avenue in Thompsonville. The parochial school currently offers instruction to students from kindergarten to the eighth grade. The St. Adalbert's gymnasium has been the home for the Enfield Deanery CCD and CYO basketball games for many years.

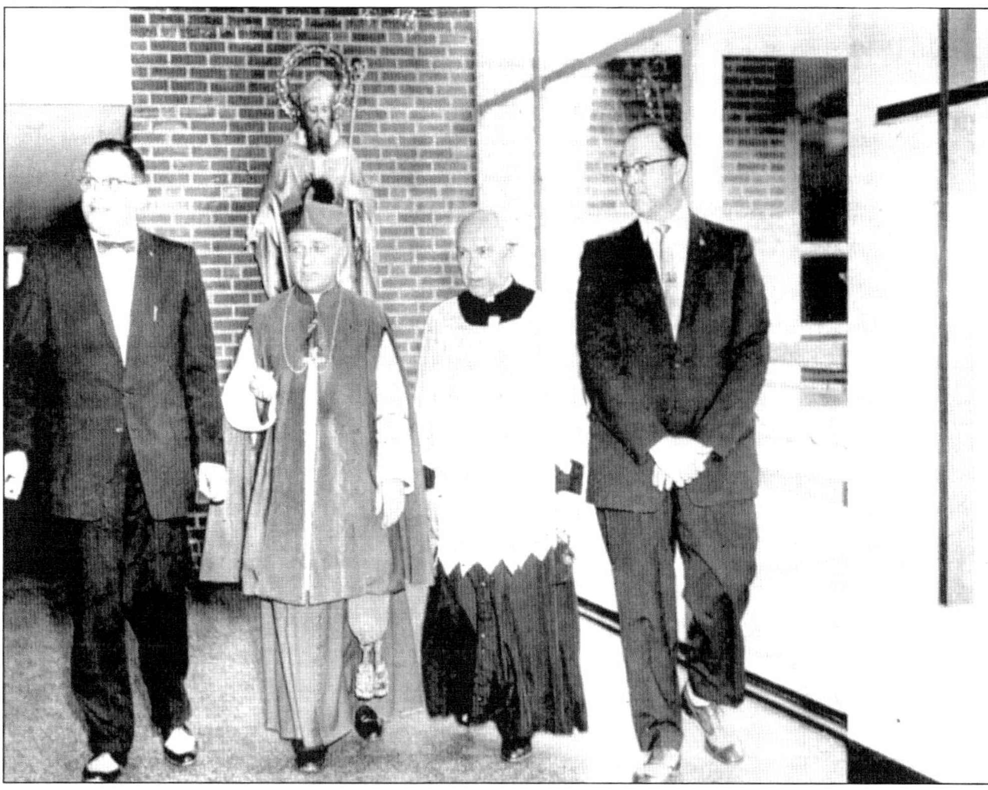

St. Adalbert's School was dedicated in September 1959. In this view, building and church officials take a tour of the new school building. From left to right are Joseph Homicki, building committee chairman; the Most Reverend John Hackett, auxiliary bishop of Hartford; Rev. Paul J. Bartlewski, pastor of St. Adalbert's; and Dominic Cimino, building architect. Rev. Paul Bartlewski served over 33 years at St. Adalbert's parish, retiring in 1972.

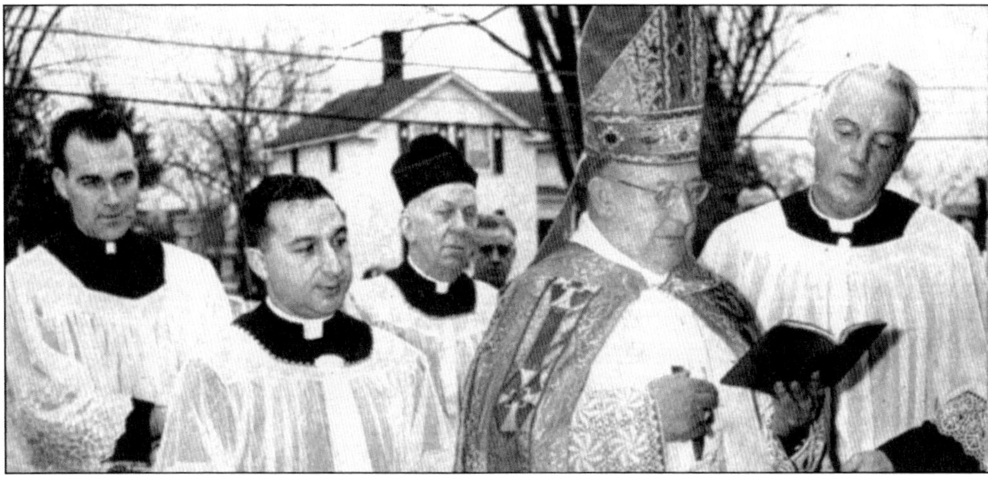

The cornerstone ceremony of the new St. Bernard's Church on Hazard Avenue was officiated by the Most Reverend Henry J. O'Brien in 1956. From left to right are Rev. Robert Kelly, Westport; Rev. Francis Fazzalaro, secretary to O'Brien; Rev. William P. Kilcoyne, pastor of St. Patrick's Church, Thompsonville; O'Brien; and Rev. Edward J. Reardon, pastor of St. Bernard's.

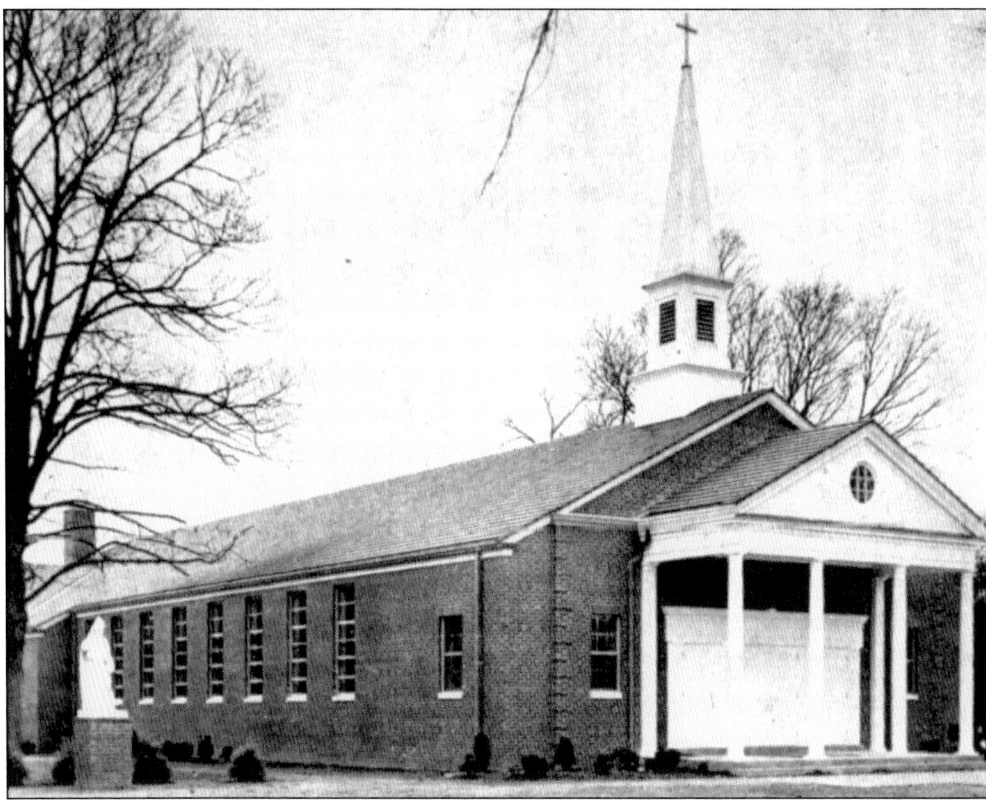

The furniture of the old St. Bernard's Church was removed by local prisoners, and the building was torn down by Labutis Construction, owned by Charles Labutis. The company also completed site work for the new church. This 1956 view shows the new St. Bernard's Church, located on Hazard Avenue. The bell inside the church came from a locomotive that ran along the Springfield branch of the New York, New Haven, and Hartford Railroad in Scitico.

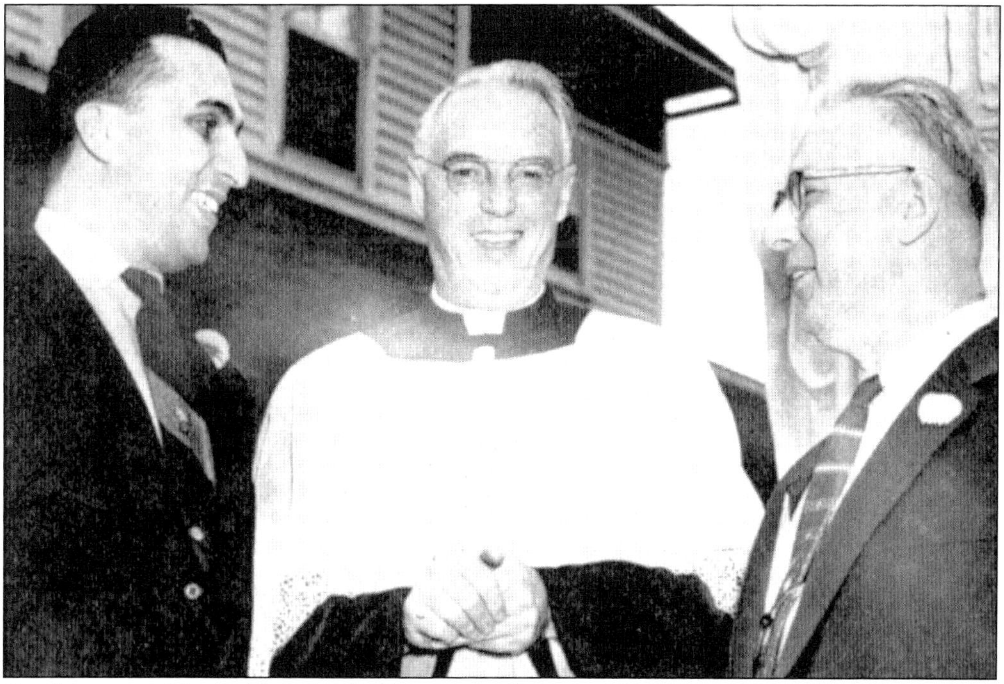

Co-chairmen of the building fund offer congratulations to their pastor on the new St. Bernard's Church in 1956. From left to right are Robert Berger, Rev. Edward J. Reardon, and Fred Stroiney. St. Bernard's School, located behind the church, now provides instruction to students from pre-kindergarten to first grade. St. Bernard's School West, located on Pearl Street (in the former St. Joseph's School), provides instruction to students from the second grade to the eighth grade.

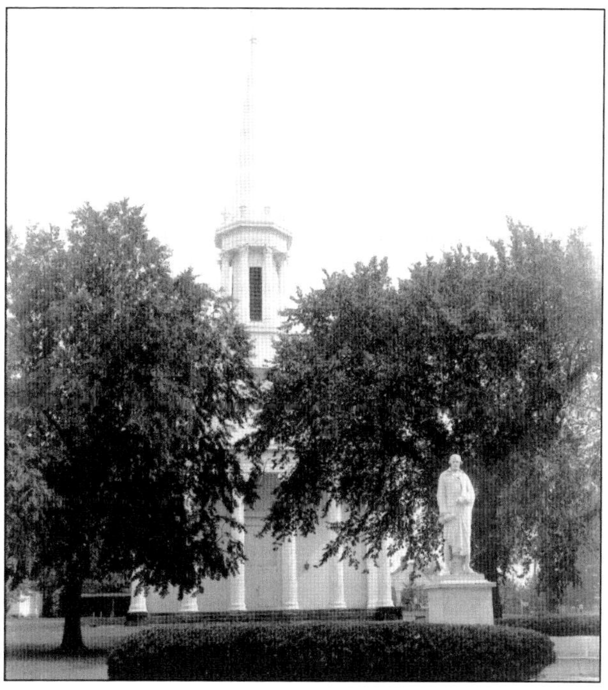

This 1960s view shows the Captain Thomas Abbey Memorial and the Enfield Congregational Church, built in 1849 at the intersection of Enfield Street and South Road. Thomas Abbey was a Revolutionary War soldier and became well known for beating his drum to summon Enfield soldiers to arms in response to the attack by British soldiers on Lexington, Massachusetts.

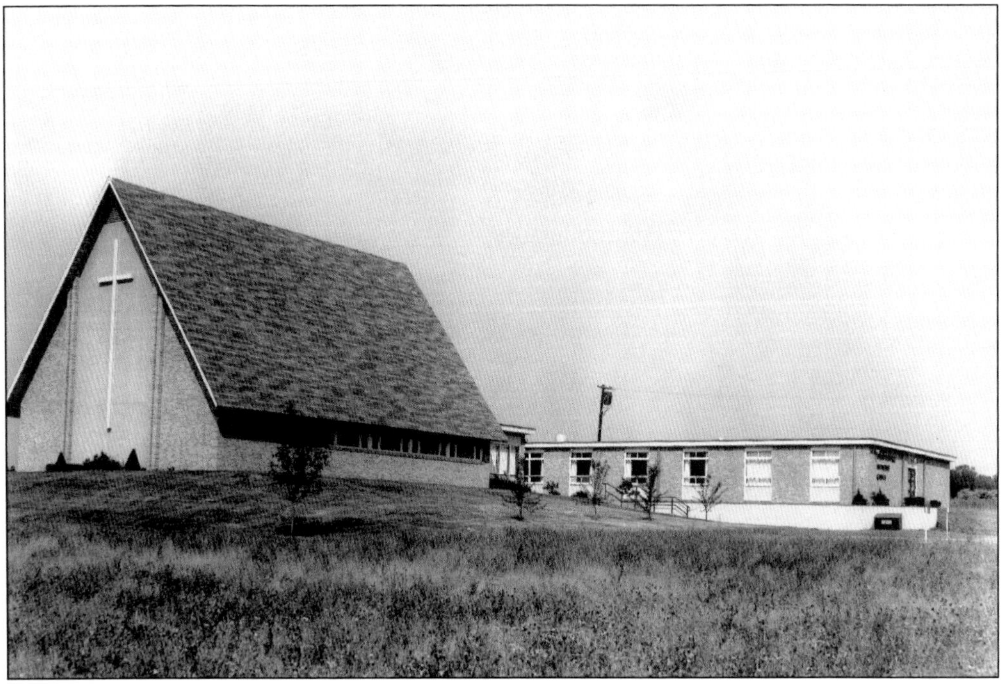

The Enfield United Methodist Church, located on Brainard Road just east of Interstate 91, is pictured in the 1960s. The congregation was organized in 1841 and adopted different locations throughout the village of Thompsonville, the last one being on High Street opposite Spring Street. The High Street building later became the home of the Amvets.

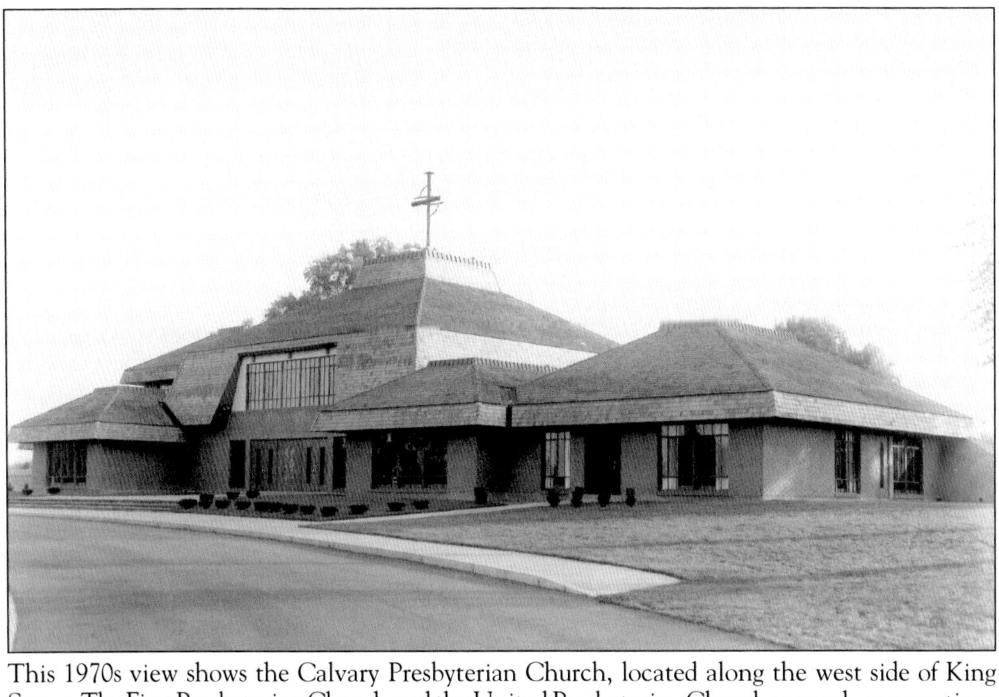

This 1970s view shows the Calvary Presbyterian Church, located along the west side of King Street. The First Presbyterian Church and the United Presbyterian Church merged congregations to form the the Calvary Presbyterian Church.

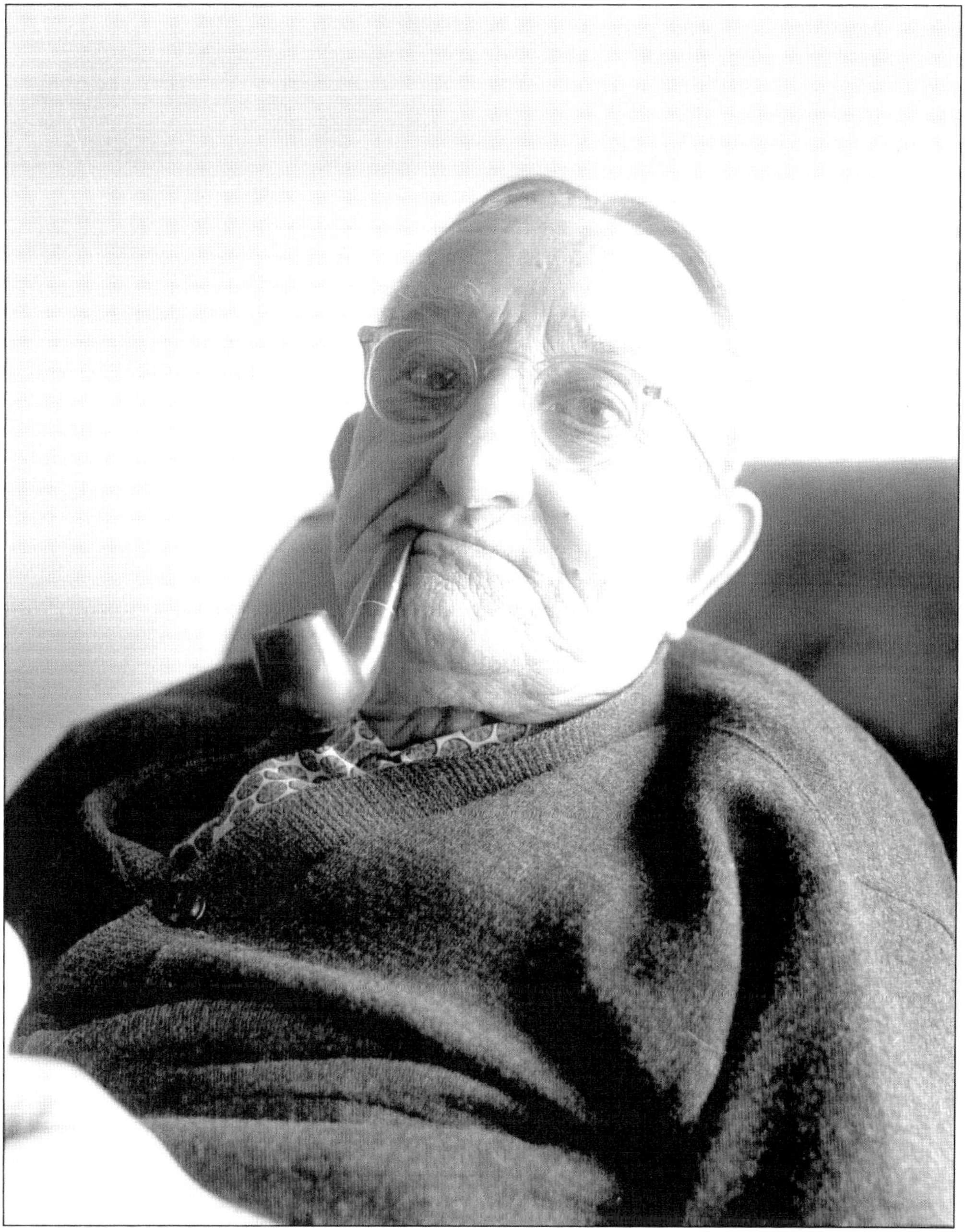

Edward J. Malley Jr. captured his grandfather James A. Malley enjoying his pipe in the 1950s. James A. Malley was born in Thompsonville in 1879, the son of Irish immigrants Patrick and Catherine (Fleming) Malley. He was a first-generation American and the youngest of nine children. He was married to the former Nellie O'Donnell and was the father of three children. He worked as a bartender at Malley's Saloon, located in the Malley Block, at the intersection of Pearl and High Streets. He was also employed for 30 years in the Axminster department of the Bigelow-Sanford Carpet Company. When he passed away at his home on Asnuntuck Street, he was 84 years old. James A. Malley's life was mirrored by many immigrants and first-generation Americans in Thompsonville.

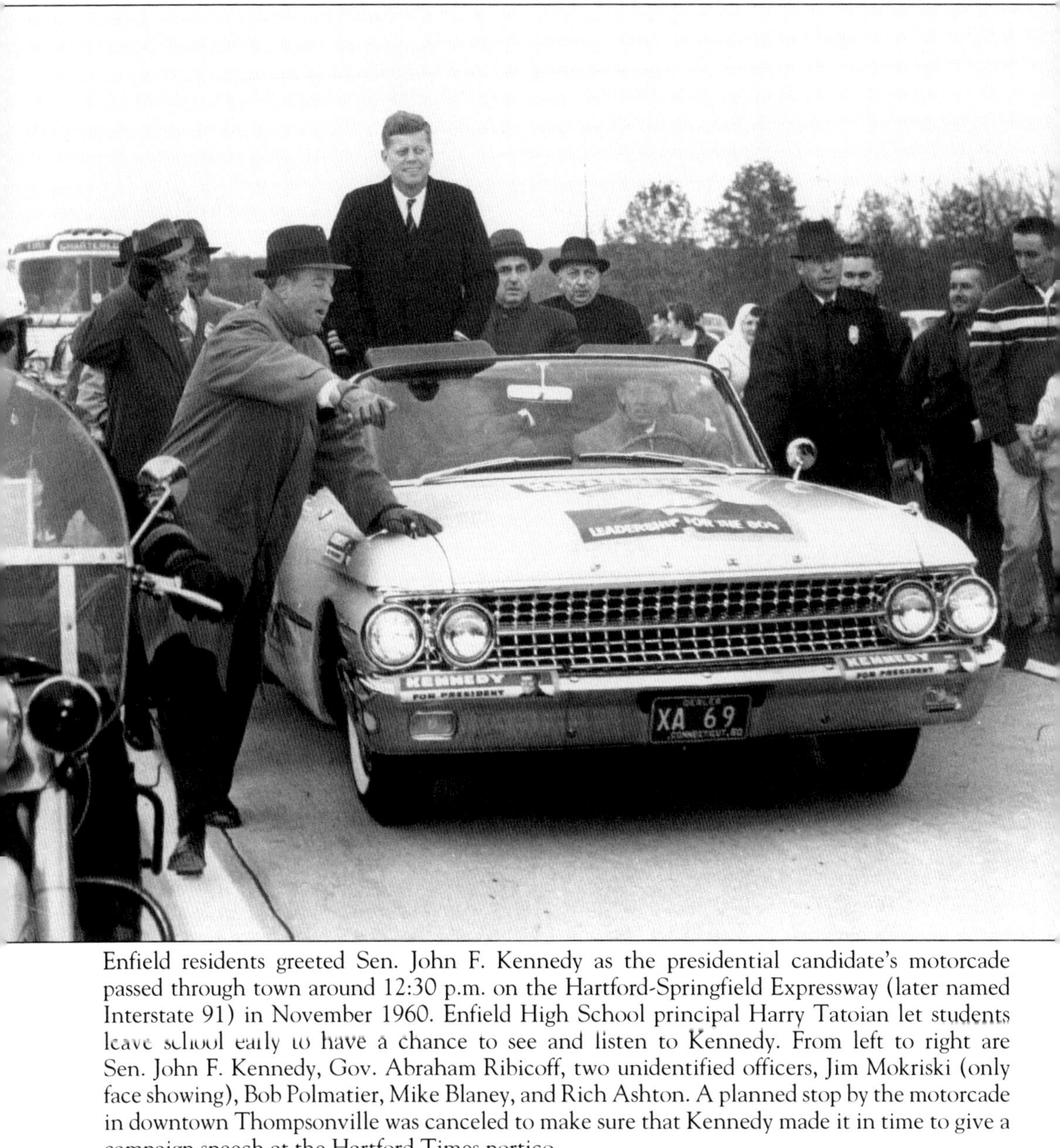

Enfield residents greeted Sen. John F. Kennedy as the presidential candidate's motorcade passed through town around 12:30 p.m. on the Hartford-Springfield Expressway (later named Interstate 91) in November 1960. Enfield High School principal Harry Tatoian let students leave school early to have a chance to see and listen to Kennedy. From left to right are Sen. John F. Kennedy, Gov. Abraham Ribicoff, two unidentified officers, Jim Mokriski (only face showing), Bob Polmatier, Mike Blaney, and Rich Ashton. A planned stop by the motorcade in downtown Thompsonville was canceled to make sure that Kennedy made it in time to give a campaign speech at the Hartford Times portico.

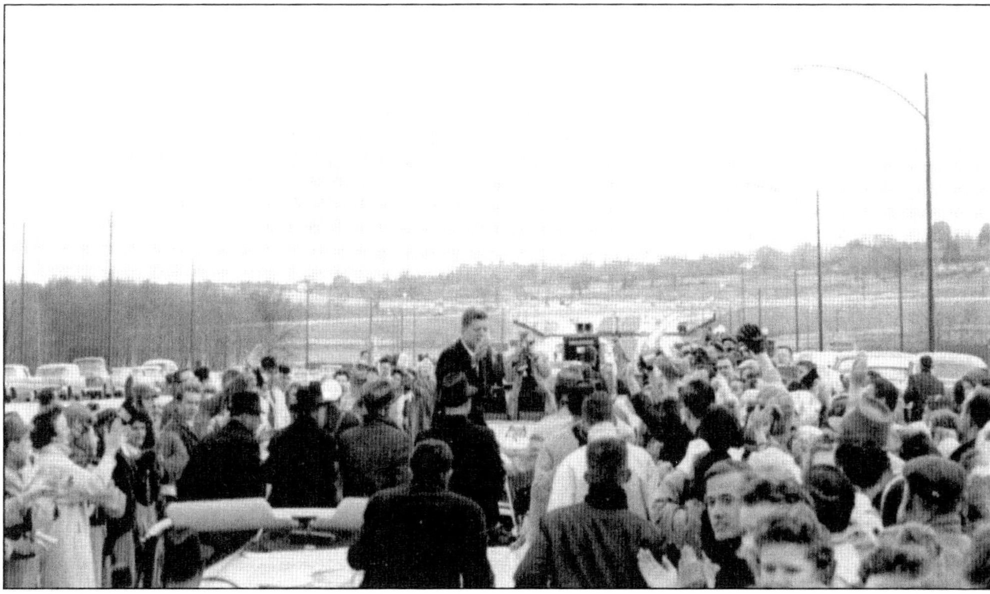

Sen. John F. Kennedy waves to the crowd standing on the Elm Street overpass. The Hartford-Springfield Expressway (later named Interstate 91) comes to a standstill as people rush from downtown Thompsonville to get a glimpse of the 1960 Democratic presidential candidate from Massachusetts.

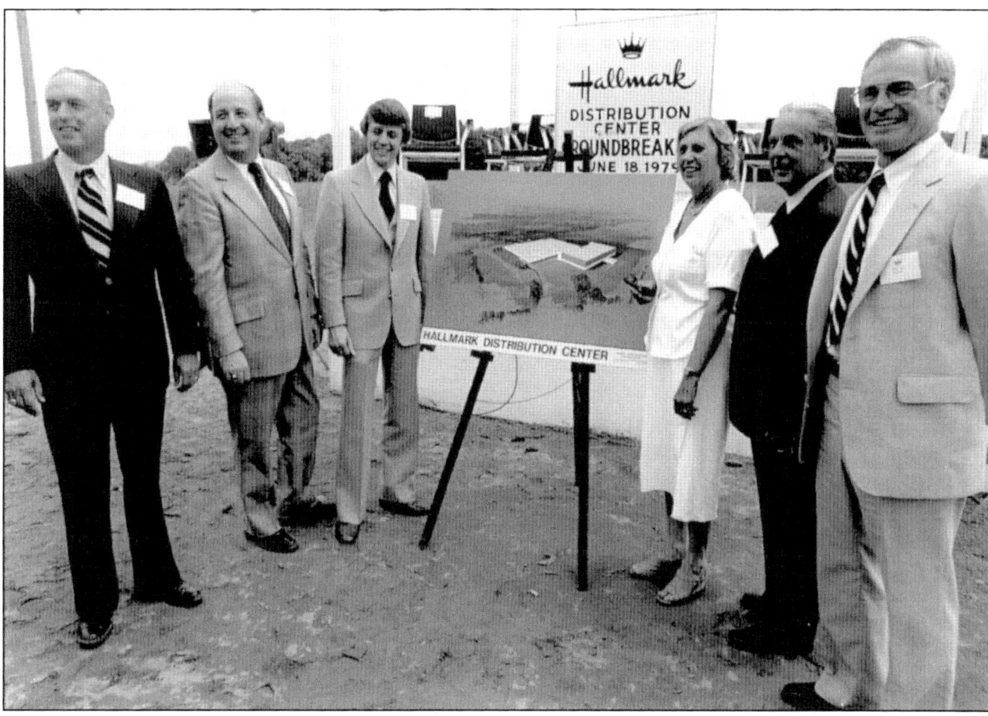

Gov. Ella Grasso stands among a contingent of local officials in the groundbreaking of the Hallmark distribution center on Bacon Road on June 18, 1979. Standing, from left to right, are Hallmark official Art Coate, Hallmark official Robert Stark, Mayor James Baum, Gov. Ella Grasso, Hallmark official Omer Muchmore, and Hallmark official Glenn Davis.

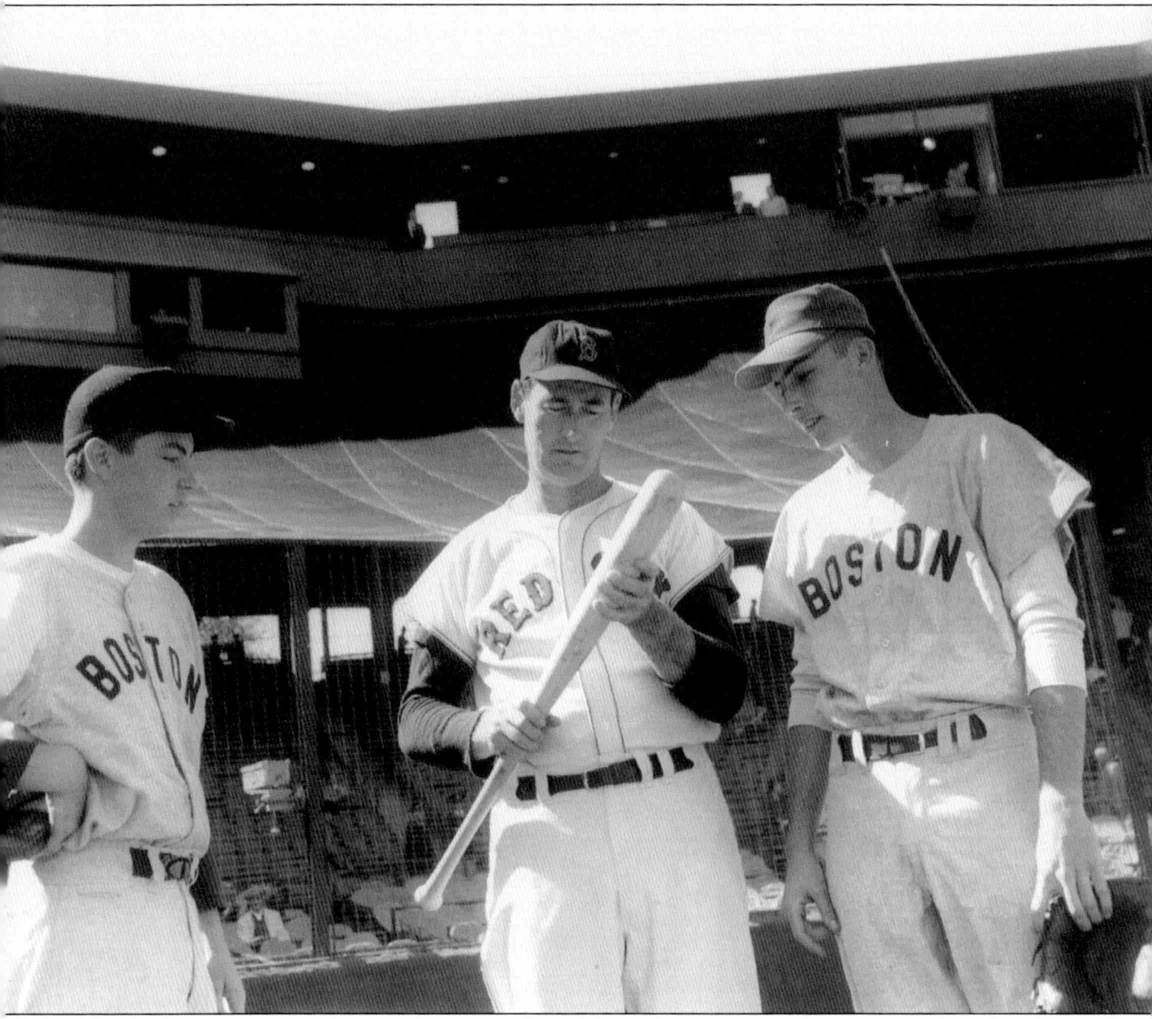

This 1957 view shows the Spanswick brothers as they listen intently to Ted Williams's wisdom on hitting at a workout with the Boston Red Sox at Fenway Park. From left to right are Jim Spanswick, a promising high school star; Ted Williams, the "Splendid Splinter;" and Bill Spanswick, a member the Holy Cross baseball team. Jim Spanswick signed with the Red Sox in 1959 and pitched in the Eastern League, retiring after five years with arm trouble. Bill Spanswick, who signed with the Red Sox in 1958, was named the 1963 Triple-A Pitcher of the Year for the Seattle Rainiers. He played for five years in the minor leagues before playing for the Red Sox.

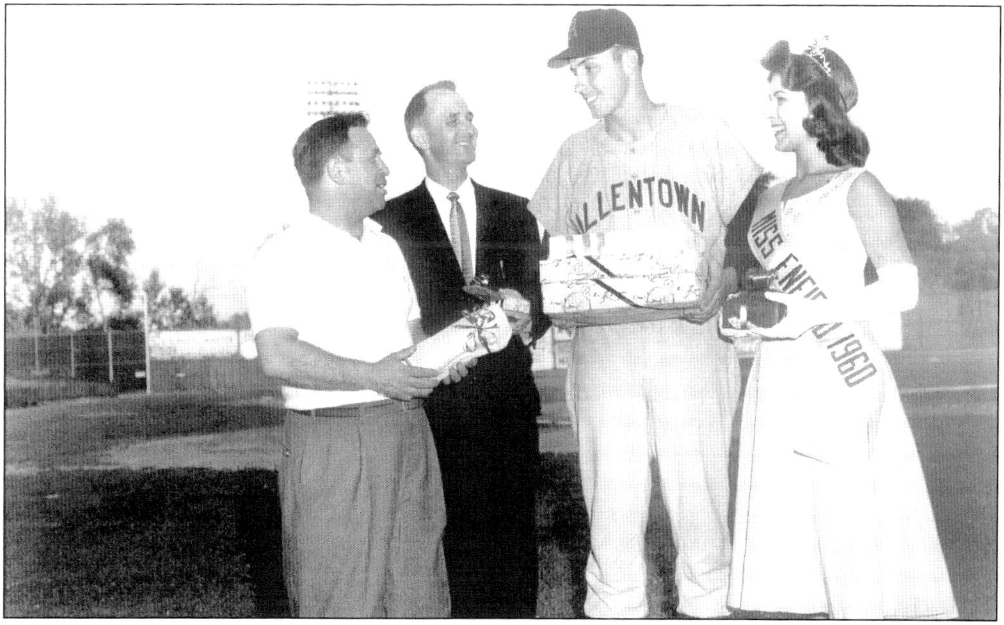

This 1960 view shows Enfield representatives with Allentown's Bill Spanswick for "Bill Spanswick Night" at Pynchon Park in Springfield, Massachusetts. From left to right are Vito Tallarita, promoter; Dr. Raymond Keller; Bill Spanswick; and Diane Whitney, Miss Enfield of 1960.

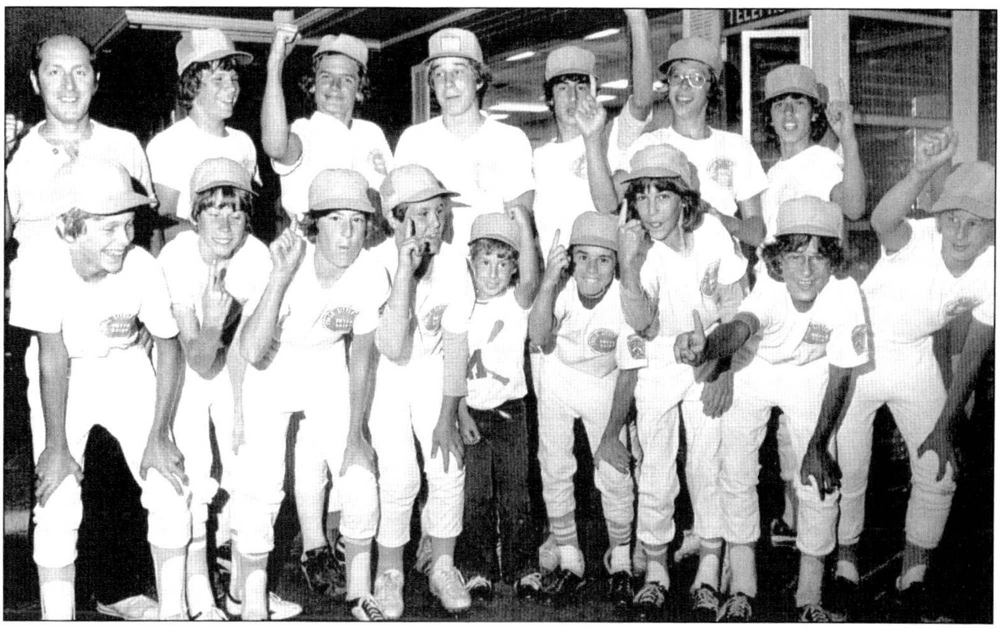
The Smyth Farm Dairy baseball team celebrated outside the Smyth Farm Dairy Bar restaurant in 1977. The Thompsonville Senior League championship team members are, from left to right, as follows: (front row) Ford Carson, Jay Messier, Chris Strapp, Randy Whynot, batboy Ralph Cerrato III, Jon LeBlanc, Brant Moskowitz, Jim Malley, and Greg Olsen; (back row) coach Ralph J. Cerrato Jr., David Morton, Marty Dupuis, Peter DeRose, Stephen Cerrato, David Korona, and Guy Tittarelli.

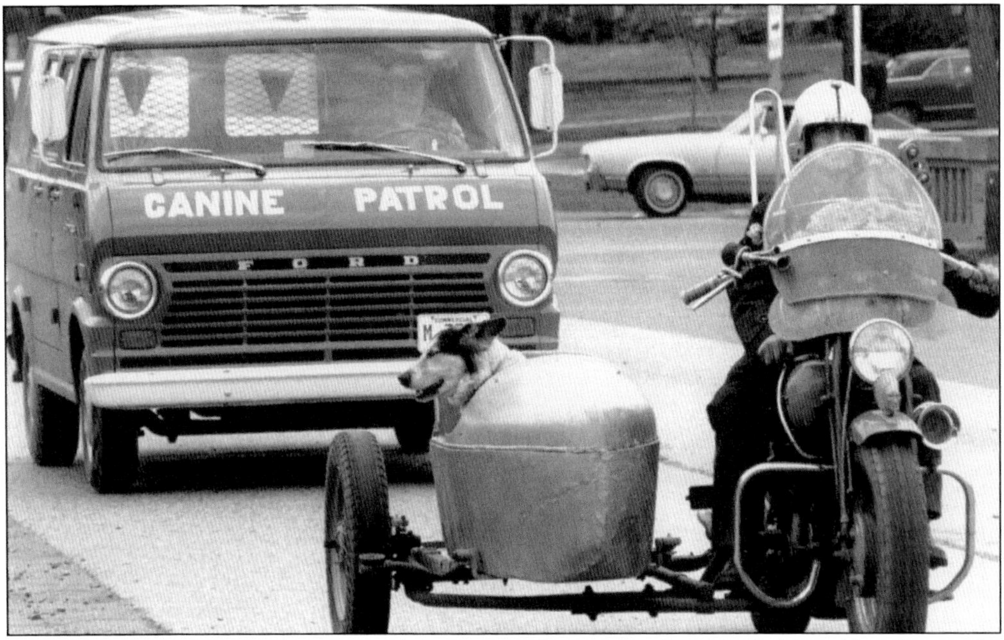

The Enfield Canine Patrol unit is in hot pursuit of Leon Greski of Suffield and his dog Lucky on Enfield Street just north of High Street in 1970. Greski was riding a 1948 Indian Chief motorcycle and welded on the tub as a sidecar. He was one of the first Indian motorcycle dealers in the area. His shop was located at 34 Pleasant Street.

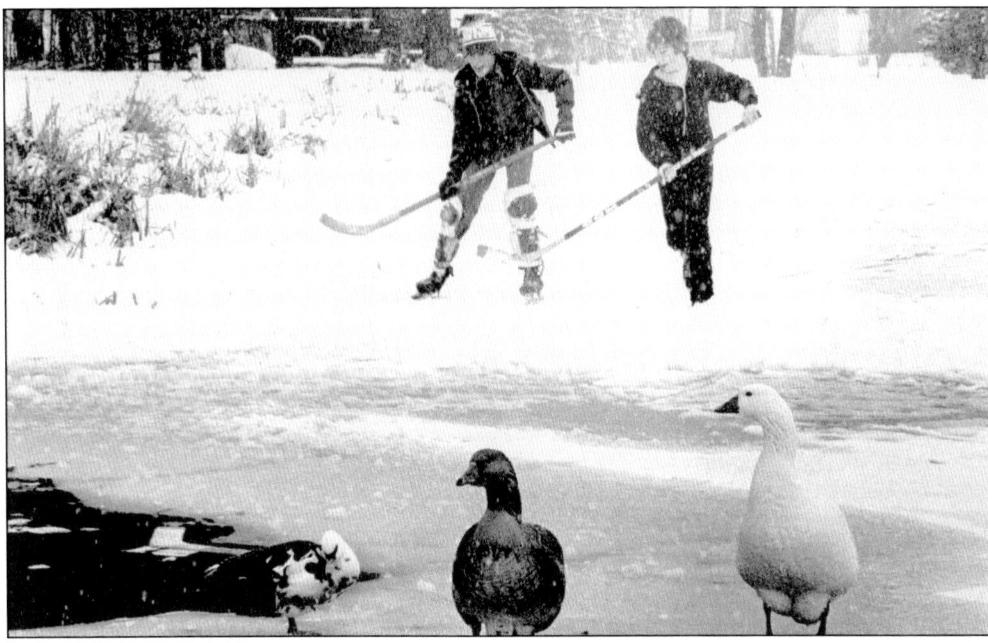

Pat McGuire (left) and Bob Mercik scramble for the hockey puck on a pond behind St. Joseph's Residence as the water fowl ignore the action in 1979. Pond hockey pickup games were very popular throughout town. Games were held on Freshwater Pond, Freshwater Brook, St. Martha's Pond, Shaker Pines Lake, Crescent Lake, the Scantic River, and Molinski's Pond off Bridge Lane and Riverview Terrace.

Six

Business and Industry

Local business and industry revolved around the carpet mills in Thompsonville. The carpet mill moved production down south in the 1950s, reducing the number of jobs and the tax base. The carpet mill closed its doors in 1971. As early as the late 1950s, Enfield town officials realized that a solid commercial and industrial tax base was necessary to provide town services. When Interstate 91 was completed in the 1950s, it provided residents with a quicker avenue to Hartford or Springfield. By 1964, it also provided the opportunity to lure major shopping center developers and highly skilled workers to prime locations along the highway. Today, seven shopping malls make up Enfield's regional shopping district.

A diversified industrial base was also needed. In 1971, residents approved the 550-acre Enfield Memorial Industrial Park. In 1980, the plan of development and zoning amendments significantly expanded industrial-zoned land along Moody and Shaker Roads and Interstate 91. Some major companies that have located in Enfield include Hallmark Cards, Lego Systems, MagnaPrint, Olympia Sales Club, the Phoenix Life Insurance Company, and Westvaco.

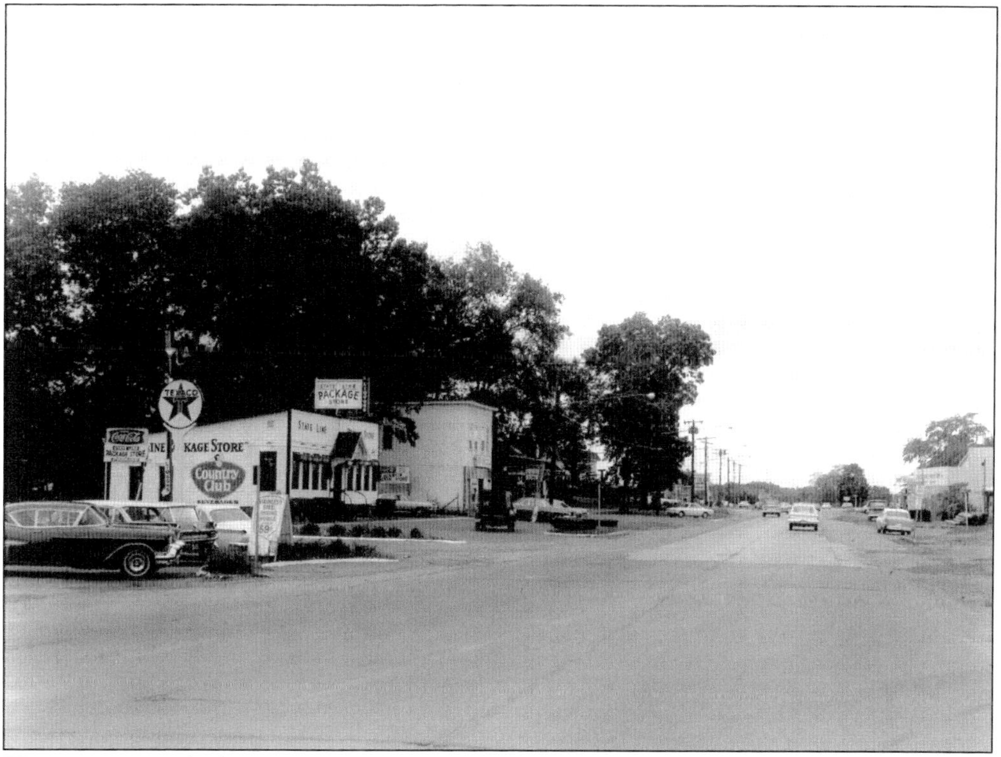

This 1960s view, looking south, shows businesses on Enfield Street at the state line. Businesses on the east side are, from left to right, George's Texaco Service, owned by George Corey; the State Line Package Store, owned by David J. Poggi; an unidentified business; and the North End Package Store, owned by Julius Drenzek.

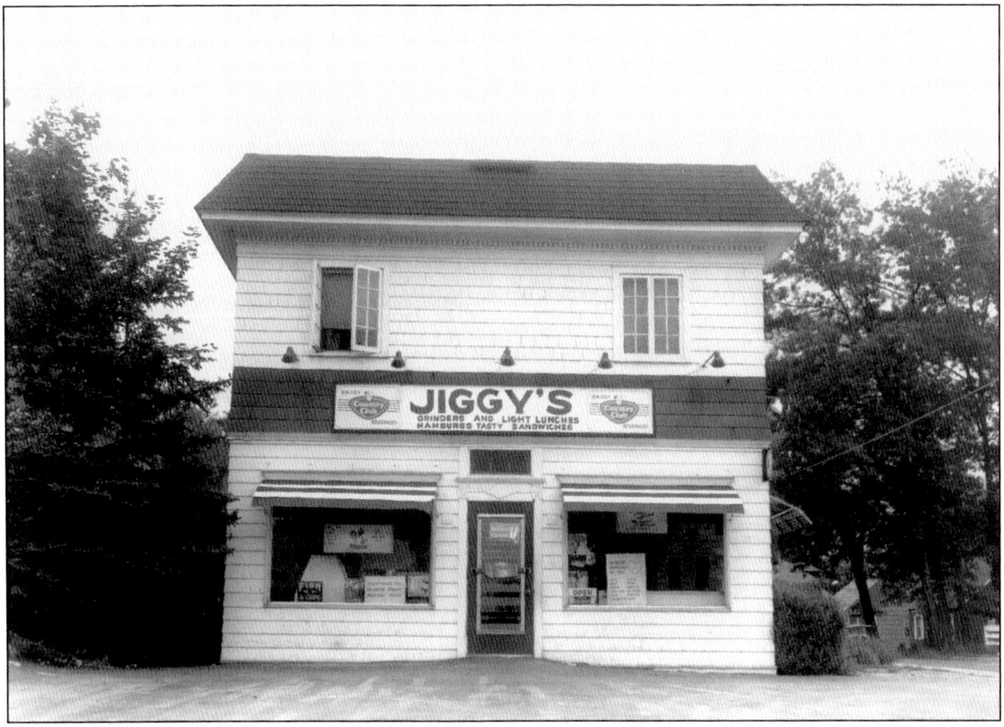

Jiggy's, located on Enfield Street at the state line, is pictured in the 1960s. The restaurant was owned by Ciro Jacaruso.

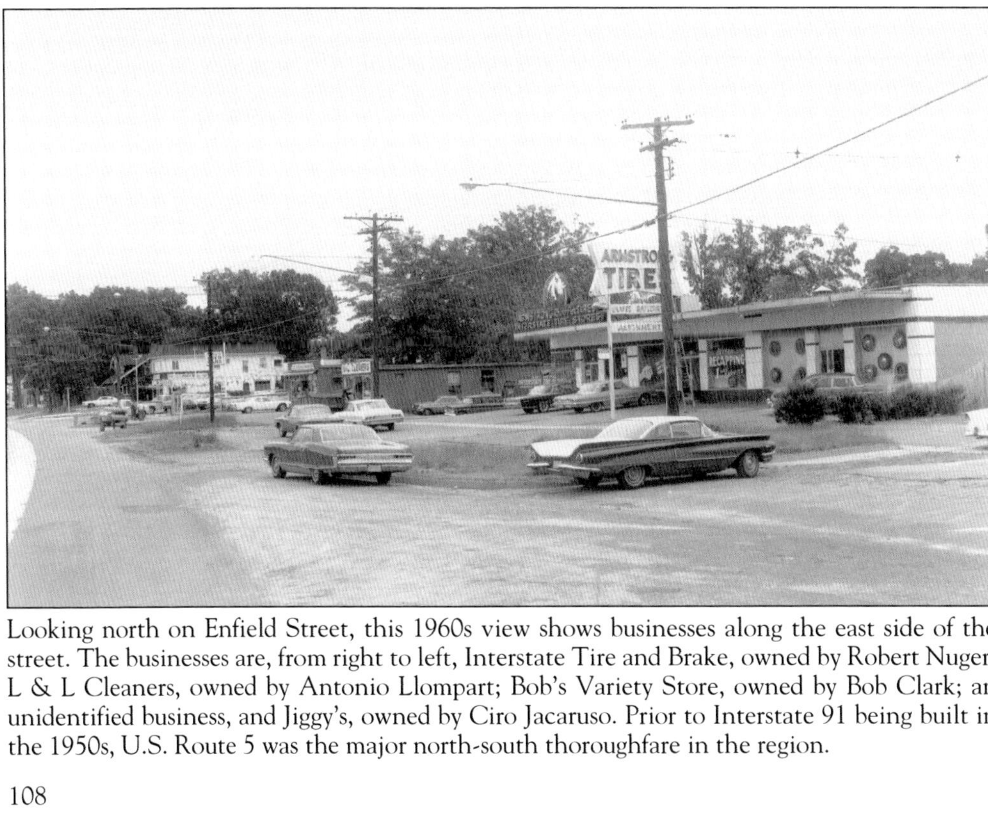

Looking north on Enfield Street, this 1960s view shows businesses along the east side of the street. The businesses are, from right to left, Interstate Tire and Brake, owned by Robert Nuger; L & L Cleaners, owned by Antonio Llompart; Bob's Variety Store, owned by Bob Clark; an unidentified business, and Jiggy's, owned by Ciro Jacaruso. Prior to Interstate 91 being built in the 1950s, U.S. Route 5 was the major north-south thoroughfare in the region.

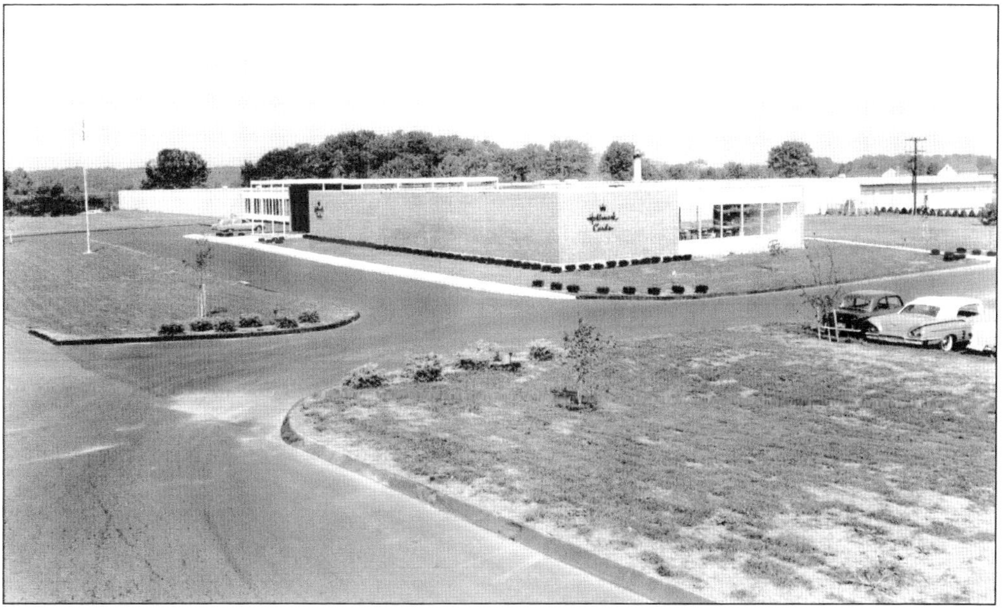

Hallmark Cards located its distribution activities to town in 1952 on Central Street. This 1960s view shows the new Hallmark Cards distribution plant, built in 1960 on Manning Road. In 1967, the company completed a $2 million addition to the Manning Road plant. Hallmark Cards expanded again, and the new distribution center groundbreaking ceremony took place on June 18, 1979, on Bacon Road. In November 2002, Hallmark Cards celebrated its 50th year in town.

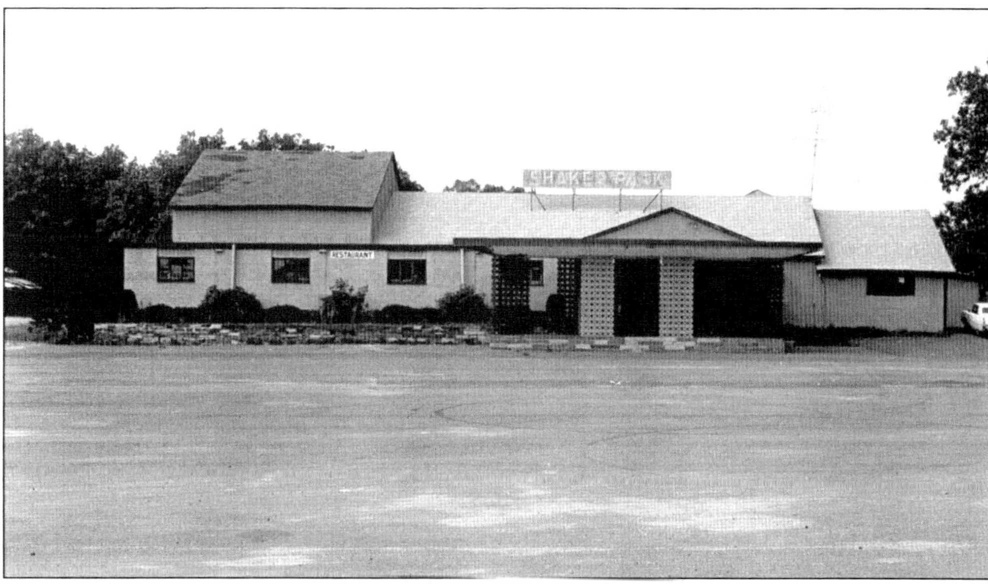

This 1976 view shows the Shaker Park Restaurant, located on on the north side of Brainard Road. Owned and operated by Joseph, "Max," Frederick, and Tadeusz Olko, the restaurant opened in the early 1950s. In the 1960s, the top music recording artists played at the club. Joseph and Max operated the restaurant and club until 1987. Shaker Park was sold to developers, and the building was torn down. Ashmead Commons condominiums were constructed in the late 1980s.

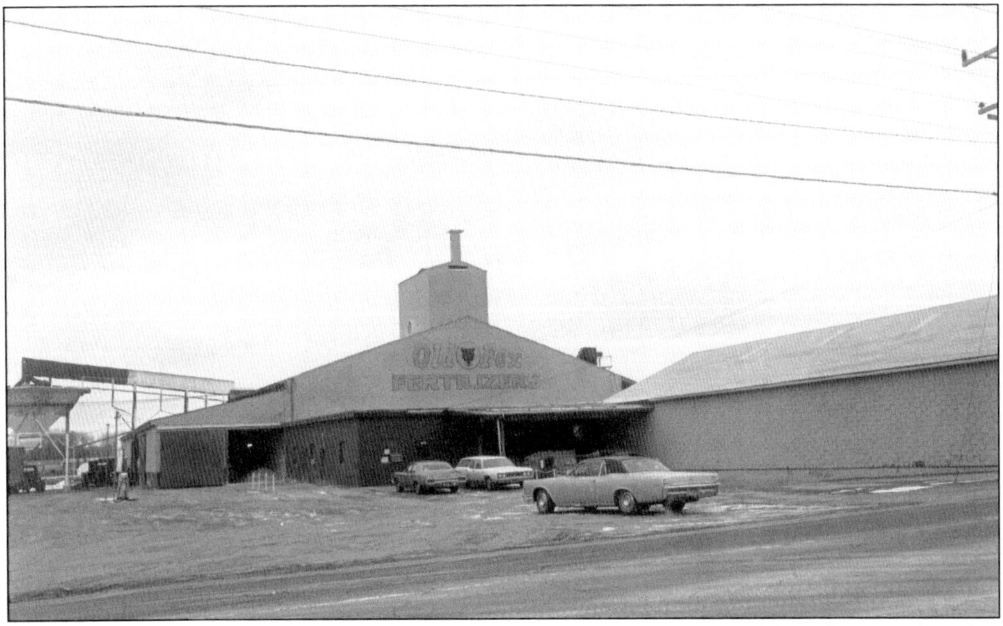

Old Fox Fertilizers moved to Enfield in the early 1960s. The company sold fertilizers and seed to area farmers until 1992. This 1974 view shows the Old Fox Fertilizers plant on Shaker Road. In 1993, the property was listed as a Superfund site. The Environmental Protection Agency cleaned up the site the same year. On July 23, 1996, an early-morning fire destroyed the building. The site remains vacant today.

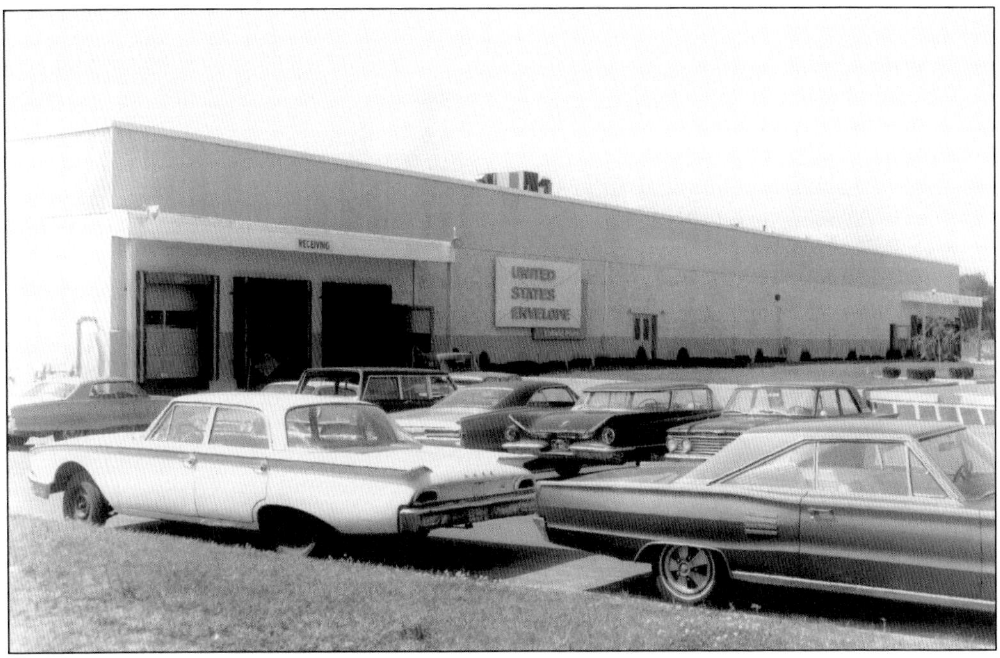

This 1965 view shows the U.S. Envelope plant on Moody Road. The site was selected in 1964, and the building was completed in early 1965. In the 1960s, the company was a major manufacturer of standard and custom envelopes, stationery, school supplies, and paper cups. In the 1980s, the company name was changed to Westvaco.

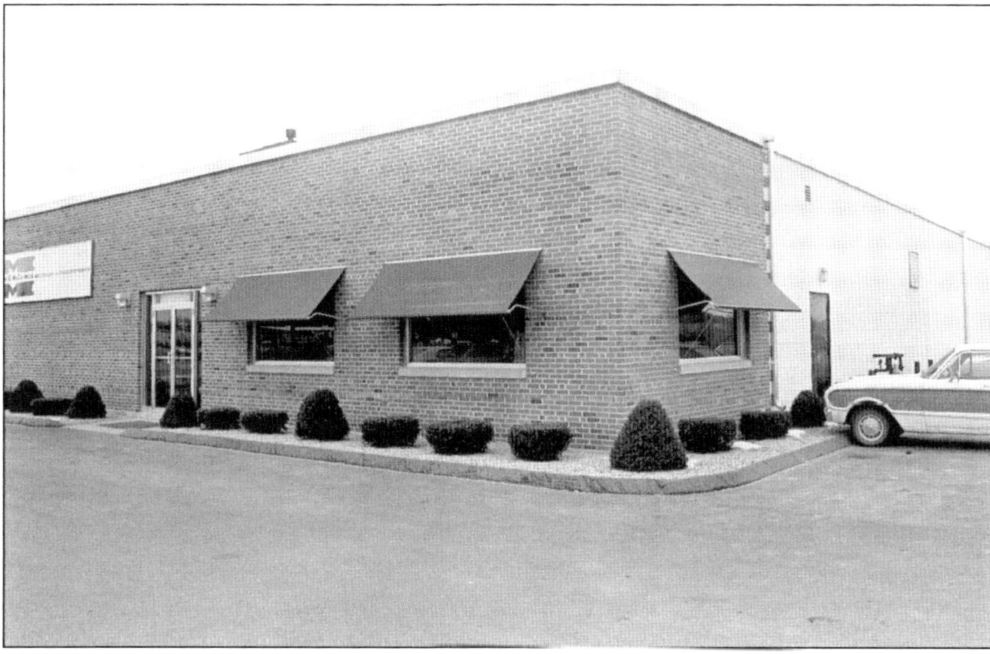

The Magnani & McCormick printing company, shown in 1974, was located on Moody Road and was owned by John Magnani and Thomas McCormick. The building was constructed in 1966, with additions completed in 1985 and 1990. In 1999, the company moved into a second plant on Pearson Way in Enfield. John Magnani is the current principal owner, and his son John P. Magnani is president of the firm. In 2000, the company name was changed to MagnaPrint.

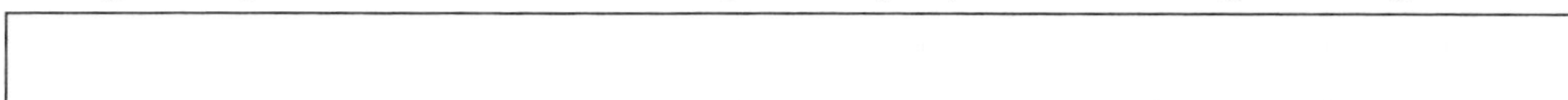

Pictured in 1974 is the Olympic Sales plant, located on Moody Road. The company relocated from Windsor Locks to Enfield in 1970 and constructed an office building on the same site in 1987. In 1990, the company changed its name to Olympia Sales. The company sells greetings cards, stationery, and paper products. Arthur O'Hara is the current chief executive officer; his son Tom O'Hara is the president.

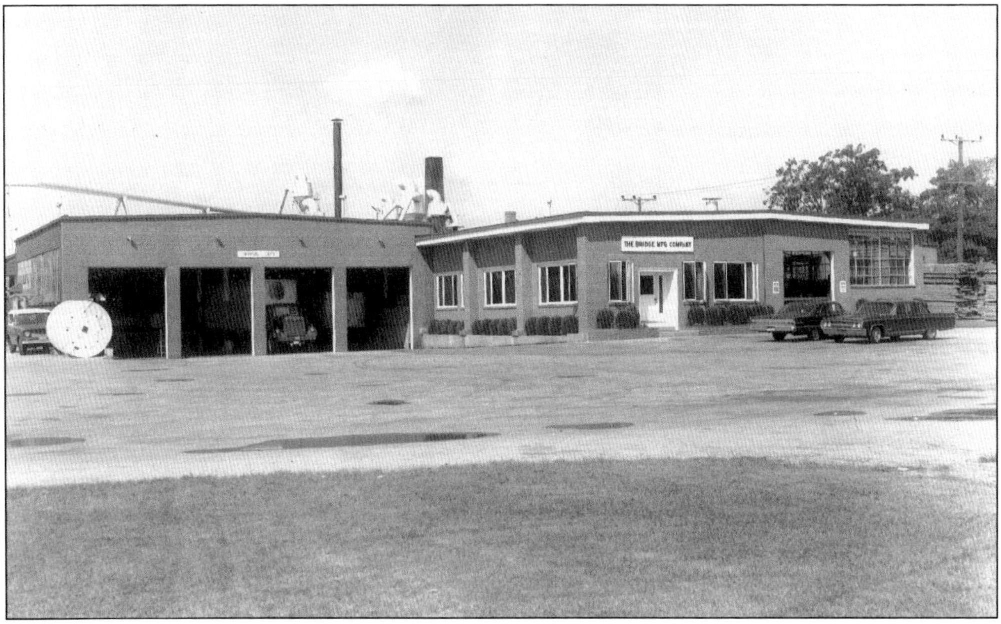

This 1960s view shows the Bridge Manufacturing Company plant, located on Randolph Street in Hazardville. Company officials in the 1960s included Douglas C. Bridge, president; Donald C. Bridge, vice president; and R. Dudley Bridge, secretary-treasurer. The plant manufactured cable reels. The company is currently owned by Carris Reels.

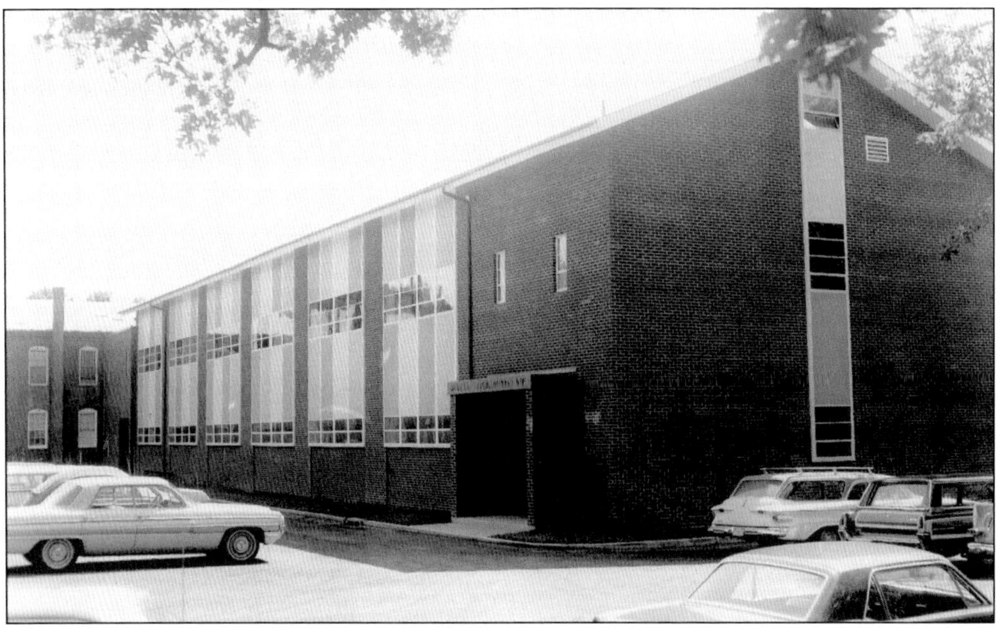

The DeBell & Richardson building, located on Hazard Avenue in Scitico, is pictured in the 1960s. The company, organized by John DeBell and H.M. Richardson in the 1940s, specialized in research of plastics and polymers. In 1972, Dr. Robert Springborn took over leadership duties of the company. In 1977, the company name was changed to Springborn Laboratories. In 1998, the company was sold and the name was changed to STR (Specialized Technology Resources). The company specializes in quality assurance and laboratory testing.

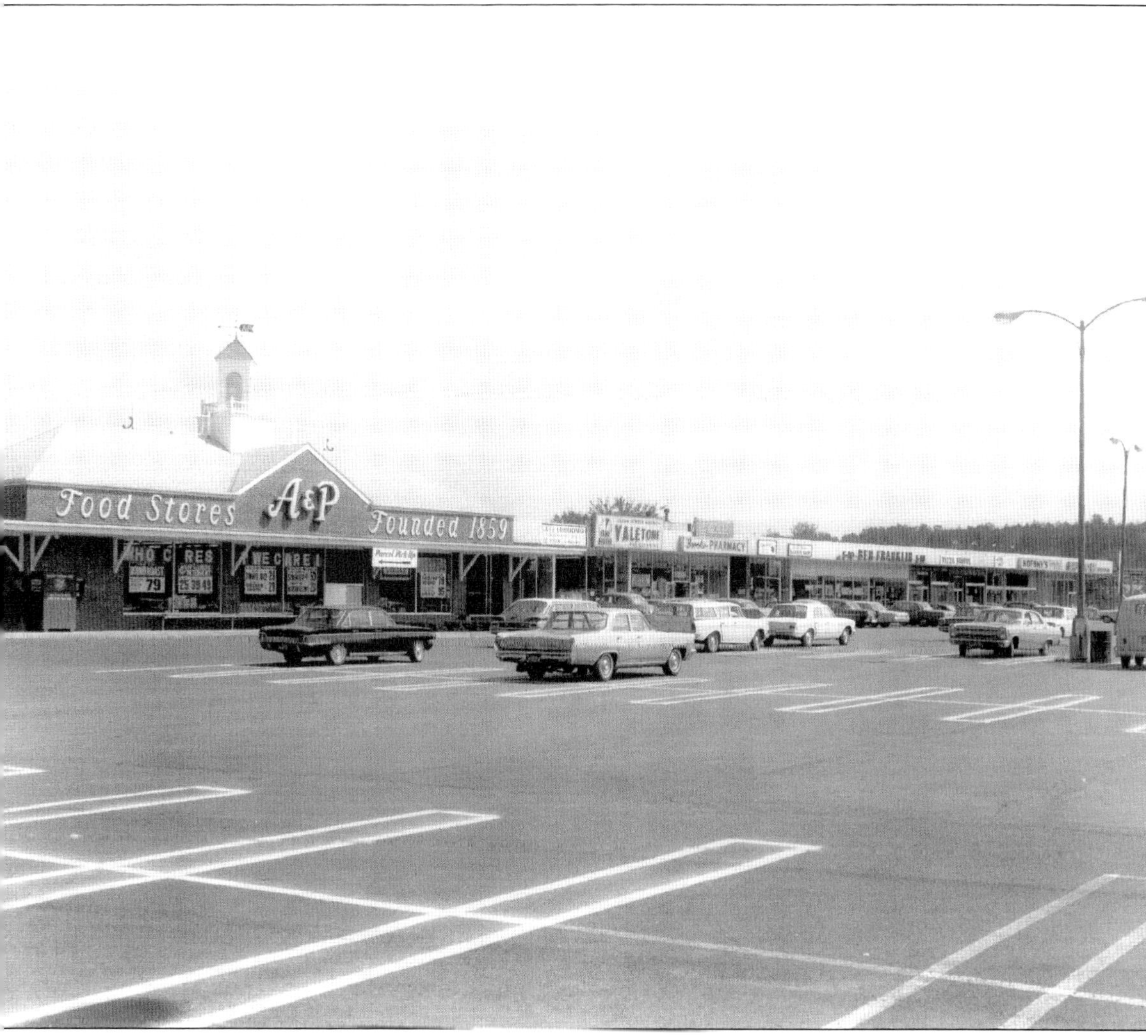

Pictured here in the 1960s is the Green Manorville Shopping Parkade, anchored by the Great Atlantic & Pacific Tea Company (A & P). The plaza was located at the intersection of Main Street (later named Hazard Avenue) and Taylor Road. It also included the Scitico Laundercenter, Valetone Dry Cleaners, Brooks Pharmacy, Gaetano's Beauty Studio, Green Manor Barber Shop, Ben Franklin, the Pizza Shoppe, Ann's Dance Studio, Kofsky's (a shoe store), and Suffield Savings Bank. The name was later changed to Scitico Plaza. Since 1977, the Scitico Market has anchored the plaza and is now owned by the D'Alessandro family.

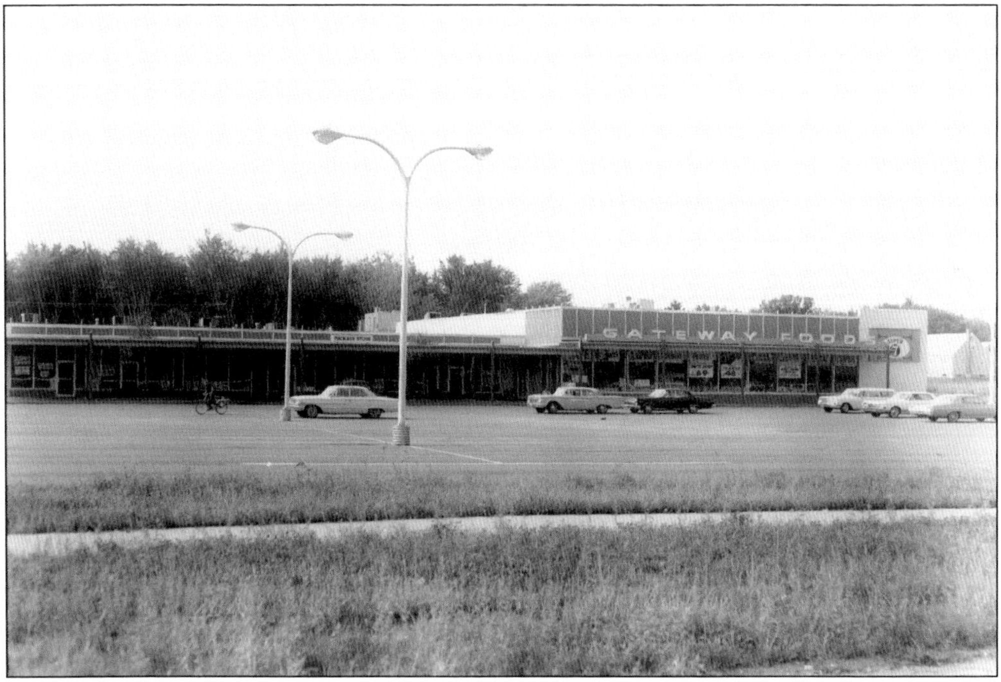

This 1960s view shows the Gateway Foods supermarket, located at the intersection of Weymouth and Steele Roads. In the 1970s, the Amber Light Lounge & Cafe was an establishment in the plaza. The current site is home to the Porter and Chester Institute.

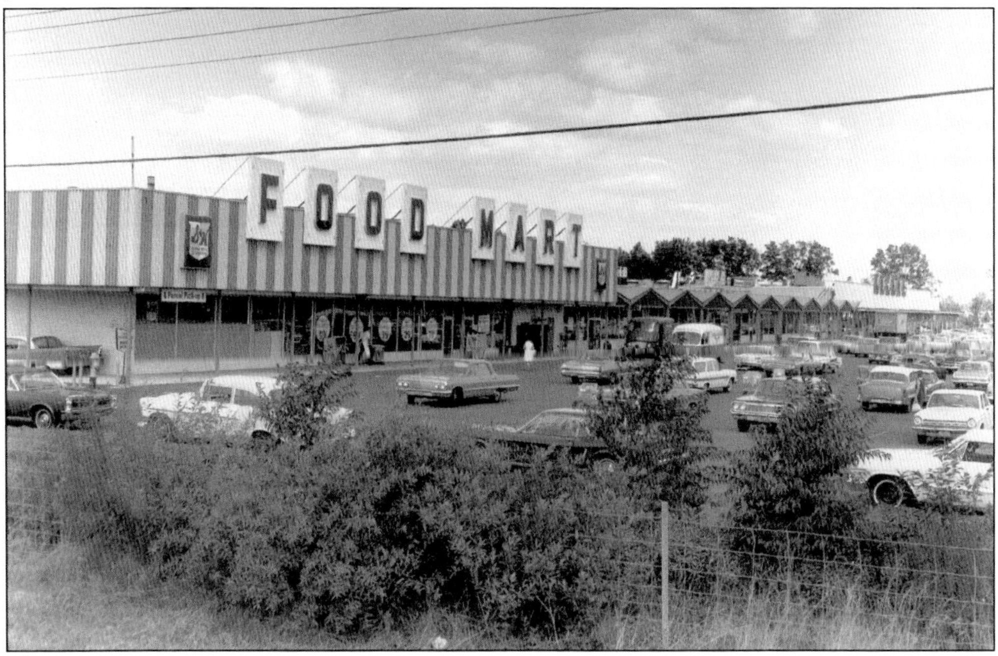

The Elm Plaza Shopping Center, anchored by Food Mart and the W.T. Grant department store, was located on Elm Street and is pictured here in the 1960s. The Food Mart supermarket has been a tenant in the plaza for over 37 years. The W.T. Grant store closed its doors in the 1970s, and the plaza was later anchored by Caldor and, currently, by Kohl's.

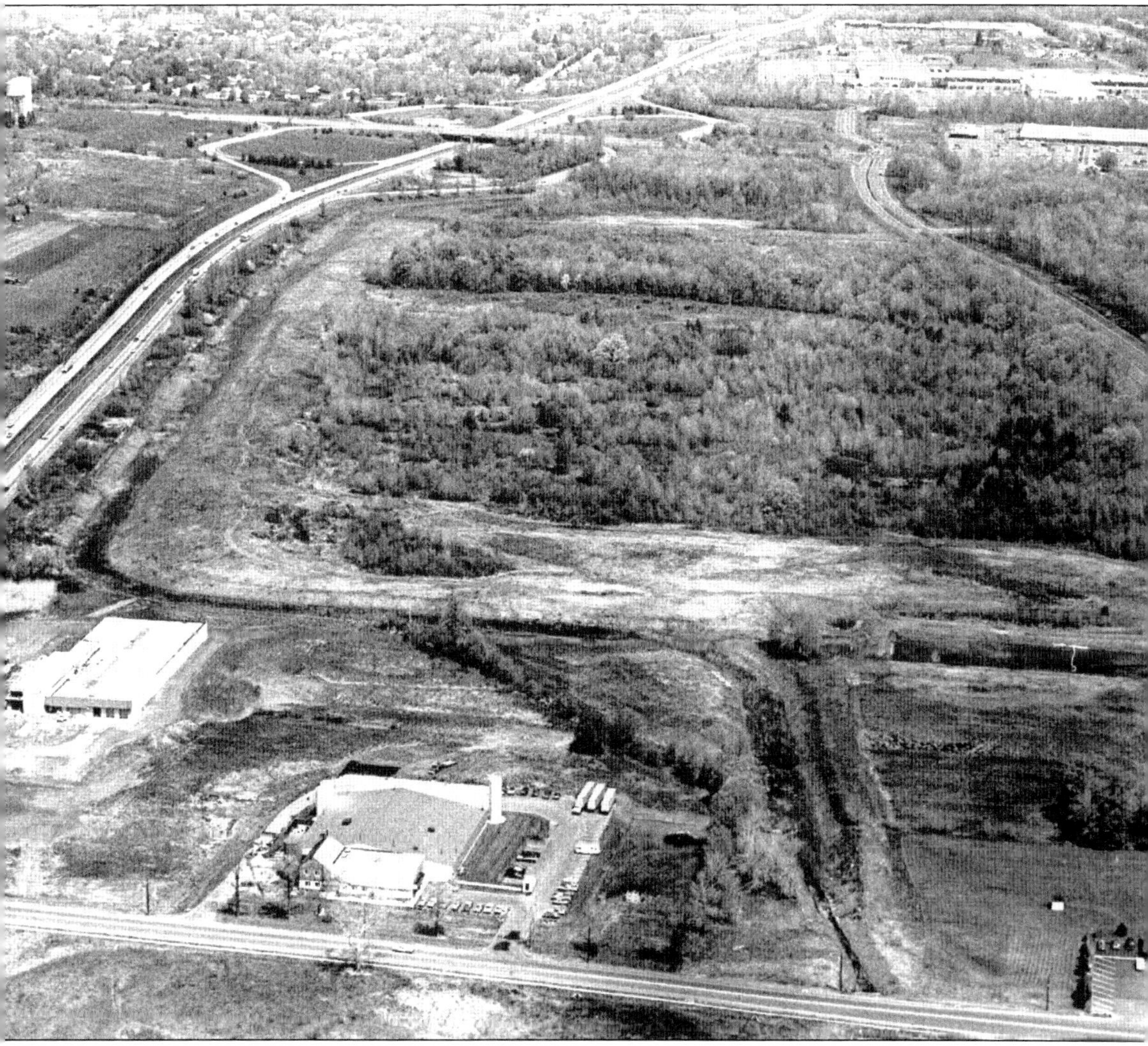

This 1970s photograph shows Interstate 91 on the left and businesses under construction in the Enfield Memorial Industrial Park in the foreground. From left to right are Toolkraft; Dairy Mart, owned by Charles Nirenberg; and the Enfield Dairy Bar, owned by John D. Cimino and located on South Road. Della Construction was awarded the contract to build the streets within the industrial park. Phoenix Avenue can be seen to the right. Three shopping malls are in the regional shopping district in the background.

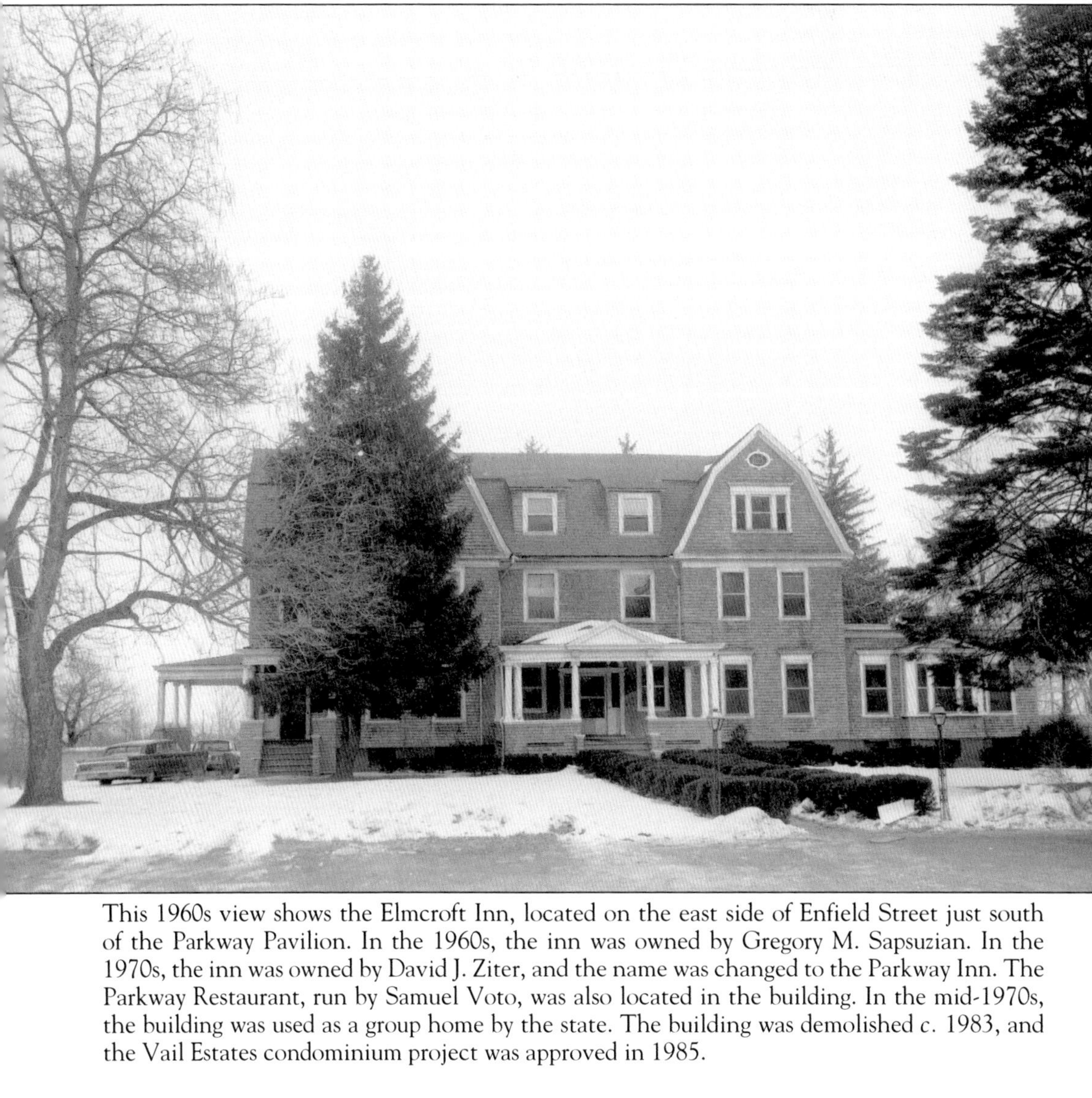

This 1960s view shows the Elmcroft Inn, located on the east side of Enfield Street just south of the Parkway Pavilion. In the 1960s, the inn was owned by Gregory M. Sapsuzian. In the 1970s, the inn was owned by David J. Ziter, and the name was changed to the Parkway Inn. The Parkway Restaurant, run by Samuel Voto, was also located in the building. In the mid-1970s, the building was used as a group home by the state. The building was demolished *c.* 1983, and the Vail Estates condominium project was approved in 1985.

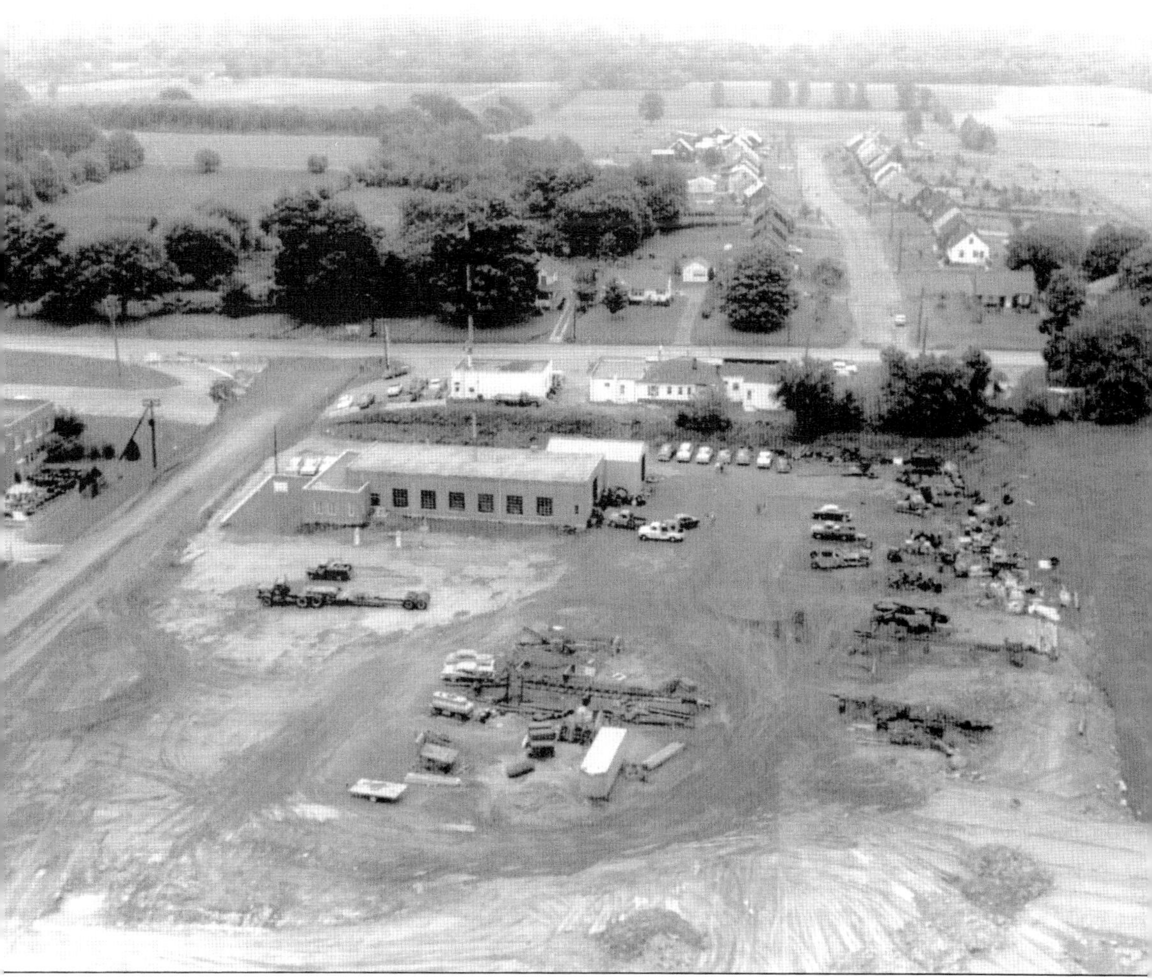

King's Korner, pictured in a 1960s view looking east, shows the Della Construction company office building and construction yard on Depot Hill Road in the foreground. In 1965, the following businesses (listed from left to right) were located on King Street: the Connecticut Light and Power Company, King's Korner Service Station, King's Korner Package Store, King's Korner Barber Shop, Sue's Luncheonette, and King Street Market grocers. The King Court subdivision is east of King Street in the background.

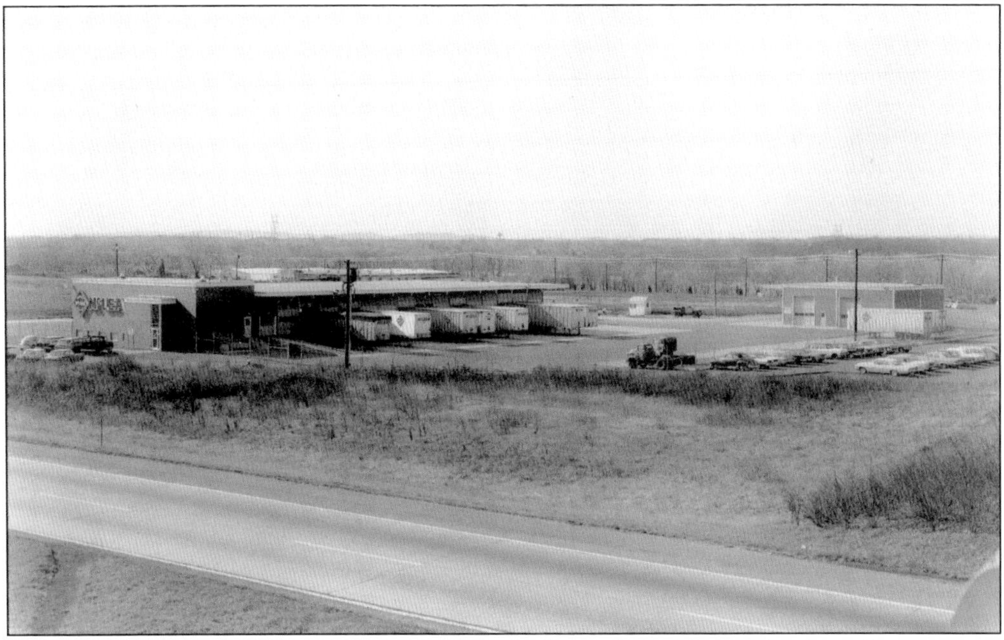

This 1965 view from the Interstate 91 overpass shows the McLean Trucking Company on Depot Hill Road. The company provided transport services in the region. The building later housed Carolina Freight Carriers and, since 1995, has been home to the ABF Freight System trucking company.

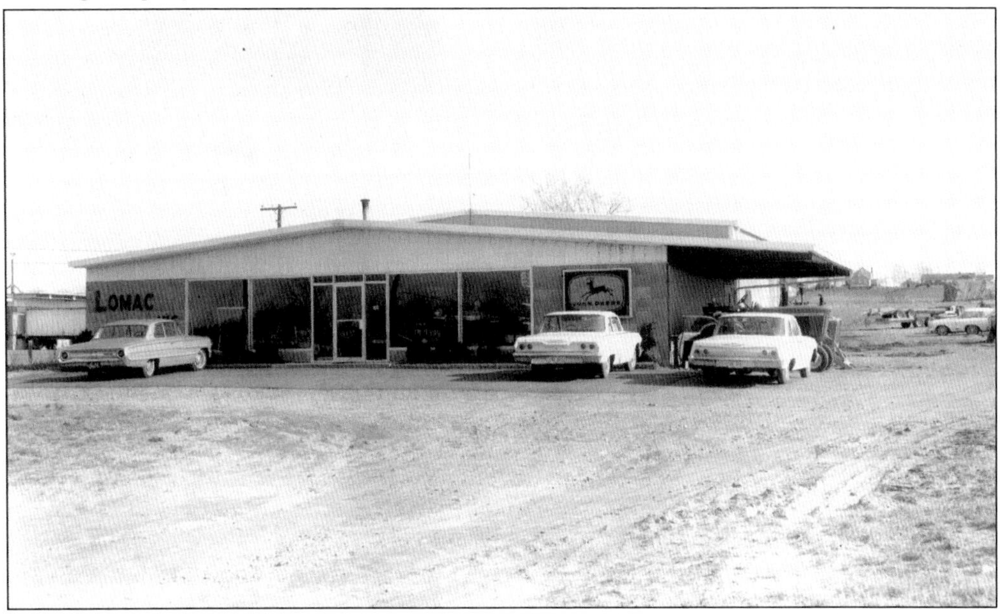

In 1963, James McKnight and Harry Lowenstein became business partners in Windsor Locks. The business name Lomac was formed from a combination of each owner's last name. In 1964, Lomac moved to a site on Depot Hill Road in Enfield. This 1965 photograph shows an exterior view of Lomac, which sold a variety of John Deere industrial and commercial equipment. The Depot Hill Road store location moved to East Windsor in 1986. The building now houses the Smyth Bus Company.

Seven

FIRE DEPARTMENTS

From the age of 15 to the end of his newspaper career, Edward J. Malley Jr. actively covered the five town fire departments in action. He captured local firefighters in action as a teenager because he always had his camera by his side. He was at the scene of some of the the worst fires in the history of the town, including the Enfield Inn fire in 1969, the Osborn Prison Farm blaze in 1971, and the Browne Building fire in 1979. The five fire departments he covered were established in Enfield by legislative act, including Thompsonville in 1839, Hazardville in 1892, Enfield in 1896, North Thompsonville in 1914, and Shaker Pines in 1941. These five fire districts remain in operation today. Enfield fire officials conduct a fire-prevention program in the elementary schools, which is unique in the state of Connecticut.

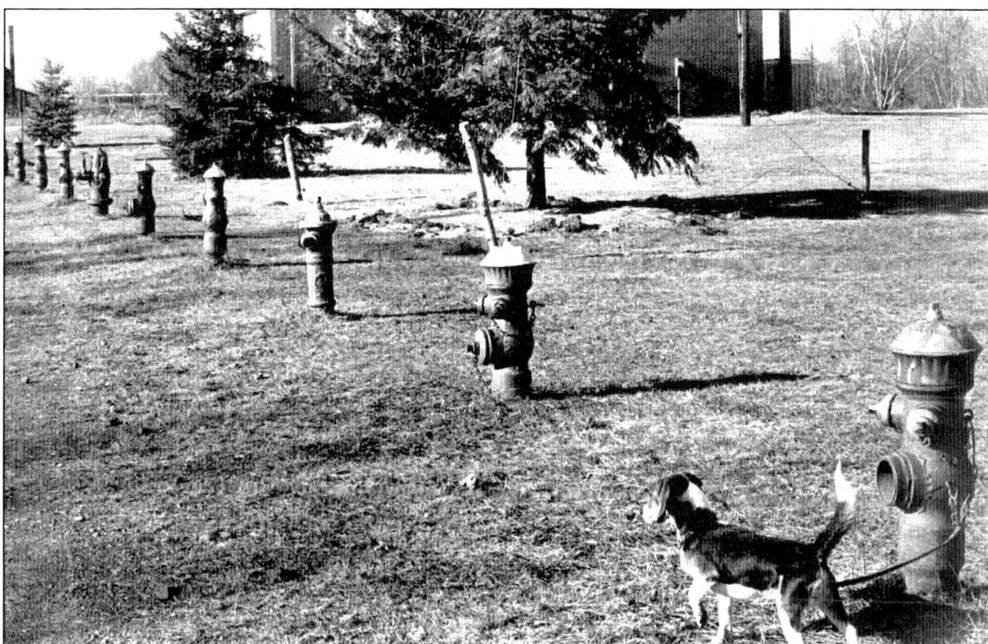

The Enfield Fire Department recycled old fire hydrants to create a unique barrier to keep motor vehicles off the grass. The old fire hydrants were installed adjacent to the Enfield Fire District Station 2 on Weymouth Road. A beagle views the landscaped area in 1971.

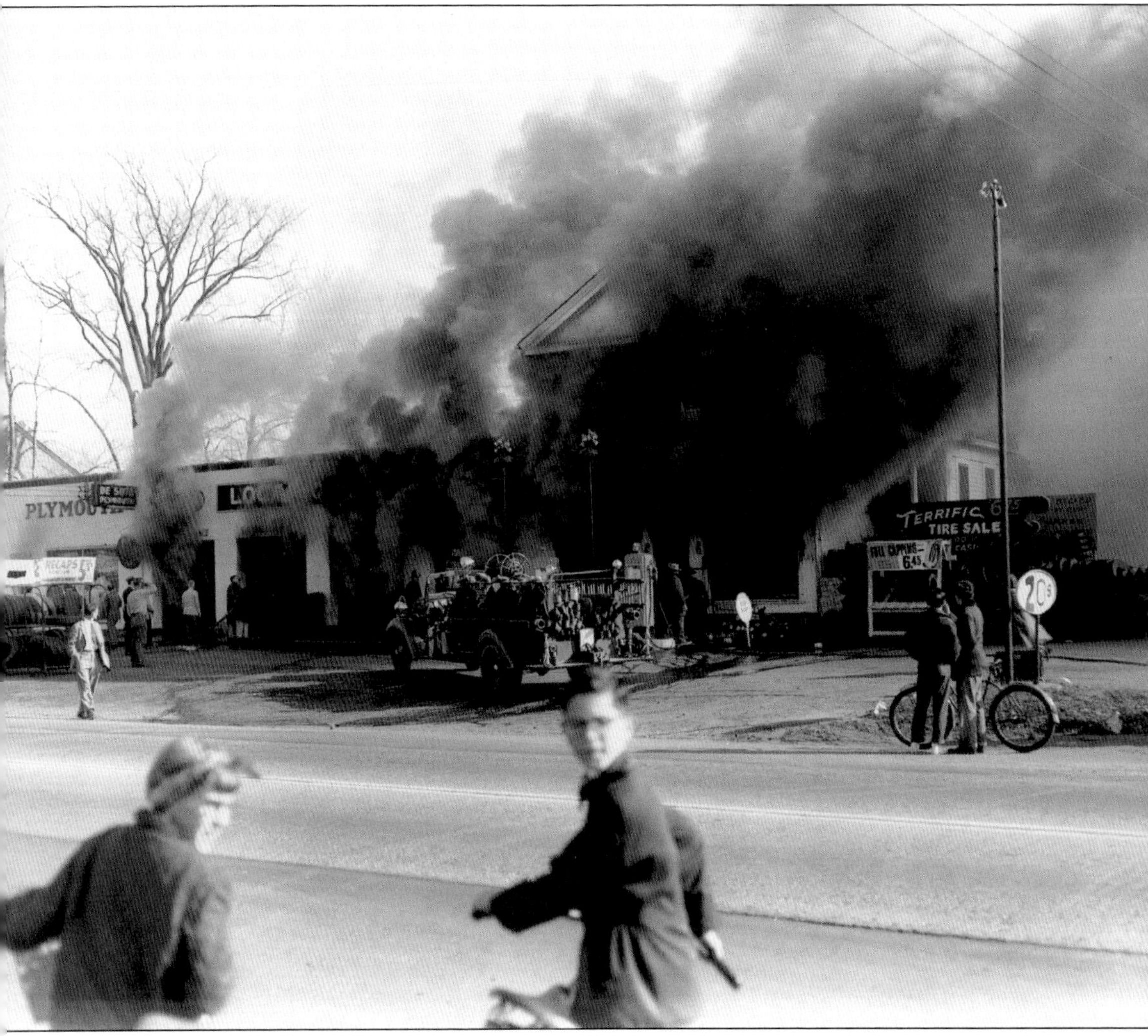

On November 11, 1953, heavy volumes of black smoke pour out of the Locario Brothers garage at the corner of Enfield Street and Enfield Avenue. The fire started from a faulty oil burner in the basement and spread to the garage and then to a second-floor apartment. The Thompsonville Fire Department, under the direction of Chief Thomas J. Furey, had the fire under control within an hour. The DeSoto Plymouth showroom next to the garage was not damaged by the blaze. The site is now home to Enfield Chrysler Plymouth.

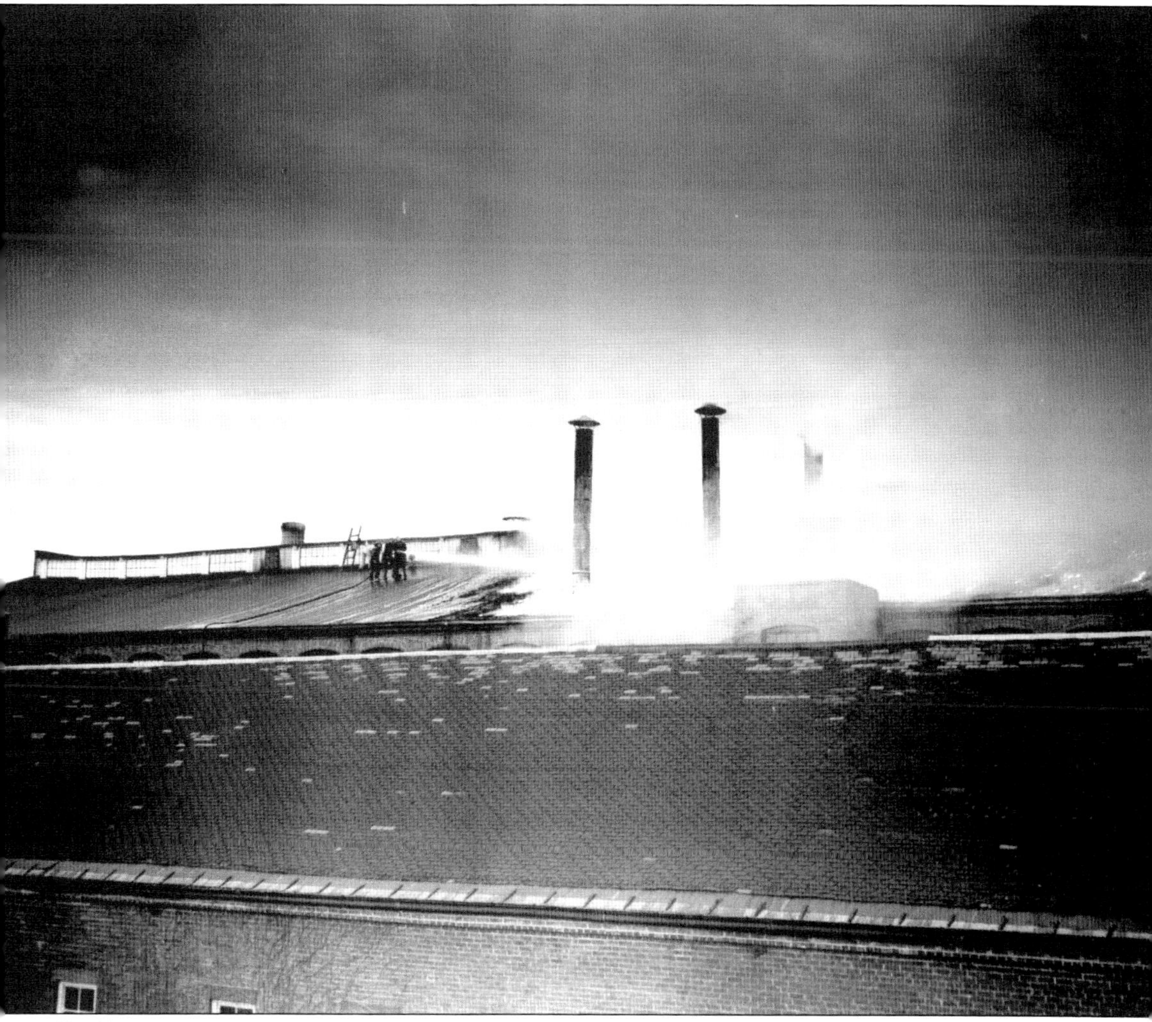

On December 23, 1953, the finishing department building roof at the Bigelow-Sanford Carpet Company went up in flames. The Thompsonville, North Thompsonville, and Enfield Fire Departments, under the direction of Chief Thomas J. Furey, confined the fire to the roof of the four-story building. The fire started in a drying machine on the fourth floor of the building. Firefighters are shown spraying down the spreading flames on the finishing department building roof.

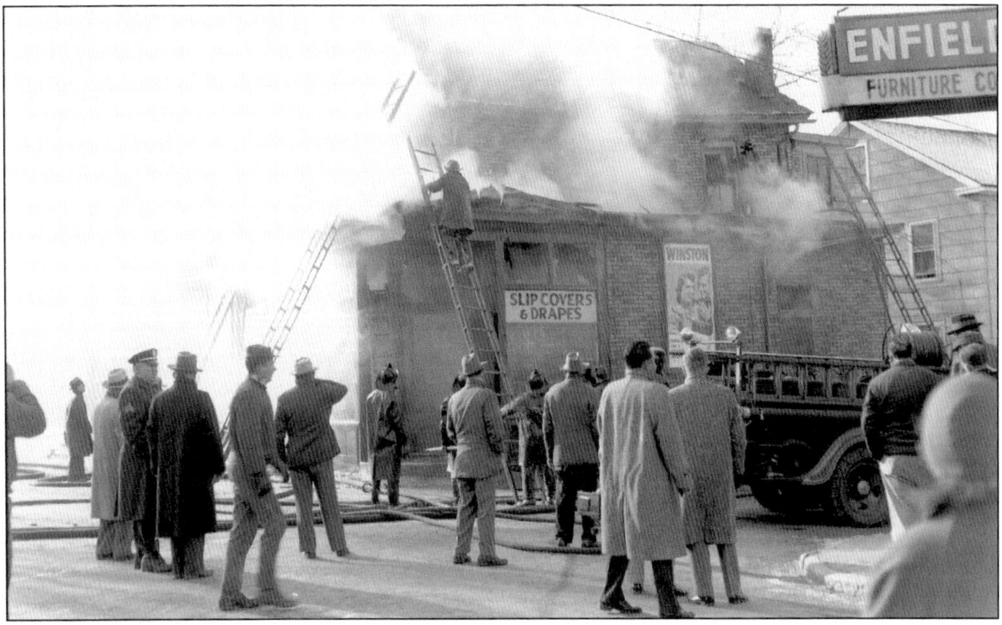

On January 2, 1957, a fire left a family homeless and severely damaged the Enfield Furniture and Upholstery Company store, owned by Peter Giaccone at the intersection of Church and School Streets. Thompsonville firemen, under the direction of Chief Judd Bourgeoise, fought the blaze under extremely cold conditions. The fire was started by a faulty heater in the store basement.

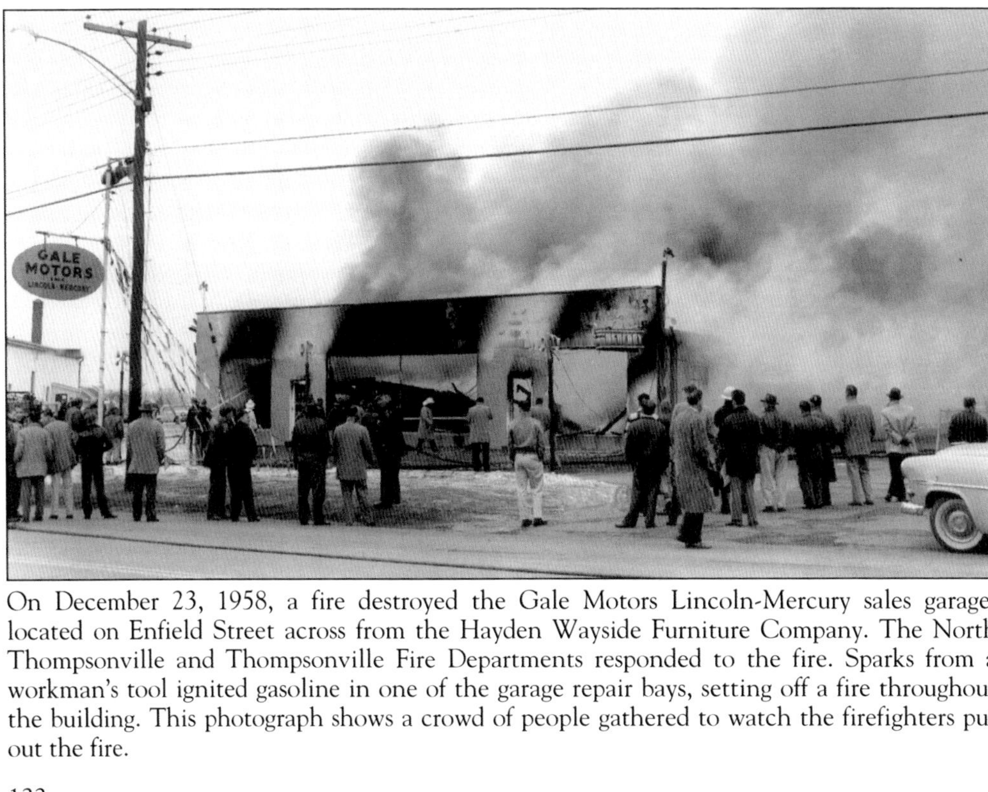

On December 23, 1958, a fire destroyed the Gale Motors Lincoln-Mercury sales garage, located on Enfield Street across from the Hayden Wayside Furniture Company. The North Thompsonville and Thompsonville Fire Departments responded to the fire. Sparks from a workman's tool ignited gasoline in one of the garage repair bays, setting off a fire throughout the building. This photograph shows a crowd of people gathered to watch the firefighters put out the fire.

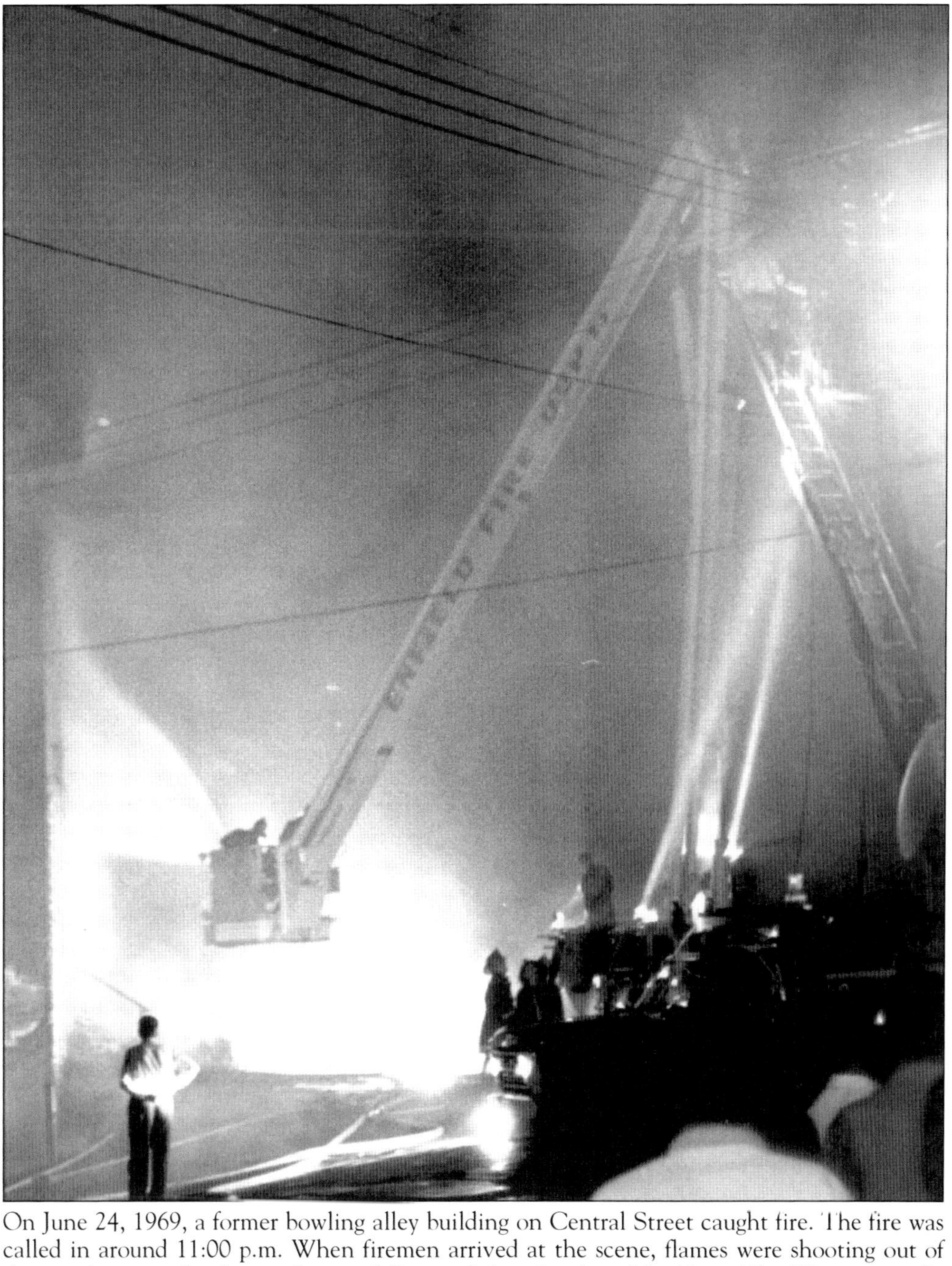

On June 24, 1969, a former bowling alley building on Central Street caught fire. The fire was called in around 11:00 p.m. When firemen arrived at the scene, flames were shooting out of the windows on the first and second floors of the abandoned building. The Thompsonville and Enfield Fire Departments, under the direction of Chief Thomas J. Furey, had the fire put out, but major damage was done to the building. This photograph shows Enfield District 1 firefighters spraying water on the flames.

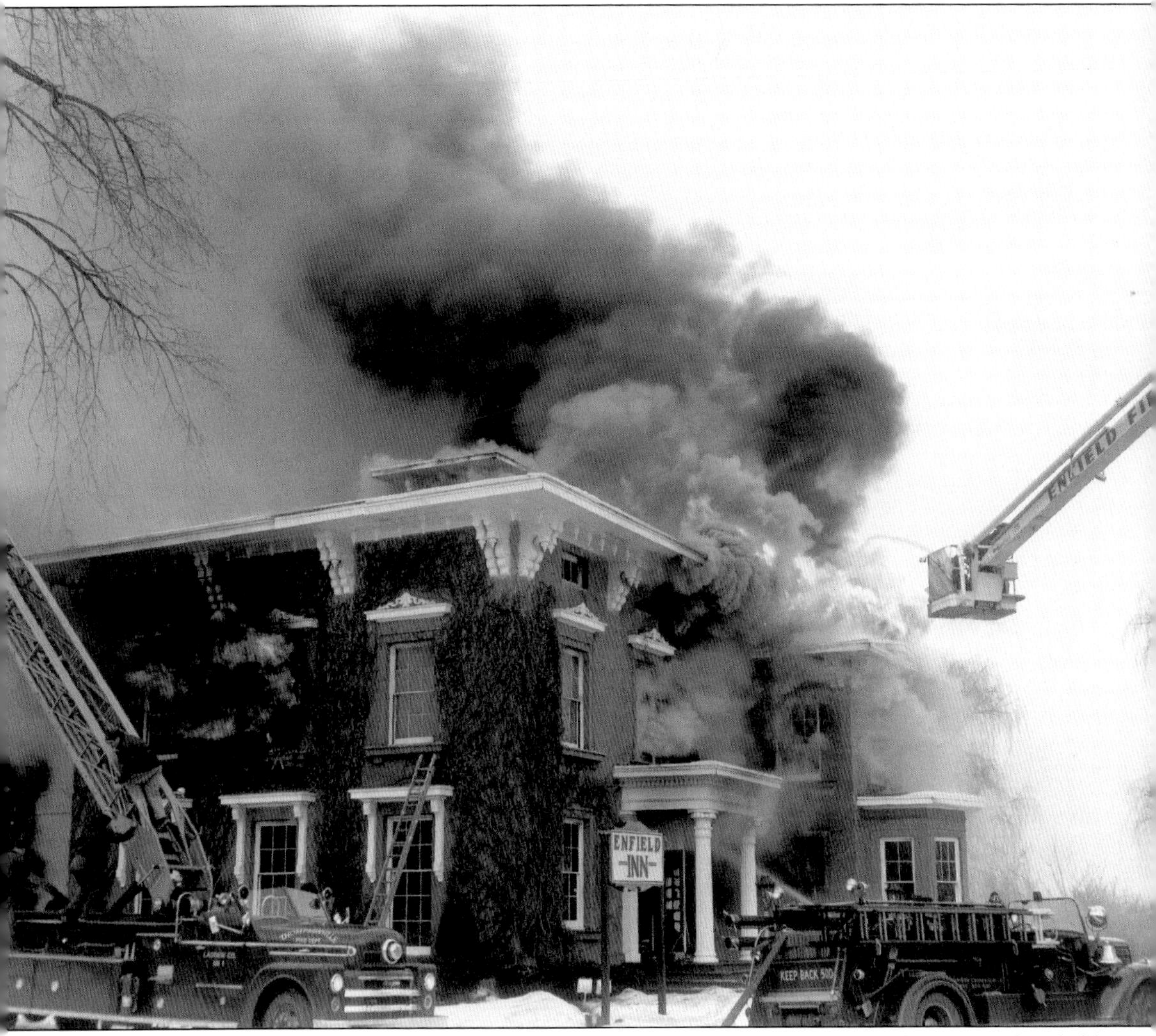

On January 3, 1969, the Enfield Inn, located across from the present-day driveway of Enfield High School, was engulfed in flames and smoke. Enfield fire chief James Richards Jr. was driving along Enfield Street when he saw the smoke and called in the blaze to the department from his truck. The fire departments of Enfield, Thompsonville, and Hazardville, under the direction of Richards, put out the fire. The fire was caused by a spark from a contractor's tool that ignited paint fumes, causing major damage to the historic inn. On the left, firefighters on the Thompsonville Ladder Company No. 1 truck get their ladder into position. On the right, Enfield District 1 firefighters spray water on the flames.

The Thompsonville Ladder Company No. 1 truck is shown in front the historic Enfield Inn as flames shoot out and billowing clouds of smoke pour out the second-floor window on January 3, 1969. The fire swept up the spiral staircase and spread quickly to the second floor. Firefighters rescued two men from the second floor.

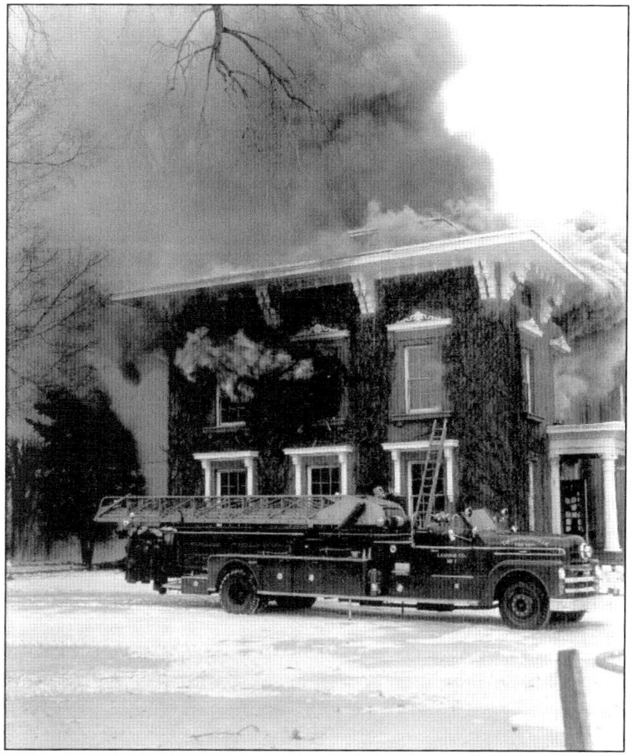

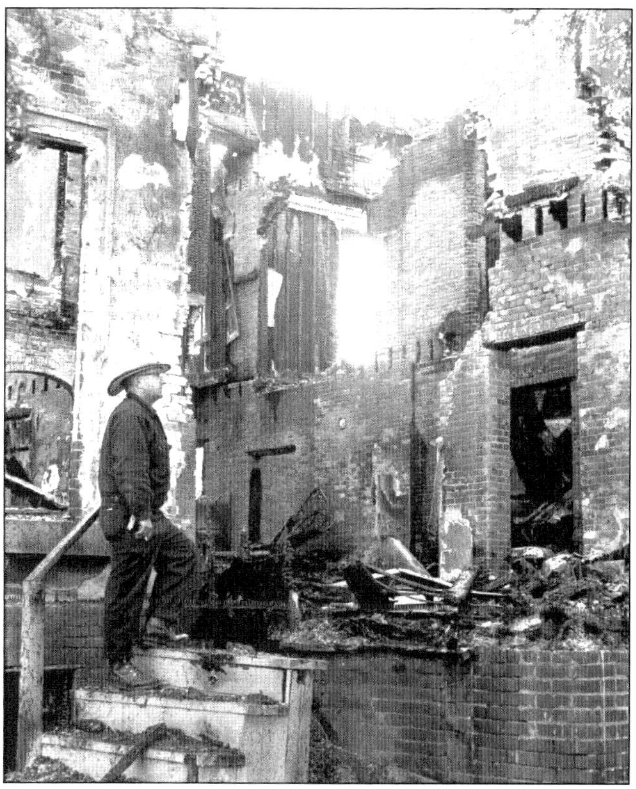

On January 4, 1969, Enfield District 1 fire chief James Richards Jr. views the damaged remains of the Enfield Inn. Richards's career spanned over 40 years. He became a member of the Enfield District 1 Fire Department in 1951 and was appointed chief on November 5, 1963. He served in this capacity until he retired on June 30, 1992. His son Edward N. Richards succeeded him as chief on July 1, 1992.

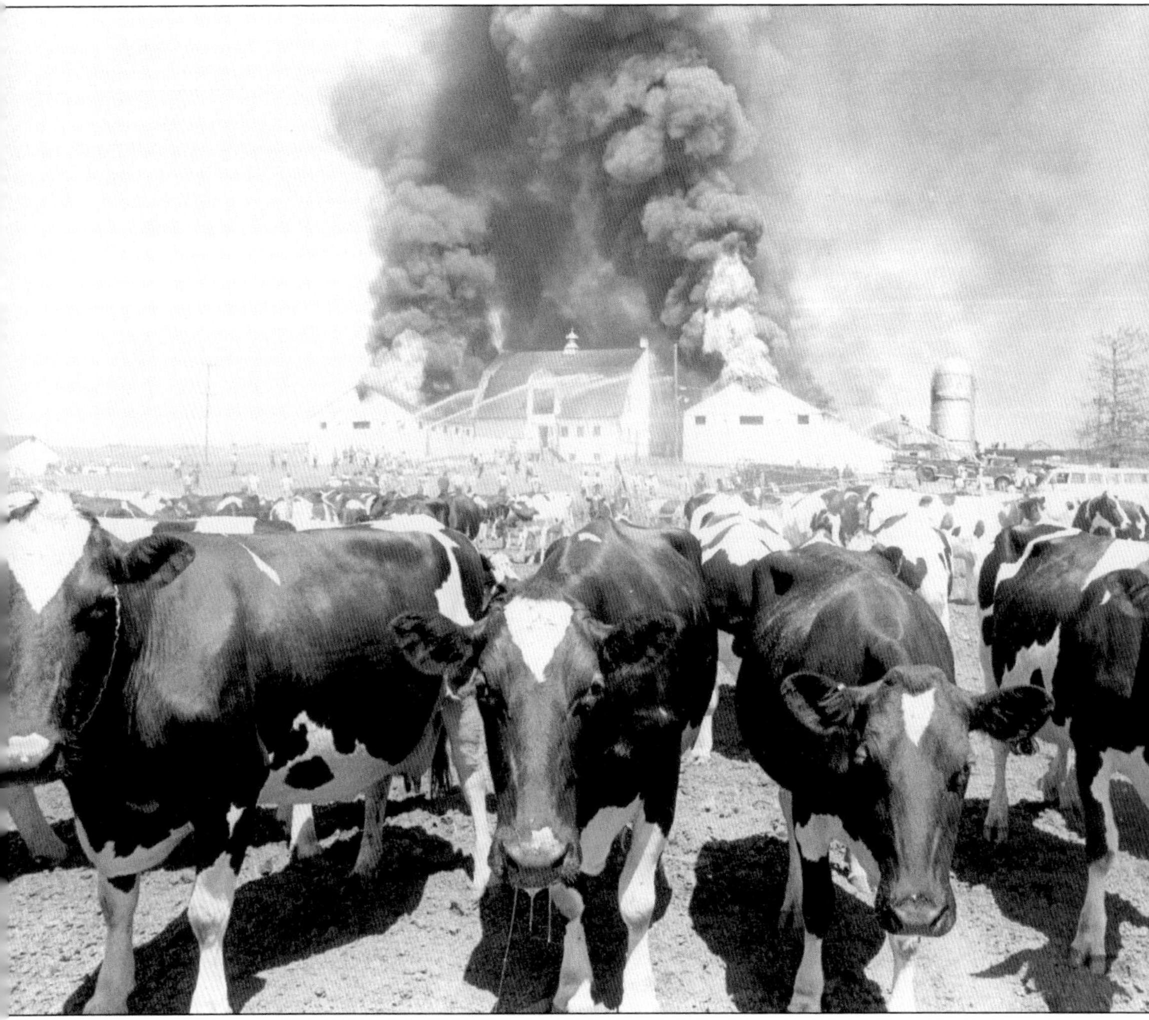

On July 8, 1971, the Connecticut State Prison's minimum security Osborn Prison Farm went up in flames. The fire was started by spontaneous combustion. The five town fire departments, the prison fire department, and two fire departments from Massachusetts responded to the blaze. The photograph shows a herd of cows walking away from their home as flames shoot out of their barns. Inmates guided 180 cows and 19 calves to safety.

An unidentified fireman is shown spraying water on one of the five silos, behind the prison's Dodge International Power Wagon. Two of the five silos were destroyed, while the remaining three were severely damaged.

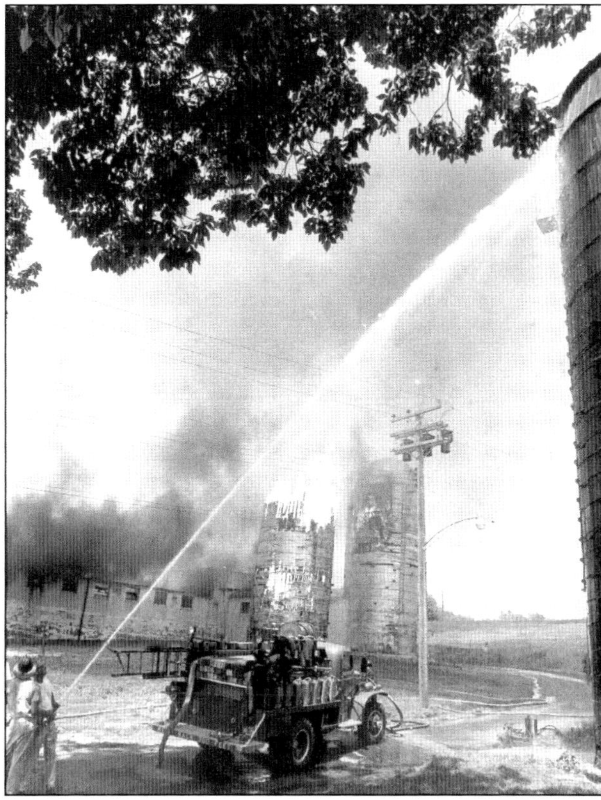

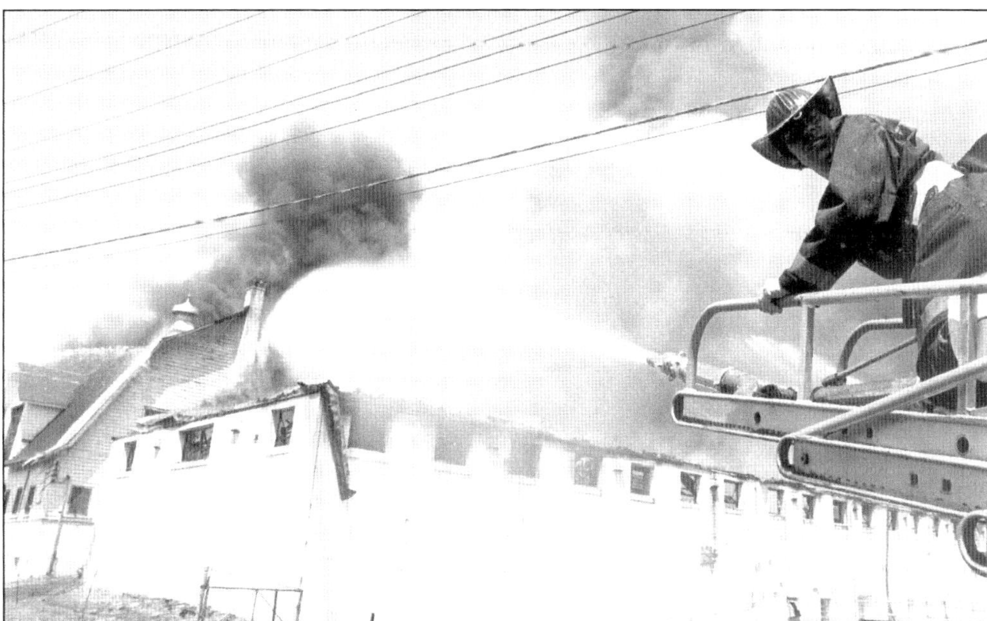

Fireman Doug Cordis of the Longmeadow Fire Department is shown spraying water on the large U-shaped barn. Damages were estimated at $100,000. The prison fire unit and inmates were responsible for saving the livestock and some of the dairy equipment.

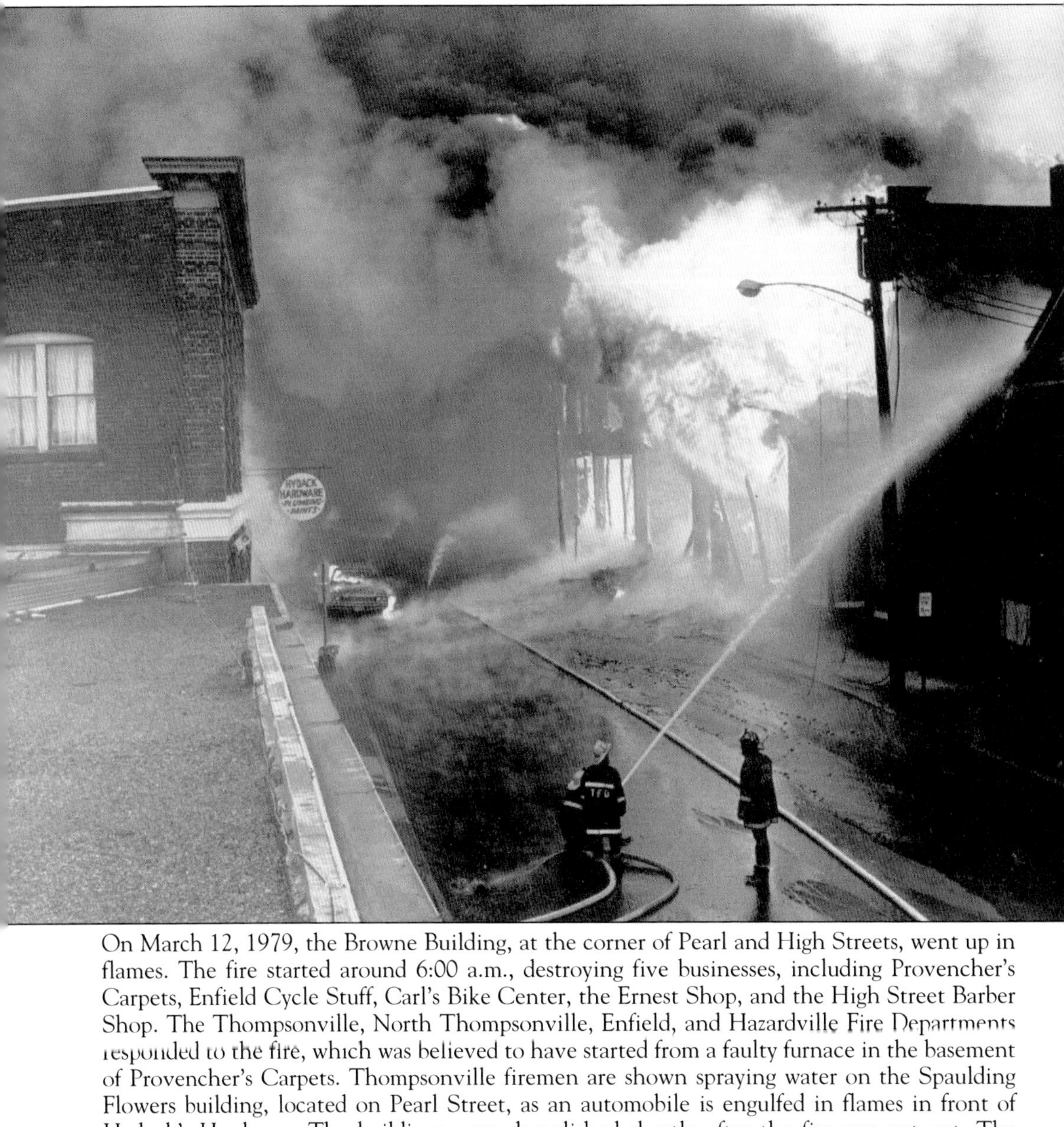

On March 12, 1979, the Browne Building, at the corner of Pearl and High Streets, went up in flames. The fire started around 6:00 a.m., destroying five businesses, including Provencher's Carpets, Enfield Cycle Stuff, Carl's Bike Center, the Ernest Shop, and the High Street Barber Shop. The Thompsonville, North Thompsonville, Enfield, and Hazardville Fire Departments responded to the fire, which was believed to have started from a faulty furnace in the basement of Provencher's Carpets. Thompsonville firemen are shown spraying water on the Spaulding Flowers building, located on Pearl Street, as an automobile is engulfed in flames in front of Hydack's Hardware. The buildings were demolished shortly after the fire was put out. The current site is a parking lot for Diana's Bakery.